365

truths

FOR EVERY
WOMAN'S HEART

OTHER WORKS BY HOLLEY GERTH

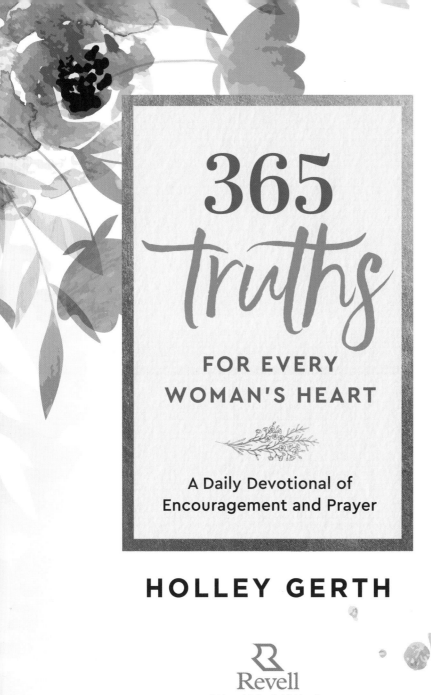

365
truths

FOR EVERY
WOMAN'S HEART

A Daily Devotional of
Encouragement and Prayer

HOLLEY GERTH

Revell
a division of Baker Publishing Group
Grand Rapids, Michigan

© 2024 by Holley, Inc.

Published by Revell
a division of Baker Publishing Group
Grand Rapids, Michigan
RevellBooks.com

Printed in China

Library of Congress Cataloging-in-Publication Data
Names: Gerth, Holley, author.
Title: 365 truths for every woman's heart : a daily devotional of encouragement and prayer / Holley Gerth.
Other titles: Three hundred sixty five truths for every woman's heart
Description: Grand Rapids, Michigan : Revell, a division of Baker Publishing Group, [2024] | Includes bibliographical references.
Identifiers: LCCN 2023053815 | ISBN 9780800738556 (cloth) | ISBN 9781493447183 (ebook)
Subjects: LCSH: Women—Religious life—Christianity. | Devotional calendars.
Classification: LCC BV4527 .G4653 2024 | DDC 248.8/43—dc23/eng/20240207
LC record available at https://lccn.loc.gov/2023053815

Interior design by Jane Klein
Cover design by Mumtaz Mustafa

Portions of this book have previously appeared in *You're Already Amazing* (Revell, 2012), *You're Made for a God-Sized Dream* (Revell, 2013), *You're Going to Be Okay* (Revell, 2014), *What Your Heart Needs for the Hard Days* (Revell, 2014), *You're Loved No Matter What* (Revell, 2015), *Hope Your Heart Needs* (Revell, 2018), and *Strong, Brave, Loved* (Revell, 2019).

24 25 26 27 28 29 30   7 6 5 4 3 2 1

Introduction

Then you will know the truth, and the truth will set you free. (John 8:32)

You are loved.

You're going to be okay.

Your future is secure no matter what happens.

What truth does your heart need to hear from God today? Perhaps it's one of these or another you'll discover in the pages ahead as you spend time growing closer to him.

You can read one devotional per day or use this book as a reference you turn to whenever you need a reminder of what's true. Each day's reading also has a Scripture, prayer, and reflection question to help you apply what you read. You can go through this book on your own or invite others in your life to join you.

Each devotional will only take about five minutes to complete. That's enough to start replacing lies with truth, strengthening your heart, and helping you find the deeper joy and purpose you sometimes long for in your life.

Are you ready for the truth to set you free in new ways, starting today? Here's my prayer for you as we begin . . .

God, I pray you will bring hope and encouragement to the one reading these words right now. Guide her on this journey, and give her heart exactly what she needs on each page. You love her so much, and I pray that she would know that in a deeper way every day.

GOD WANTS TO SPEAK TO YOUR HEART

In the beginning God created the heavens and the earth.... And God said, "Let there be light," and there was light." (Genesis 1:1, 3)

The God who spoke the world into being wants to speak to *your* heart today. With so many voices competing for your attention, he is inviting you to take a few moments to be still and listen.

When pressure tells you to try harder, God reminds you that you're already accepted.

When insecurity says you're not enough, God reassures you that you're deeply loved.

When fear whispers you can't handle what's ahead, God promises to take care of you.

God said, "Let there be light," and he is still saying "Let there be . . ." in your life. Let there be peace. Let there be hope. Let there be grace. Let there be light in your darkest places, in your most difficult moments. He will bring his best for you into being.

God welcomes you into his presence just as you are right now. His voice is one of compassion, not criticism. He will speak only life-giving words to you. He calls you by name. He knows your desires. He understands your needs.

You're not here by chance; this moment is a divine invitation into deeper intimacy with the one who joyfully created you. His Word is forever true, and he has so much to say to you.

God, I love you and I want to listen to your voice above all others each day.

. . . .

What's one truth your heart needs to hear?

Day 2

GOD IS WATCHING OVER YOU

The Lord will protect your coming and going
both now and forever. (Psalm 121:8 CSB)

As I wait for my flight, I watch the parade of people. Where have they come from? Where are they going?

I realize all over again in that moment God knows the answers. He sees every detail of our lives. He's been with us in every step we've ever taken. This reassures me because no human knows what's ahead. There are certain to be blessings and moments of happiness. There will also be hard days and shed tears.

God will watch over it all. Every coming and going. Every beginning and end. Every dream come true and heartbreak. He has done this for all of history. He is doing so today. He will continue to do so every day of your life.

Here are three certain things about your future:

1. God will be there.
2. You will be loved.
3. Nothing will be too much for you and Jesus to overcome together.

You may not know exactly what's ahead of you, but you can be certain of who is with you. You are not a random passenger, nameless and unknown in the crowd of humanity. The one who travels with you isn't afraid of your tears, overwhelmed by your struggles, or hesitant about entering into your happiness and celebrations.

We are beloved children of the God who breathed life into our lungs and who numbers every hair on our heads. So let's go boldly into the next moment with the confidence that all things are possible and that, in the end, all will be made right.

God, thank you for watching over all the hellos and goodbyes,
highs and lows, comings and goings in my life.

. . . .

Where are you going with God today?

YOU CAN HAVE HOLY CONFIDENCE

> *Bring my sons from afar*
> *And my daughters from the ends of the earth—*
> *everyone who is called by my name,*
> *whom I created for my glory,*
> *whom I formed and made. (Isaiah 43:6–7)*

For years I tried to prove I was enough. Perfect enough. Good enough. Experienced enough. Smart enough. Pretty enough. But it's only when we come to the place where we can finally say, "I'm not enough but Jesus is" that our hearts get free.

The reality is we will always fall short of the expectations of others and ourselves. But it doesn't matter because our extraordinary God, our gracious Savior, declares we are beloved and chosen and empowered anyway.

The world tells us we need to have self-esteem, but what we really need is holy confidence.

Self-esteem says we can do anything we want.

Holy confidence says we can do all things through Christ.

Self-esteem says we can belong in the right crowd.

Holy confidence says we belong to the Creator of the universe.

Self-esteem says our worth comes from what's external.

Holy confidence says our worth comes from what's eternal.

We are daughters of God created in his image. We are chosen to be part of his plan. We are promised that we will have everything we need for all he has called us to do. We have been forgiven and set free. This is the source of our hope. This is our security. This is why in spite of our weaknesses and failures, we can walk in holy confidence today.

> *God, thank you for offering me so much more than self-esteem.*
> *Help me walk in holy confidence today.*
>
> ....
>
> What helps you have holy confidence?

IT'S OKAY IF YOU'RE NOT OKAY

In all these things we are more than conquerors through him who loved us. (Romans 8:37)

When we're having a tough day, we can feel as if we're failing. But really, we're just fighting hard. So remember this: you're doing better than you know, you're loved more than you can imagine, and you're going to get through whatever is in front of you today.

There is nothing you will face today that's bigger than your God. No problem. No struggle. No opposition. He can't be defeated, and therefore you can't be defeated either. Yes, there may be some battles. You may even be wounded. But you will not be overcome.

He's in the hospital room when the test results come. He's in the meeting when the announcement is made. He's in your living room when the person you love slams the front door and walks into the night.

He's there in the middle of it all, standing with you on the battlefield, promising you that the war isn't over, that the enemy will not win in the end.

It's okay to let the tears stream down your face, to pound your fists against your pillow, to feel tired or sad or confused. In the middle of it all, hold tightly to what's true and refuse to let anyone or anything take it from you.

You're not weak; you're a warrior fighting a hard battle.

Your story isn't done; God is still doing a good work in your life.

It's not over; you're an overcomer with hope and a future.

God, give me the strength to keep fighting, the courage never to give up, and the faith to stand firm no matter what happens.

. . . .

How have you been a warrior who's fighting hard?

YOU'RE LOVED ANYWAY
AND ALWAYS

Nothing can ever separate us from God's love. (Romans 8:38 NLT)

I stand at the kitchen stove and stir butter around in a warm pan with a spoon. My mind feels mixed up too. I close my eyes and whisper the prayer I'm learning to cling to in these moments: "God, what do you want to say to my heart today?"

Usually a Scripture comes to mind. Sometimes I remember encouraging words from a wise friend. But this time a new phrase comes instantly: *I love you anyway.* Tears fill my eyes because it's exactly what I need to hear. My struggles sometimes make it seem as though God must be upset and far away. But he is still right there with me. And he is still for me.

When we battle depression, God loves us anyway.

When we fight anxiety, God loves us anyway.

When we mess up, God loves us anyway.

When we face doubts, God loves us anyway.

When we forget who we really are, God loves us anyway.

When we're weary, God loves us anyway.

Whatever we're struggling with today, God loves us anyway.

Do you ever have thoughts like *If people really knew all of me or what I'm going through, they might not love me the same?* Me too—it's such a human thing to do. But thankfully, it isn't true.

I carry my plate to the table and whisper, "God, help me truly believe I'm loved by you right now just as I am." My prayer is the same for you. May we be confident we're loved anyway. May we be certain we're loved always, especially today.

God, I'm so grateful that nothing can separate me from your love.

. . . .

What's a reminder of God's love in your life today?

GOD WILL LIFT YOU UP

But you, Lord, are . . . the One who lifts my head high. (Psalm 3:3)

We often go through life with our hearts downcast. We don't even have the energy to try anymore. We feel alone. And then God does something that's beyond our comprehension. He comes to us in infinite love and tenderness. *He lifts our heads.*

When we look down, it's usually because we're feeling shame, sadness, or insecurity. God wants to change all of that by reaching out to touch our lives and hearts. When someone lifts up your head, it's an invitation for eye contact. It's a way of clearly showing, "I see you. I'm here with you. I want to connect with you."

What else happens when we lift our heads? Our perspective changes. We may have been staring at the place where we feel stuck and the difficulties right in front of us. But when we look up, we can see God is in that place with us. We can even dare to look over his shoulder and catch a glimpse of the future he has for us. We know we're going to be okay.

Right in front of you is a Savior who wants to lift your head and heal your heart. Can you feel his touch and hear his voice? Both are full of love for you. Wherever you are today, he's with you.

*God, I trust that you see me, you understand,
and you know what I need.*

· · · ·

What's a recent time when you felt down and God lifted you up?

YOUR FAITHFULNESS IS ENOUGH

Well done, my good and faithful servant. (Matthew 25:21 NLT)

What does God see as success? *Faithfulness.*

This is not the answer our world would give. We'd be told fame or material possessions, staying young forever, or getting to sit at the cool table are markers of success. But in the Gospels, the master doesn't say, "Well done, my good and famous servant." He says, "Well done, my good and *faithful* servant."

Faithfulness doesn't make headlines. We're not likely to get awards, applause, or even an abundance of "likes" for it. But faithfulness is quietly, often invisibly, life altering and world changing.

If you're putting pressure on yourself today to do more, be more, achieve more, then pause and take a deep breath. *Just be faithful.* If you're comparing yourself to others in life or ministry and feel you're falling short, refocus on your own journey. *Just be faithful.* If you're striving for perfection and trying to make everyone happy, let go of those unrealistic demands. *Just be faithful.*

We don't need big resolutions. We don't need to check every item off our bucket list. We don't have to prove our worth. Instead, we can simply say, "Jesus, I will do what I can, where I am, in this moment to love you and others today. Then I will do it again tomorrow."

That's faithfulness.

That's powerful.

That's enough for a lifetime.

God, I ask for the courage and wisdom to simply do what I can, where I am, with what I have today.

. . . .

What's one small way you can love Jesus and others where you are, as you are, with what you have today?

YOU BELONG TO THE FATHER

You have always stayed by me, and everything I have is yours. (Luke 15:31 NLT)

The older son is busy working hard in the fields when his prodigal little brother shows up. It seems big brother is likely the striver and performer, the perfectionist of the family. He has done his part. He has sacrificed. He has held it all together.

He doesn't want to go inside the party celebrating the return of the prodigal. This is not the way he believes life works. In his world, you hustle for your worth. You trade effort for affection. You earn everything that's given to you.

So the older brother stands outside, alone. That's why what comes next is so beautiful to me. "His father came out and entreated him" (Luke 15:28 ESV). The word *entreated* means to ask someone earnestly. The father wants his son to come into the house, the place of belonging, into a space of grace.

Then the father calls the older brother "dear son" (v. 31 NLT). It is a reminder of his true identity. When we are hustling and working hard, we can so easily forget who we are and how much we're loved.

The father also says, "You have always stayed by me, and everything I have is yours" (v. 31 NLT). In other words, "Remember our relationship. Remember you have no reason to strive, nothing to prove."

The story ends, and we don't know if the older son ever chooses to go in. But I know this: today I'm stepping back into the house. Today I'm choosing to belong. Today I'm going to believe what the Father says to and about me.

*God, thank you for inviting me out of striving
and into your abundant grace.*

. . . .

How does your heart need grace today?

GOD'S PRESENCE
WILL GUIDE YOU

Whenever the cloud lifted from above the tent, the Israelites set out; wherever the cloud settled, the Israelites encamped. (Numbers 9:17)

I'm with two friends, and we're talking about seasons of transition. Tears come to my eyes as I say, "I don't know what's next." They nod in understanding. I've been walking through a challenging season, and certainty about the future eludes me.

One reason I've struggled with where I am is because I was taught God's path for me is like a straight line I must figure out and follow. If I deviate at all from it, then I'm out of his will. But in this season, someone else's unhealthy choices knocked me off the path I thought I was supposed to follow. Have you been there too?

This made me worry that somehow anything ahead would always be plan B, because hadn't plan A been destroyed? But in the conversation, I realized that the path of God for my life isn't about specific details. The path of God for my life is about his presence.

When the Israelites traveled to the promised land, God's presence was their personal GPS. When the cloud of his presence lifted from the tabernacle, they set out. When it stayed, they encamped. In other words, what mattered most was *going with God*.

I look at my friends again, take a deep breath, and speak the truth that's sustaining my soul: "I don't know 'what' but I do know 'Who' and that is enough for today."

God, thank you that the one constant in my life is your presence and what matters most is that wherever I go, you will be with me.

. . . .

How can you sense God's presence in your life in this season?

GOD HAS NOT FORGOTTEN YOU

In the course of time Hannah became pregnant and gave birth to a son. (1 Samuel 2:20)

Hannah longed for children, and yet her arms remained empty. When God finally granted her request, the child she became pregnant with grew up to be Samuel, one of the greatest prophets to serve Israel.

Scripture says about Hannah, "The Lord remembered her" (1 Sam. 1:19). Surely God hadn't ever forgotten Hannah or her request! When I looked deeper into the Hebrew meaning of the word *remembered*, I discovered it more specifically means looking on someone with kindness and granting a request. We can feel forgotten too when it seems God isn't answering our prayers. But God is always aware of every detail of our lives.

I went through a season like Hannah when my husband and I struggled with infertility for almost a decade. We faced grief, losses, and hard questions that didn't seem to have answers. Several years into our journey, God placed a dream in our hearts to one day adopt an older child who'd had a difficult background or aged out of the foster system. He brought our daughter Lovelle to us when she was twenty, and she's been in our lives for almost a decade now. She got married not long after she met us and had two little ones, so we get to be Nana and Poppi too!

You and I have not been forgotten. God isn't ignoring our needs or waiting for us to be perfect before he answers our prayers. Instead he's working out his plans for us long before we ever catch a glimpse of what he's doing. We are remembered.

God, thank you for remembering me too and working out your plans for my life.

. . . .

How has God remembered you?

GOD HELPS YOU WITH STRESS

Peace be with you, dear brothers and sisters. (Ephesians 6:23 NLT)

Stress itself is neutral. We experience stress in hard times but also in positive situations like getting married, having a baby, being promoted at work, and moving to a new place. Stress is part of every worthwhile endeavor—from adjusting to change, to making a new friend, to winning an Olympic gold medal.

In other words, stress actually has a purpose. It points out what matters most to us. It helps us identify possible threats. It prepares us for action. *Our natural human stress response is God-given.* He hardwired it into our brains and bodies. We need it to survive.

But we're fallen, broken people in a fallen, broken world, and sometimes a response that's intended to be helpful becomes a hassle and a headache (literally). Thankfully, God also gives us what we need to manage our stress, to make it work for us rather than against us.

Understanding stress matters because stressed-out people often experience guilt or shame about the way they feel. Or they become determined to get rid of stress completely. But what we really need is to know how to make stress work for us, to keep it from wearing us out and bossing us around.

Think of your natural stress response like a wild horse. It can trample your yard and throw you into the dirt. But it can also be tamed. And when that happens, it has surprising potential to help you move forward in life. What makes the difference? *Who's in control.* God will help you show your stress who's boss.

God, you don't condemn me for experiencing stress; instead, you come alongside me to lead me back toward peace.

· · · ·

What have you been taught about stress that might not be true?

GOD WILL GIVE YOU PEACE

In peace I will lie down and sleep,
for you alone, LORD,
make me dwell in safety. (Psalm 4:8)

Hard days can tempt us to place our security where God never intended it to be. We grasp at money, relationships, or even self-reliance to make us feel safe. It's a human response to reach out for what's tangible and what seems like it will give us peace.

We try to find a way to stay standing. We want to hold on to what's in front of us with all our might. The psalmist offers us a different approach: "In peace I will lie down and sleep, for you alone, LORD, make me dwell in safety" (Ps. 4:8).

In other words, release control. Realize that you can't keep yourself safe. You can't fix this problem. You can't be strong enough on your own. Next time you want to stay up and strive, lie down in peace instead. It's a strange paradox. It's often in the moments when we feel weakest and most vulnerable that God exerts his strength on our behalf.

Lay your head on his chest. Tell him you're afraid and weary. Tell him what you need. Then let your heart rest. You are in God's care, and your security is with him—the one who will never let you go, who can keep you through the darkest night until the dawn.

God, please help me rest in you. Hold me close and fill me
with peace in the way only you can.

· · · ·

What's worrying you right now, and how do you need God's help?

YOUR FAILURE CAN BE SUCCESS

When I am weak, then I am strong. (2 Corinthians 12:10)

"Go to failure." I tilt my head in confusion. I'm being instructed to *fail*? I'm used to hearing encouragement to push for success. But in this scenario, failure *is* success.

I'm standing in front of a bar with weights on each end. I'm supposed to lift them, do a squat, add more weight, and repeat the process until I find the maximum I can lift. Why? Because my "failure point" today is the starting place for growth tomorrow. Once I know what I can handle, I can start improving from there.

Think of a heavy situation in your life. You gave it everything you had. You used all your strength. You dug deep and pushed hard. Then at some point you gave out, you just couldn't do any more. You likely saw that moment of feeling weak as a failure. But it was *success*. You chose to "go to failure," which means you made every effort.

After we "go to failure" it's time to pause for recovery. We can ask, "What worked well and what do I want to do better next time?" Then we try again—and eventually we fail again. This isn't a reason to criticize ourselves; it's a reason to say, "I'm growing. I'm getting stronger. I'm making progress."

Success is not the absence of failure; it's the presence of perseverance in the face of it. The moments when you feel weakest are often the ones when God is most able to work in your life.

*God, give me the courage to "go to failure" and
the wisdom to see the success in doing so.*

. . . .

When have you "failed" in a way that made you stronger?

YOUR WAITING TIME ISN'T WASTED

> *Wait for the Lord;*
> *be strong and take heart*
> *and wait for the Lord. (Psalm 27:14)*

Each year pairs of geese create nests by the ponds in our neighborhood. I'm amazed by how the mamas faithfully stay on their nests day after day even when it seems like nothing is happening. They sit through storms, wind, and the heat of the sun. They are wise enough to know that soon all of that stillness and waiting will be worth it.

Some seasons in our lives feel like this too. We want to see results. We want to hurry the process. But because God never wastes anything, there is great value in where you are right now.

Sometimes what we see as wasted time is actually the training ground for what God has in store for us. The lessons we learn and the obstacles we overcome equip us for growth and prepare us for how God wants to use us next.

There are so many times in his plan when what looks like "wasted time" is actually necessary for preparation or part of a greater purpose. Jesus being a carpenter, Moses in the desert, Sarah not becoming pregnant until late in her life—all are examples of God working in the delays.

Right now you may feel frustrated or stuck. But God won't let any hurt or hard time go unused. He is working, even now, to use all of your circumstances in ways you can't yet see.

God, help me to trust that you are working in each moment, redeeming everything in my life, turning my future into what you want it to be.

· · · ·

How might God be working in your life in ways
you can't fully see yet?

JESUS WILL QUENCH YOUR THIRST

The water I give them will become in them a spring of water welling up to eternal life. (John 4:14)

The Samaritan woman's thoughts are interrupted by a man's voice. "Will you give me a drink?" She knows by his accent that he's Jewish. His people and hers don't mix.

But he says something that grabs her attention: "Everyone who drinks this water will be thirsty again, but whoever drinks the water I give them will never thirst" (John 4:13).

This is what we all want, isn't it? To never be thirsty again. She reveals the hope tucked away in her drained-dry heart: "I know that Messiah is coming" (v. 25). She doesn't expect his reply: "I, the one speaking to you—I am he" (v. 26).

It's the first time Jesus has ever revealed his true identity to anyone. And the woman who went to the well as an outcast suddenly becomes a chosen messenger. She hurries back to town and extends a surprising invitation: "Come, see a man who told me everything I ever did. Could this be the Messiah?" (v. 29).

I like to imagine the Samaritan woman listening to Jesus with the crowd of people from her town. The sun is still high in the sky, but she now has a smile on her face. Perhaps a man taps her on the shoulder and offers her a cup of water with a wink. This time she has a different response. She can finally say along with all those who have found soul satisfaction in Jesus, "No, thanks—I have everything I need."

God, thank you for being the one who satisfies my soul thirst.

. . . .

What are you thirsty for today that Jesus can give you?

JESUS IS THE AUTHOR
OF YOUR STORY

Looking unto Jesus the author and finisher of our faith. (Hebrews 12:2 KJV)

In our modern world, *author* has limited connotations. It's used almost exclusively for those of us who write professionally in some way. I dug deeper and discovered "an author is a person who starts or creates something (such as a plan or idea)."[1]

Jesus is not only the author; he is also the finisher. This resonates with me because it means no matter what happens, he is the only one who can put "The End" on the final page of this world. But even then it will not truly be the end. It will only be the beginning of another, even better story—one that goes on forever with us and with him.

When I think of Jesus as the author in this way, something inside me gives a sigh of relief. Because it means I don't have to hold the pen of my own life, and I can be certain of the One who does. I know he is good and faithful. I know he is wise and kind. I know he is untamable and victorious always. He is not a careless creator. He will take care of every syllable and sentence, every dash and comma.

We are not random scribbles on a page. We are not notes jotted down, then crumpled up and tossed away. "We are God's masterpiece" (Eph. 2:10 NLT).

He is not finished with history yet. He is not finished with our stories either.

God, you are the author behind the story of everything, and you live in me. I give you the pen of my life today.

. . . .

How do you see God's hand in your story?

GOD EMPOWERS YOU

"You will not succeed by your own strength or by your own power. The power will come from my Spirit," says the Lord of heaven's armies. (Zechariah 4:6 ICB)

In the past, the strategy I've usually decided on in tough moments can be summed up in six words: *Be good. Do more. Try harder.* I convince myself that if I'm perfect and hustle enough and make things happen, then somehow it will all turn out okay. But this strategy has been failing me. I think of a recent evening when I went to bed feeling worn and weary.

Sometime past midnight I woke up in the dark and words from Zechariah 4:6 came to my heart: "You will not succeed by your own strength or by your own power." I'd been acting like everything depended on me, but it wasn't about my strength, power, or ability to make anything happen.

When I looked up the verse the next morning, I noticed it ends this way: "says the Lord of heaven's armies." I'd been worried because I thought the battle was completely up to me. And all the while I had the Lord of heaven's armies willing to fight on my behalf.

Whatever you're facing today, you don't have to handle it on your own either. It's not about our effort; it's about the faithful, unstoppable force of our God. We are his beloved daughters. We are more than conquerors. Nothing is too difficult for us because nothing is impossible for the God within us. *He will do it.*

God, I ask for your Spirit to empower me today in ways beyond what I can see.

. . . .

What have you been trying to do in your own strength that you need God's power for today?

GOD WILL MEET YOU
WHERE YOU ARE TODAY

Then the Lord God called to the man, "Where are you?" (Genesis 3:9 NLT)

After Adam and Eve eat the forbidden fruit, God doesn't abandon them. In his great tenderness, he asks them a question, "Where are you?" Adam responds, "I heard you walking in the garden, so I hid. I was afraid because I was naked" (Gen. 3:9–10 NLT).

We've been responding in similar ways ever since. We may not do so physically, but we hide emotionally. We pretend we're okay. We're fine, just fine. We hold it together on the outside while on the inside we're falling apart.

Author and researcher Brené Brown says, "Shame hates it when we reach out and tell our story. . . . It can't survive being shared. Shame loves secrecy. The most dangerous thing to do after a shaming experience is hide or bury our story."[1] God goes looking for us because he doesn't want us to stay in our shame. He wants to be in it with us because he's relentlessly for us.

God is asking you today, *Where are you?* No matter the answer, he already knows. What he's really asking is *Are you ready to let me meet you where you are today?* God wants to free you from shame, deliver you from fear, and bring you to a new place of freedom. He's calling to your heart even now. He loves you even in every moment. It's time to come out of hiding.

God, I'm so grateful you want to meet me where I am today.

· · · ·

Where is your heart today?

GOD IS THE STRENGTH
OF YOUR HEART

My flesh and my heart may fail,
but God is the strength of my heart
and my portion forever. (Psalm 73:26)

Even on our worst days we are daughters of God. We are more than conquerors. We can't be defeated. We are women of destiny with a power within us greater than we can even imagine.

One of the greatest victories we can win for our heavenly Father is to refuse to live in insecurity. Oh, we call it "humility," but I think that may be just another deception of the enemy. True humility—the kind Jesus demonstrated—is fully knowing who we really are and then choosing to love and serve from that place. And holy confidence is an act of war against the enemy of our hearts.

We're beautifully dangerous women when we know deep down we're loved. Because then we have the kind of courage that changes the world one heart at a time.

We are significant threats when we understand we have valuable gifts within us. Because then we actually dare to offer them.

We are wild warriors when we realize we are stronger and braver than we've yet to see. Because then we stop cowering and start swinging our swords.

So let's stop beating ourselves up and instead start beating the real opponent. Let's walk in truth and boldness. Let's carry ourselves like the beloved, strong, fiercehearted daughters of a mighty King. The enemy already knows who we really are—let's make sure we truly do too.

God, you are my strength, the source of my identity,
and my hope for the future.

. . . .

What's really true about you today?

YOU CAN MAKE A NEW START

For the LORD your God is God in heaven above and on the earth below.
(Joshua 2:11)

These words in Joshua 2:11 are spoken by Rahab, a prostitute in a pagan land who becomes part of the story of God's people. She protects Israelite spies who are gathering information before a battle against her city. She says, "Swear to me by the LORD that you will show kindness to my family, because I have shown kindness to you" (2:12). Rahab and the spies make a plan for her to hang a scarlet rope from the window to identify her home (a symbol many scholars believe foreshadows the blood of Christ).

Rahab's story in the book of Joshua ends with, "and she lives among the Israelites to this day" (6:25).

Although a former prostitute and a gentile, Rahab found grace and acceptance with the people of Israel. Because she dared to believe life could be different, Rahab the prostitute became the mother-in-law of Ruth, the great-grandmother of King David, and one of the only women named in the lineage of Jesus (Matt. 1:5–6). The scarlet cord she stretched out her window reached through generation after generation and still gives us hope today. No matter where we come from or what we have done, God is always willing to give us a new beginning and a place in his extraordinary, eternal plan.

God, thank you for welcoming all people to come to you.

· · · ·

How does it help you to know God chooses
and uses unexpected people?

GOD WANTS TO FILL YOU UP

"My food," said Jesus, "is to do the will of him who sent me and to finish his work." (John 4:34)

I walk through the door bone weary, head throbbing, searching for the nearest flat surface so I can sink into silence. I feel depleted, drained, tired in a way that makes my heart echo with emptiness.

On another day I walk through the door worn out but not worn down, ready for a nap but also ready to get up and go for it again, smiling even through the physical fatigue that tugs at every part of my body. My energy tank is empty but my heart is full.

One task depleted me—like a sugar crash after too much junk food. The other filled me up—like a satisfying meal that makes you lean back in your chair and sigh with new strength. Here's the catch: both looked like great opportunities on the outside. But one was not for me.

What God truly has for us to do on this earth will fill us up deep inside. Oh, yes, we will get tired sometimes along the way. We will have struggles and face obstacles. But what he has for us is not meant to leave us continually empty.

Be careful if you're working hard "for God" and your heart feels hungry all the time. Stop and ask him, "Is this really, truly what you have for me? Have I taken in or taken on something you never intended?" God offers something better than a busy, full life. He offers life to the full.

God, give me the wisdom to know what you truly have for me to do.

· · · ·

What fills you up (even if it's hard and tiring sometimes)?

Day 22

GOD WILL HELP YOU PERSEVERE

Endurance develops strength of character. (Romans 5:4 NLT)

Have you ever taken steps only to find yourself stalled, detoured, or behind? When we begin something, we picture the path in our mind and it is perfect. No delays. No obstacles. No setbacks. But that is never how moving forward works.

The real path, the one that will actually get us where we want to go, is always harder than we imagined, slower than we hoped, and longer than we first planned.

When we realize this, it's easy to be discouraged. "Things aren't the way they should be," we tell ourselves. But this is the way things always are in a world that's imperfect. It doesn't mean we've done anything wrong. It isn't proof that we won't get there. It's not a sign to stop.

What needs to be adjusted isn't our plans—it's our expectations. Keep the dream, chase the goal, go for it with all your heart. Just know that it's going to look different from the perfect vision in your mind. When it does, adjust accordingly and then take the next small step.

If you are not where you thought you'd be now, it doesn't mean you're failing. It means you are trying to move forward in a place that is not heaven. What matters isn't perfection; it's perseverance.

Every path has its obstacles.

Every journey has its detours.

Every place worth going will be harder to get to than it first seems.

You're making more progress than you know. You're so much closer than you can see. You're going to get there right on time.

God, you are the one who empowers me to persevere.
Help me keep moving forward today.

. . . .

What is the next step God is asking you to take today?

YOU ARE LIVING IN THE IN-BETWEEN

*Then I saw a new heaven and a new earth, for the old heaven and
the old earth had disappeared. (Revelation 21:1 NLT)*

As I drive, my thoughts zip down a two-lane road in my mind. In one lane,
I'm thanking God for answered prayers and desires granted. In the other
lane, I'm feeling frustrated that my day-to-day reality doesn't always line up with
the magnificent vision I have in mind. I long to see a sign from God that one day
those two lanes will merge. When will that finally happen?

It seems God has an answer for me. Um, heaven.

Oh, right. I should have seen that one coming.

We live in a paradox. We are not home yet. And on the journey to where we're
going, what we can dream up and what actually unfolds in our lives are never
going to align perfectly.

If we demand that our perfect vision be fulfilled, then we will never be satisfied. Not with our dreams. Not with our marriage. Not with our job. Not with
our church. Not with ourselves.

What can we do to avoid that? First, we can accept that we will live between
those two lanes all of our lives here on earth: the ideal and the real, the eternal
and the everyday. Then we intentionally thank God for what's less than perfect,
and at the same time we keep pressing toward the vision he's placed in our
hearts.

We live in the paradox. We release our expectations and yet we continue
to look to the future with expectation. One mile, one day, one dream at a time.
Yes, all the way home.

God, help me live with both gratitude and hopeful expectation today.

. . . .

What are you grateful for and what are you hoping for today?

YOU CAN TAKE TIME TO HEAL

O LORD, if you heal me, I will be truly healed. (Jeremiah 17:14 NLT)

I'm sitting cross-legged on the floor like a kindergartner, talking to Jesus and telling him how overwhelmed I feel. Inside, words reverberate through me . . . *Bigger. Better. More.*

In other seasons, words like these might have felt motivating. But in this one, they feel like a weight I don't have the strength to carry. But isn't this what is expected of me?

Then these words come to my heart: *This isn't a season for growth. This is a season for healing.*

I inwardly feel the weight drop from my shoulders and soul. Yes, that's exactly it. Some seasons are for expanding, climbing, doing more. Other seasons are for turning inward, recovering, being made whole again.

If you are in a season of healing rather than a season of growth today, that is okay. It's more than okay; it's beautiful and necessary. Without healing, we won't be ready for what's next. Without healing, we'll limp when we could be soaring. Without healing, what we're called to do isn't sustainable for a lifetime.

If we need to heal, it doesn't mean we've failed—it means we are humans living in a fallen world. Things happen. Hearts break. Relationships falter. Mistakes get made. Battles are fought. Needing healing is nothing to be ashamed of; instead it's a tender invitation from the heart of one who loves us enough to not let us live in pain.

There will be other seasons. There will be growth again. For now, slow down and settle in. Let the healing begin.

God, give me wisdom to know when it's a season for growth
and when it's a season for healing.

. . . .

How is God healing you?

YOU'RE WORTH THE WORK

Jesus replied, "My Father is always working, and so am I." (John 5:17 NLT)

I've talked with many women who have believed this lie: "I'm not worth the work." I've been there too. How about you?

Maybe someone who should have seen you chose to look away. Maybe someone who should have been there decided not to stay. Maybe someone picked harmful habits over healing, and your heart was collateral damage. Maybe you were blamed, avoided, neglected, overlooked, or abandoned.

Do not let someone's unwillingness to do their work be a reflection of your worth. Your worth comes not from the responses of others but from who God says you are. God did the work for you—he came to a manger, died on a cross, and rose again.

God pursues you. God cherishes you. God sacrifices for you. God endures discomfort for you. Love does the work—even when it's hard.

Here's what the Jesus who loves you says today: *You are worth the work.* He left heaven and came to earth for you. He showed up. He endured the discomfort. He faced the difficulties. He cried salty tears and sweat drops of blood for you. He knows you fully and loves you completely. He will never blame, avoid, neglect, overlook, or abandon you.

Your worth is not defined by the way someone else's brokenness might have made you feel.

Your worth is defined by your maker. It is declared by your Savior. It is secure forever, and no one can take it from you.

You are worth the work today—you always have been, you always will be.

God, thank you for all the work you have done on my behalf and the worth you have given me.

· · · ·

How has God worked in your life?

Day 26

YOU ARE A CITIZEN OF HEAVEN

We are citizens of heaven, where the Lord Jesus Christ lives. And we are eagerly waiting for him to return as our Savior. (Philippians 3:20 NLT)

My husband and I recently visited Canada for a few days. Imagine if we had stepped into a coffee shop and the baristas had asked, "Who are you?" and I had answered, "I'm a Canadian, y'all." They would have taken one look at my touristy tennis shoes and listened to my Southern accent, then shook their heads in bemused disagreement.

I imagine you would do the same because you understand this: there's a difference between a visitor and a citizen. And "we are citizens of heaven," declares the apostle Paul (Phil. 3:20). Your circumstances may change, but who you truly are remains forever the same. Your identity is eternally secure in Christ.

What words have you been using to describe who you are based on where you are in life right now? Stressed? Depressed? Alone? Whatever comes to mind is where you are, not who you are. It's your current location. To help shift your perspective, rework those words as phrases that show they aren't part of your identity. For example, "I'm going through a stressful time right now" or "I have experienced a divorce."

Once you know who you're not, it's time to ask God one of the most important questions of all: "Who am I?" Perhaps there's no more important time for seeking these answers than when we're in the middle of a bad day or a hard season. We lean into God's heart and ask, "Who am I *in spite of this*? Tell me what's true about me no matter what happens."

*God, nothing that happens to me in this life
can change who you say I am.*

. . . .

Who does God say you are?

YOU HAVE A PURPOSE

I cry out to God Most High,
to God who will fulfill his purpose for me. (Psalm 57:2 NLT)

When life comes along and slaps us silly, it can feel as if God's purpose for us has now been canceled. But nothing can stop his purposes for us. Scripture is full of stories in which people found themselves in difficult circumstances that turned out to be part of God's mysterious plan.

Joseph's brothers sold him into slavery because of their jealousy. Then his master's wife falsely accused him, and he landed in prison. But God acted on his behalf, and he ended up second in command of the whole country, which enabled him to save the lives of God's people during a famine.

Esther got drafted into the royal harem along with hundreds of other women. Taken away from everything she knew, she had one shot to win the king's favor. She did so and became the next queen, which eventually gave her the opportunity to rescue the Jewish people from a wicked man's plot.

Jesus himself faced death on a cross, which seemed like the ultimate defeat. Instead of being welcomed as Savior, he experienced betrayal, mistreatment, and abandonment. Yet three days later, he victoriously and joyfully rose again to rescue us all from death.

God's purpose for you *will* prevail. In all of history, no person has ever been able to thwart God's ultimate plan. He isn't shocked by the brokenness of this world or even by your personal failures. He can redeem and reroute as much as is needed to get you to the destination he has in mind.

God, thank you that nothing and no one can destroy
your purpose for me.

· · · ·

How have you seen God work out his purpose for you?

YOU HAVE HOPE
AND A FUTURE

"For I know the plans I have for you," says the LORD. *"They are plans for good . . . to give you a future and a hope." (Jeremiah 29:11 NLT)*

God chose for you to be here at this moment. He's watching over your life with love. He's sending others to encourage you. Even now he's working out his good plan for your life. What's ahead for you will not be a surprise to him.

On the days when life is hard, he will give you strength.

In the times that are happy, he will rejoice with you.

Even in the middle of what seems ordinary, he will do extraordinary things.

The hairs on your head are all numbered. The cares in your heart are all known. You will never be alone. If it ever feels like that isn't true, come back to these words and let them remind you.

God's heart and character will never change. Nothing can separate you from his love. He is always with you and for you.

Your past is full of grace. Your future is full of hope. Your day is full of possibilities.

God, you are my Creator and the one who knows every detail of my life. I choose to trust you with my past, present, and future.

. . . .

What detail of your life do you want to entrust to God today?

YOU DON'T HAVE
TO CARRY SO MUCH

My yoke is easy to bear, and the burden I give you is light. (Matthew 11:30 NLT)

I'm sitting in a booth at a coffee shop with two friends. We're talking about what the future holds, where we'll go from here, and what we want to leave behind.

One friend says, "I've found new clarity about my purpose, and I'm going to let certain things go." She asks us to bear witness as she writes these distractions down, then tells us she's going to bury them in a degradable box in the ground. "I'm laying them to rest," she says.

What struck me was that nothing she wrote down was a *bad* thing, just a few professional hopes, goals, and dreams. They simply weren't the *best* things for her. We're allowed to pause and ask, "What feels heavy in my life that I might not have to carry anymore?"

I understand many things in life aren't optional. We all have our have-tos that can't be delegated or ignored. I'm talking about what weighs us down that God never asked us to pick up. Maybe it's a lie we've believed. Maybe it's a yes we said years ago out of guilt that we simply keep saying because we're afraid to stop. Maybe it's a dream that had its season, and now it's time to move on.

If you had a box like my friend, what would you put in it? What's one thing you'd like to bury and leave behind forever?

Each day is an opportunity to reset our souls, rethink our lives, and perhaps travel a little lighter than we did before.

God, thank you that your yoke is easy and your burden is light.

. . . .

What's weighing you down that you want to give to Jesus today?

YOU HAVE SOMETHING TO GIVE

A poor widow came and put in two very small copper coins, worth only a few cents. (Mark 12:42)

A widow steps into the temple court and takes in the familiar scene before her. The two small coins she's carried with her seem to burn into the palm of her hand. Who is she kidding? No one needs what she has to give. But this is an act of trust, love, and obedience. She is saying to God, "All I have, all I am is yours."

As she turns back, she sees she's not the only one who has been watching the offerings. A group of men are observing as well, and one with kind eyes gives her an understanding smile. She hears him say to those gathered around him, "Truly I tell you, this poor widow has put more into the treasury than all the others. They all gave out of their wealth; but she, out of her poverty, put in everything—all she had to live on" (Mark 12:43–44). Where has she seen him before? Oh, yes, this is Jesus! The one many believe to be the Messiah. He has noticed her. He has seen the sacrifice. He grasps the true value of what she's giving. Even if no one else understands, his affirmation somehow seems like enough.

The widow with two coins understood there's only one thing we can give to God that he doesn't already have: *our hearts*. That means we all have something valuable to offer. And with him, a little can be so much more than we see.

God, all I have and all I am is yours.

. . . .

What is God asking you to give him today?

GOD SEES EVERYTHING
IN YOUR LIFE

But God heard the boy crying, and the angel of God called to Hagar from heaven, "Hagar, what's wrong? Do not be afraid!" (Genesis 21:17 NLT)

Hagar, the Egyptian servant of Abraham, bore him a son when his wife, Sarah, couldn't conceive. Eventually, Sarah demands that Hagar and Ishmael leave.

Hagar wanders in the desert. When her water is gone, she places Ishmael in the only bit of shade she can find. She sits down a short distance away and cries.

"But God *heard the boy crying*, and the angel of God called to Hagar from heaven, 'Hagar, what's wrong? Do not be afraid!'" This verse doesn't say, "God heard Hagar crying." He knows Hagar's tears aren't her greatest concern; instead, it's the pain of her son.

As Hagar listens to God, her perspective shifts. Then God opens Hagar's eyes. She sees a well full of water, quickly fills her water container, and gives the boy a drink. From a human viewpoint, there is no way out of this situation. But when Hagar sees circumstances and the people she loves as God does, everything changes.

When we're anxious about those we love, it feels as if their well-being depends on us. We have to keep them safe. We have to ensure they make the right choices. We need to control what happens. But the story of Hagar and Ishmael reminds us that God is ultimately in charge of those we love. He is their protector. He is their provider. He is the one who will meet them in the dry, desert places where there seems to be no hope.

God, thank you for loving the people in my life even more than I do.

. . . .

When have you seen God take care of someone you love?

YOU CAN THINK BEYOND FIGHT-OR-FLIGHT

Let God transform you into a new person by changing the way you think. (Romans 12:2 NLT)

The fight-or-flight response is the brain's natural reaction when we experience a threat. But are fight and flight really our only options? Thankfully, no. Our brains have two other responses to stress that can prove much more helpful.

The first is the challenge response. Think of a time when you were afraid but also determined to take action. Examples would include an athlete before a big game, a presenter preparing to give a speech, or a parent handling a crisis involving their child. The difference in the challenge response is that we tell ourselves "I've got this" or, as believers, "I've got this because God's got me."

Making a plan or asking ourselves, "What's one helpful action I can take right now?" helps our brains move into the challenge response.

The second alternative our brains have to stress is called tend-and-befriend. We see this during any disaster when the helpers appear. When we assist others, our brains release oxytocin, which is sometimes called the cuddle hormone. It bonds us to others, and it's good for us personally; it can literally strengthen our hearts. Asking, "Who can I help right now?" helps shift our brains out of fight-or-flight mode.

We all experience fight-or-flight response, but we don't have to stay in it. God takes care of the birds and flowers outside my window. He also takes care of us—including giving us remarkable, adaptable brains.

God, thank you for giving me a brain that can respond and adapt in many ways to whatever happens.

. . . .

What's a time when you chose the challenge or tend-and-befriend response?

YOU DON'T HAVE TO BE "GOOD ENOUGH"

When I tried to keep the law, it condemned me. So I died to the law—
I stopped trying to meet all its requirements—so that I might live
for God. (Galatians 2:19 NLT)

One morning I realize that to be "good enough" by my own standards I would have to be perfect. I am not perfect. I never have been. I never will be on this side of eternity. The same is true for you. We need a solution besides trying harder, and Paul offers one in Galatians 2:19.

Paul is writing these words to people who have been trying to be good enough too. He is telling them what I've come to see: I will never meet the impossible standard of perfection. His answer is not to pat them on the back and tell them they're nice people anyway. No, his response really comes down to two words— but Jesus.

I'm not good enough. But Jesus.

I fall and fail and make mistakes. But Jesus.

I didn't get everything right today. But Jesus.

What we need is not more self-esteem. We need to fully understand that our hope and identity and security rest only in our Savior—in what he did for us on the cross and through his resurrection and in who he says we are as a new creation.

Maybe your life could use a little more peace today too. What our hearts struggle with may be different, but who rescues us is the same. We are the beloved and this is our hope, our anthem, our heart-shout that rises above the wind within—but Jesus.

God, thank you that Jesus frees me from all condemnation
and sets me free to live in grace.

· · · ·

What do you need to say "but Jesus" to today?

YOU HAVE TIME

A time to cry and a time to laugh.
A time to grieve and a time to dance. (Ecclesiastes 3:4 NLT)

My counselor looks at me and says, "This is part of the grief process." She's repeated this numerous times over the past few months as I've worked through an unexpected loss in my life. She's said it when I've cried, gotten angry, felt joy, and circled back to all of those again.

Here's what I'm learning: as humans we want our stories to be neat and tidy, but that is not the way our hearts work. When a moment of sadness or anger hits me, I often think, *I don't have time for this!* But wise Solomon said there is a time for everything.

To heal well, to live fully, we need to make time to cry and time to laugh, time to grieve and time to dance. If we cry and grieve but never let ourselves feel joy, we'll end up depressed and weary. If we only give ourselves time to laugh and dance, we'll miss out on the healing and comfort that harder moments bring. Someone once told me that when we refuse to experience negative emotions, we limit our ability to feel positive ones too.

We serve a God who knows what it's like to live on this earth, who wept at the tomb of a friend and turned water into wine at a wedding. He experienced loss and deep love, died on a cross and rose again. We will have highs and lows, ups and downs, tragedies and triumphs too. There is a time for all of them.

God, help me to make time for whatever is
most needed in my life today.

. . . .

What do you need to make time for in your life today?

YOU CAN HAVE TRUE CONFIDENCE

Now faith is confidence in what we hope for. (Hebrews 11:1)

My husband reads those ancient words still alive today. I hold my hand up for him to pause. "Wait," I say, "read that part again." I think in my non-morning-person fogginess I must have heard it wrong. He repeats, "Faith is confidence."

Huh. I heard right after all. But those words made me wonder what I hadn't been hearing at all for all my life. Of course faith is the secret of confidence. Why had I never made the connection before?

I tend to think of faith as external while confidence comes from within. But isn't that where faith really comes from too? From our hearts and the one who dwells within them?

I sit back on the couch, cross my pajama-pant-covered legs, sip my coffee. It feels like a big moment. Because this changes everything. It means not only that I can be confident but also, if it's part of faith, that I'm commanded to be confident.

Confidence isn't prideful. In the kingdom of God, it's actually a synonym for humility. The very act of faith means bowing our hearts to another, and only the humble can do so.

I can be confident. You can be confident.

We can walk through this world with heads and hearts held high as daughters of the King (who wear pajama pants and don't get up on time and are beautifully messy inside and out). Yes, just as we are.

Will you join me? Let's say together that we will dare to live with faith, confidence, and joy. Right here. Right now. And forever.

---

*God, thank you that true confidence comes from trusting in you.
I choose to do so today.*

. . . .

How does your faith help you have confidence?

GOD IS WORKING
ON YOUR BEHALF

You intended to harm me, but God intended it all for good. (Genesis 50:20 NLT)

Betrayed by his brothers, sold into slavery, wrongfully imprisoned—Joseph's life is filled with hardship. But God continues to guide Joseph, and he not only becomes a powerful ruler but sees his family restored.

When we experience hard circumstances, anxiety tries to lie to us. It tells us, "Things are bad, and they're only going to get worse." Maybe anxiety whispers, "You can't handle this." Or it accuses us, "If your faith was stronger, then you wouldn't be going through this right now."

Joseph certainly had reason to believe these lies. He could have listened to anxiety and become hopeless. Instead, he chose to see God's hand even in the most difficult places.

Joseph took heart by continuing to trust that God was at work even when all the outward evidence seemed to indicate otherwise. He saw beyond what was possible from a human perspective and believed God would get him through whatever came.

Because Joseph persevered, God used him to save the lives of thousands of people, including his family. What seemed like pointless pain served a greater purpose. Whatever you're going through today, whatever anxiety is trying to say, God is still working in your life. Even when you can't yet see his hand, he's accomplishing his good plan to give you hope and a future.

God, thank you for working all things together for good in my life.

. . . .

What's a hard circumstance in your life that God used for good?

GOD'S COMMANDS
CAN BE DELIGHTFUL

Trouble and distress have overtaken me,
but your commands are my delight. (Psalm 119:143 CSB)

I've thought of commands as measuring sticks held in the hands of harsh people. I've seen them as sources of shame and guilt. I've imagined them to be restrictive. But I've never thought of them as delightful. As I consider this, I realize I have been thinking of human rules that I've been told I must keep to be accepted. What the psalmist exclaims about instead are the commands that come from God's heart.

Someone once asked Jesus, "Which command in the law is the greatest?" (Matt. 22:36 CSB). The answer Jesus gave was all about loving God, others, and ourselves. With that context in mind, the psalmist isn't saying "Trouble and distress have overtaken me, but your rules are my delight." No, the meaning is more like "Trouble and distress have overtaken me, but your ways of love are my delight."

Finding joy in God's commands means remembering we're loved by him no matter our circumstances or struggles. And choosing to extend that love to those around us regardless of theirs. Even daring to love our messy, complicated selves in the middle of it all.

The ultimate goal of a command is connection. If God's commands have felt like a burden to you, a source of condemnation or shame, then perhaps you're ready for a different perspective too. Let's look at God's commands in a new way today—through the eyes of love.

God, your commands are my delight because they come from love.

· · · ·

What's a loving command from God that makes your life better?

YOUR HOME DOESN'T NEED TO BE PERFECT

Share with the Lord's people who are in need. Practice hospitality.
(Romans 12:13)

Lydia was a prominent businesswoman selling purple dye in Philippi. The author of Acts says, "She invited us to her home. 'If you consider me a believer in the Lord,' she said, 'come and stay at my house.' And she persuaded us" (16:15).

Lydia could have said something like . . .

"I have a guest room that looks like a page from a magazine. Come and stay at my house."

"I can whip up meals better than a chef at a fancy restaurant. Come and stay at my house."

"I have children who are going straight from kindergarten to college because they're so smart and well-behaved. Come and stay at my house."

Instead she simply says, "If you consider me a believer in the Lord, come and stay at my house." In other words, *what matters most about where I live is that the presence of Jesus is in it.* That's good news for us. It means we don't have to decorate beautifully, cook fantastically, and entertain effortlessly before we invite others into our space. (It also means we don't even need an actual house. A dorm room, apartment, high-rise building, hut, or wherever else God has us will work just fine too.)

True hospitality just means opening our homes the same way we open our hearts. Jesus dwells in both, and he'll take care of what matters most.

God, help me to practice hospitality in ways that reflect your heart.

. . . .

When has someone shown you hospitality?

YOU HAVE A FOREVER HOME

This world is not our home; we are looking forward to our everlasting home in heaven. (Hebrews 13:14 TLB)

Raindrops scatter across my windshield as I drive home from a speaking engagement, and the thoughts within my mind feel much the same. Questions haphazardly come: *Should I have said that? Was I helpful? How did it really go?*

I pull into my garage and the sound of the storm lessens. It seems a stillness begins to settle within me too. I picture the corner of my couch where I curl up to spend time praying. And these words come to my heart: *When all is said and done, I get to go home to Jesus.*

In the moment I mean that in the most literal way. I'm thinking of a cup of tea, a warm blanket, and time for him to bring my still-racing heart back to its usual rhythm. But I smile as I realize the words are true for eternity too. No matter what happens in this life, when all is said and done, we get to go home to Jesus.

I open the door of my house, and it seems to invite me in like an old friend. I find my quiet spot and take a deep breath. I close my eyes and all the questioning stops. I remember again that I am loved, not because of what I do but because of who I belong to.

The saying goes, "Home is where your heart is," but I find comfort in knowing home is also who is within my heart. As I whisper a prayer while the storm subsides, I know Jesus is there.

God, I'm so grateful that my ultimate destination is going home to you.

. . . .

What are you looking forward to in your forever home?

Day 40

GOD REMEMBERS YOU

God will never forget the needy;
the hope of the afflicted will never perish. (Psalm 9:18)

When life gets tough, we can feel as if God has forgotten us. We wonder if perhaps his schedule just got a bit busy. Maybe he placed us where we are and then got distracted by something else.

But none of those things are true. You serve a God who has the hairs on your head not only numbered but memorized. He knows the details of your life even better than you do. He never loses touch with your heart. And because of that, you can always have hope. Because even if you can't see what God is doing, you can trust he is already acting on your behalf. Nothing is too difficult for him. No challenge is too big. No detail is too small.

The opposite of forgetting is thinking of someone. And God is thinking of you. The God who spoke the world into being, who holds the stars in place, who sent his Son because he loved you so much is thinking of you. Right now. In this moment. In *every* moment.

Pause for a moment and let that reality take hold of your heart. You are not alone. You are not overlooked. You are not forgotten.

You never have been.

You never will be.

You are always on God's mind.

And he is always on your side.

God, thank you for thinking of me, remembering my needs,
and working to meet them even when I can't yet see or
understand what you're doing.

. . . .

Who is on your mind today, and how can you remind them
that God is thinking of them too?

GOD CAN HANDLE YOUR QUESTIONS

The angel of the LORD appeared to him and said, "Mighty hero, the LORD is with you!" (Judges 6:12 NLT)

This is a strange greeting, considering Gideon is hiding when he hears it. Gideon's response seems even stranger. He doesn't fall down in awe but launches into a series of questions. Gideon also says God has abandoned his people and handed them over to their enemies, and he asks for a sign.

So God zaps Gideon with a lightning bolt and picks someone else. The end.

Thankfully, that's not the way it goes. Instead, God does something interesting with anxious Gideon. He doesn't explain or defend himself. Instead, he keeps using "I" statements.

"I am sending you." (v. 14)

"I will be with you." (v. 16)

"I will stay here until you return." (v. 18)

God knows what Gideon needs most isn't information; it's knowing who he can trust even when there are no easy answers.

When we find ourselves in a place of fear like Gideon, we can bring God our concerns, hurts, worries, and the ways we wish things were different. He's a safe place for all our emotions and uncertainty. Then he says to us as he said to Gideon, "Go with the strength you have" (v. 14). Why? Because the strength we have is *his* strength. We may always question what's going on around us, but we can also always trust the One who lives within us.

God, give me the strength and courage to do what you are asking of me today.

. . . .

What worries do you want to give to God today?

Day 42

JESUS WILL FEED YOUR SOUL

Jesus declared, "I am the bread of life. Whoever comes to me will never go hungry." (John 6:35)

In John 6:1–15, with only five loaves and two small fish, Jesus provided a meal for thousands of people. He broke the bread, gave thanks, and satisfied a crowd with leftovers to spare.

Only a few verses later, he says, "I am the bread of life. Whoever comes to me will never go hungry." The statement is separate from the feeding scene. But the two stories are still connected, and when we look at them together we see a truth we all need to know: Jesus is enough for everyone. He is the bread broken and passed out to the hungry.

He doesn't act stingy and say, "Sorry, there's only enough of me for a few people." No, he tells everyone to come. He gives himself over and over again. He is a God not of scarcity but of abundance.

God has every hair on our heads numbered. He knows every care on our minds. He orchestrated our first breaths and will be there for our last. He knows the cravings and the longings and the emptiness inside every human heart, and he says, "Come and eat your fill."

He is not a God of soul starvation but of salvation. He is not cutting portions; he is passing out extra helpings. He is not giving us meager handouts; he is giving us his very self. And there is more than enough for us all.

God, I want to receive whatever it is you want to give me today, and most of all I want more of you.

. . . .

How do you need Jesus to feed your soul today?

YOU'RE NOT THE ONLY ONE

There is no condemnation for those who belong to Christ Jesus. (Romans 8:1 NLT)

This is the secret the enemy of our hearts would like all of us to believe: *you're the only one.* But, of course, *we're not the only one.* We're humans and this is the way of us. Trying to impress. Numbing our pain. Tending our secrets like a night garden. We do this out of guilt and shame. Shame is ultimately the belief that we are unlovable. And because of this, love is the only way to break shame.

Freedom begins with simply being willing to say, "This is where I've been. This is where I am today. This is where I hope, by the grace of God, to be tomorrow." It means admitting this first to ourselves, then to Jesus, and then with courage and discernment to at least one other being who has a beating, wandering heart like ours.

To heal, we risk the small, huge step of being honest. We embrace the awkward. We step off the pedestal. We share that we're not fine with a friend over coffee or shout and cry on our knees in front of the God who loves us as we are. We also celebrate unexpectedly and dance like no one's watching and throw the confetti at midnight. We embrace all the parts of our unexpected, mysterious, still-being-written story.

We do this because we understand that strong, brave, and loved sometimes looks like just the opposite.

And that's beautiful.

God, you know everything about me and you love me anyway.
Give me the courage to embrace my story,
even the parts I wish were different.

. . . .

Pause for a few moments and tell God how you really are today.

YOU WILL BE WITH GOD FOREVER

We will be with the Lord forever. (1 Thessalonians 4:17 NLT)

At the time I'm writing this, the life expectancy worldwide is seventy years for men and seventy-six for women.[1] This means we have, on average, about 27,740 days on this earth. Those days will start with a sunrise and end with a sunset, be filled with loving and working, laughter and tears, the cold of ice cream and the heat of summer.

Each day will also be filled with the presence of God. We tend to think of forever as something that starts when we get to heaven. But when God says he will be with us, he doesn't just mean in the then and there. He means in the here and now of every moment too.

Wherever you are right now as you're reading these words, God is with you.

Wherever you were in your darkest moment, God was with you.

Wherever you will be in your time of greatest joy, God will be with you.

When you took your first breath, God was there.

When you finally let go of this life, God is going to welcome you into the next.

Wherever you have been, wherever you are, wherever you will be—God is there too.

Forever is not something you have to wait for to begin. Forever is in the middle of your kitchen. It's in the grocery store. It's around the table. It's at your meeting. It's in the hug of someone you love. Forever is an endless river of God's presence, and we're already standing in it.

God, thank you that forever is already mine
and you are with me always.

· · · ·

How do you see glimpses of the eternal in your everyday life?

GOD ISN'T AFRAID OF THE DARK

God is light, and there is no darkness in him at all. (1 John 1:5 NLT)

God isn't afraid of the dark. He is not scared of the secret places in our hearts. The ones that haven't seen daylight for years. The kind with the locks on the doors. The sort that we don't say out loud or even fully admit to ourselves.

God isn't afraid of the dark. He is not running scared from the tragedies in our lives. He's not backing away from the brokenness and the bitterness and the shattered dreams. He's not intimidated by the monsters under our beds or inside our minds.

God isn't afraid of the dark. He's not avoiding the struggles or the addictions. He's not waving his hands in surrender to the enemies of our souls. He is not saying, "This is too much for me."

God isn't afraid of the dark. He isn't afraid to step right into it. Not afraid to even dwell in the middle of it. Because he is light and in him there is not darkness at all. This means darkness can surround him and he cannot be defeated or diminished by it.

God isn't afraid of the dark. In the beginning he spoke life-words into it and said, "Let there be light." Then he came as a baby into a midnight world and announced his arrival with a shining star. He conquered death in a dark tomb and rolled the stone away, making a way into the brightness for all of us.

God isn't afraid of the dark. This means we don't ever have to be either.

God, I'm so grateful that you bring light even to the darkest places in my life.

. . . .

Where do you need God to bring light in your life today?

Day 46

GOD WILL MAKE A WAY FOR YOU

The LORD himself will fight for you. Just stay calm. (Exodus 14:14 NLT)

The people of Israel are free. After generations of slavery, God has delivered them from the Egyptians through Moses. Then they hear an unmistakable sound in the distance—chariot wheels. The Egyptian army is coming for them.

Moses tells the people, "Don't be afraid. Just stand still and watch the LORD rescue you today. The Egyptians you see today will never be seen again. The LORD himself will fight for you. Just stay calm" (Exod. 14:13–14 NLT).

When anxiety tries to overcome us, we can follow Moses's example. Try going through the process Moses used with a situation that causes anxiety in your life.

1. Acknowledge your fear.
2. Slow down and take a deep breath.
3. Speak truth to your anxious heart.
4. Remember that the battle isn't yours.
5. Take one small step of obedience.

God then tells Moses to instruct the people to get going, which is interesting because he has just finished telling them to stand still. We can be still on the inside while taking helpful, obedient action on the outside.

Most of us have heard the story of what happens next. God parts the waters of the Red Sea and the Israelites walk through it. The outcome in our lives might not be as dramatic, but the truth of this story is the same: *God will make a way*. He will lead us out of anxiety and into peace. He will guide us beyond fear and into courage. He will replace our questions with the certainty of his unfailing love.

God, no circumstance is too challenging, no obstacle too big, no situation beyond your solutions.

. . . .

What situation does today's message apply to in your life right now?

NO GIANT IS TOO BIG FOR GOD

But if I win . . . then you will be our servants and serve us. (1 Samuel 17:9 CSB)

The words in 1 Samuel 17:9 are spoken by the giant Goliath in his showdown with David. This isn't a battle for territory, it's a battle for *freedom*. We, like the people of Israel, can be at risk of serving the giants in our lives. But it doesn't have to be that way. When David courageously chose to fight Goliath, he used three strategies that we can use to protect our hearts in this hard season too.

First, don't listen to the voices telling you it's impossible. When David shows up, no one believes this battle can be won. But like David, we only need to listen to one voice—God's.

Next, go to battle in the way that fits you best. Saul offered David his armor. After trying it on, David quickly finds it isn't the right fit for him. Do what works for you. God has equipped you with what you need, even if it's different from how others have done it.

Finally, don't go in your own strength. "David said to the Philistine, 'You come against me with a sword, spear, and javelin, but I come against you in the name of the Lord of Armies, the God of the ranks of Israel'" (v. 45 CSB). It wasn't simply the stone from David's sling that defeated Goliath; it was the power of God working in the situation.

What do you want God to free you from today? Tell God about the biggest giant in your life. As long as you're still fighting, you're winning—and you'll have victory in the end.

God, give me the victory I need today.

. . . .

What's a giant in your life that you're battling today?

GOD IS YOUR STRENGTH IN WEAKNESS

My strength is made perfect in weakness. (2 Corinthians 12:9 NKJV)

You may think you have nothing to offer. You may want to run and hide. You may tell yourself, "I'll only be in the way." But still God asks, quietly and persistently, "Will you let me use you, right here and right now?"

Your weaknesses and struggles are not reasons for him to give up on you. Instead, they're opportunities for you to show his strength in ways you simply can't on your best days. The apostle Paul wrestled with "a thorn" in his flesh (2 Cor. 12:7). We don't know what it was exactly, only that it was an ongoing source of difficulty for him. He begged God to take it away, and many of us are familiar with the divine response. God said, "My strength is made perfect in weakness" (v. 9 NKJV).

In other words, the very places and times when you feel God can use you least are when he may actually shine through you most.

When God uses us in those moments, it's humbling because we realize *it never really has been about us.* Hopefully that leads to a new sense of freedom. We can stop our striving. We can give up working so crazy hard to change the world. We can release our plans and instead open our hands to God.

We are made in the image of the God who created the universe, and there is a part of who he is that only gets shown through who we are. Sometimes that happens through our strengths. But sometimes it's through our cracks that his light shines the brightest.

God, thank you for showing your strength through my weaknesses.

. . . .

How have you seen God's strength in your weaknesses?

YOU CAN TRUST IN GOD

I trust in God, so why should I be afraid?
What can mere mortals do to me? (Psalm 56:4 NLT)

W hat can mere mortals do to me?" My answer to David's question is quite a long list. Mere mortals can reject, shame, abandon, and hurt me (just as a start). Mere mortals even tried to kill David on multiple occasions.

Yesterday on a walk through our neighborhood, I prayed about a relationship where I'd recently gotten hurt. I found myself running imaginary scenarios through my mind where that happened again. I felt desperate to find a way to fix this situation, control the outcome, make sure I was going to be protected.

"God," I whispered, "I'm living in so much fear in this relationship. Please help me live in faith instead." David discovered what I'm still learning: trust in God is the antidote for the fear of people.

Trust that God is in control.

Trust that he is working out his plan.

Trust that he loves me more than I can imagine.

Trust that he loves every person in my life even more than I do.

Trust that no matter what mere mortals do, he will be my ultimate security.

Is living this out easy? No. Even as I type these words I hear an inner protest, *But what if . . . ?* Trust is not an emotion; it's a practice. It's a place we go home to a million times. It's a decision that often seems irrational but is essential if we're to have any peace in this world.

What can mere mortals do to me? Nothing that is too much for God to handle.

God, help me trust in you instead of fearing people today.

. . . .

What helps you trust God instead of fear people?

YOU CAN CHOOSE GROWING OVER GRASPING

You will grow as you learn to know God better and better. (Colossians 1:10 NLT)

I'm standing on the shore of the ocean, the light just coming through the clouds. Sandpipers run at the edge of the waves, seagulls fly overhead, pelicans dive for the water as they search for breakfast. The God who cares for the sparrows surely watches over all of these too.

I see growth everywhere I look in the place but I don't see grasping—the continual pursuit of more, more, more.

Growth is about quality. Grasping is about quantity.

Growth is a process. Grasping is an event.

Growth is internal. Grasping is external.

Growth is a natural response. Grasping is often a fear-based reaction.

Growth is a work God does in us. Grasping is what we do to prove our worth.

Growth is about aligning with the divine. Grasping is about making sure I get what's mine.

Growth starts with surrender, with releasing control. Grasping starts with fear, with trying to take control.

God's creation is a reminder that we are part of a greater purpose, a grander design. We don't have to make anything happen; we only need to remember we're part of what has already been happening since the start of time.

God cares for the sparrows and the seagulls, the sandpipers and the pelicans, the humans standing along the shore too. We are all part of the beautiful work of becoming that he began in Eden and will complete in eternity.

God, I pray that you will help me choose growing over grasping today.

. . . .

What's one way God is growing you?

YOUR LOAD CAN BE LIGHTER TODAY

Come to me, all you who are weary and burdened, and I will give you rest. (Matthew 11:28)

Sometimes when I speak at events, the organizers have women do scavenger hunts through their purses as a fun way to start the evening. A woman from the stage calls out random items: "four or more tubes of lipstick," "thirty-two cents in change," and "driver's license that's about to expire."

The first person to find that item wins. Purses are pulled out from under tables, and in the chaos contents are thrown everywhere. Pacifiers. Calendars. Receipts. Wrappers. Tissues. Mirrors. By the time the activity is done, the table is covered with visual reminders of how busy and complicated a woman's life can be.

If you're like me, much of what would come out of your purse would be related in some way to trying to be perfect. I've gone through seasons when my calendar was full of things I felt obligated to do because it helped me meet some standard. My ever-present, ever-being-reapplied makeup is an attempt at our culture's version of beauty. The receipts might show purchases that were more about making an impression than what I really wanted.

Carrying all of that can begin to weigh a girl down. But Jesus wants us to trade our purses of "perfection" for a much lighter load instead. He offers us security in place of striving. Full hearts instead of full schedules. Receiving instead of trying to buy our way to acceptance. We can carry less when we become convinced we're cared for more than we can even imagine.

God, help me to let go of anything that is weighing me down.

. . . .

What do you *not* want to carry with you today?

Day 52

YOU'RE ON A MISSION

Jesus said to them again, "Peace be with you. As the Father has sent me, I also send you." (John 20:21 CSB)

*M*issionary simply means someone who has or is on a mission. If that's the case, then we all bear that name. We are each called to love God and others.

Yes, let's give special care and honor to those for whom it is also an occupation. But let's not forget we also have been sent. We were sent the second the first spark of life flickered in our mother's womb. *To this earth.* And now to wherever we are today.

So let's take off our shoes and our misconceptions and declare that this is holy ground. Because God is here. He is in this moment. Perhaps even more miraculous, *he is in us.* And that is what he wants us to bring to wherever we are, wherever we go—not our talent or our goodness, our knowledge or our niceness. *God himself.*

Do you want to know where God is asking you to serve and bless and bring him glory right now? You only need to look down at the one-foot square of humble, sacred earth beneath your feet. The only place on this spinning globe where both you and God are present in this moment.

God, thank you that I don't have to get on a plane or go far away to live out your mission for my life. I can do so wherever you've placed me today.

. . . .

How can you be a missionary by loving God and others wherever you are today?

CREATING ONE-ANOTHER RELATIONSHIPS

Carry one another's burdens; in this way you will fulfill the law of Christ. (Galatians 6:2 CSB)

"Carry one another's burdens" says Galatians 6:2. The word *burden* in the original language describes excessive heaviness, like a boulder. It's something no one can bear alone, and we're to help each other with those needs. But verse 5 also says, "Each person will have to carry his own load." The word *load* refers to something like a pack carried by a soldier on a march.

It's easy to try to earn love and affection by helping others, and we are called to serve each other. But a relationship in which one person is always giving and the other taking isn't healthy or sustainable. We're made for one-another relationships, not one-sided. These relationships are reciprocal, both people benefit—and so does the kingdom as a whole.

We can pause and ask, "God, is this person's need a boulder or a pack? Are you asking me to meet this need? And if you are, how can I do so from a place of believing I'm *already* loved?"

I've heard people say, "But Jesus gave everything for us when he went to the cross." Yes, and he also asks everything *from* us: "If anyone wants to follow after me, let him deny himself, take up his cross daily, and follow me" (Luke 9:23 CSB). The model Jesus gives us isn't sacrificing everything for others and neglecting ourselves or never asking for anything in return. Our relationship with him is "one another" too.

Let's choose to love *and* be loved.

God, help me to create one-another relationships where I can love and be loved.

. . . .

What's a burden you can help someone with, and what do you need too?

GOD GIVES YOU A NEW SONG

The LORD is my strength and my song. (Exodus 15:2 NLT)

Standing on the other side of the Red Sea, finally safe from the Egyptian army, Moses and the Israelites do more than breathe a sigh of relief; they *sing*. It's the first song ever recorded in the Bible.

Singing can not only help us recover from stress but also give us more courage and holy calm in anxiety-provoking situations.

You don't need to be a musician to get the physical and spiritual benefits of singing. I'm a *terrible* singer. I've even been known to mouth the words to songs in church to spare those around me (don't tell). My version of using singing to help with anxiety looks like turning on my favorite tunes as I get ready in the morning and sometimes singing along. I listen to music when I run and might join in if no one is around. Or if I'm driving to a meeting or event that makes me nervous, I occasionally belt out some fear-fighting lyrics in the privacy of my car.

All throughout Scripture, people sing—in times of difficulty, joy, sorrow, victory, fear, and everything in between. We can join David in saying,

> He has given me a new song to sing,
> a hymn of praise to our God.
> Many will see what he has done and be amazed.
> They will put their trust in the LORD. (Ps. 40:3 NLT)

God, give me a new song to sing, one of calm and courage.

· · · ·

What's one way you can use music to encourage yourself today?

YOU HAVE A FIRM FOUNDATION

*No one can lay any foundation other than the one we already have—
Jesus Christ. (1 Corinthians 3:11 NLT)*

It's still dark when I pull up to SafeKeepers, the self-storage business my husband, Mark, and I own. We completed phase one over a year ago, it filled up, and now we're building phase two. This morning the foundation is being poured.

Mark has been here since midnight, and I hand him breakfast as he explains the process to me. The foundation matters more than anything else. It needs to be strong enough to withstand the weight of whatever is placed on it. The foundation also needs to remain steady when the earth beneath it shifts. Different people and things will come in and out of our buildings every day, but the foundation will remain the same.

Having Jesus as our foundation means that we have security in an insecure world. We have stability even in seasons of uncertainty. It means we are always supported by something so much stronger than our human frailty.

Throughout our lives, what stands on this foundation will change. Relationships, things, jobs, houses, accomplishments will all come and go. But what matters most will remain. "Even a tornado could hit this building and the foundation would still be here," Mark says.

You have a foundation who is loving, wise, and good. He is strong, solid, and immovable. You can place all your weight on him, all your burdens. You don't have to build your life on your humanness, on dirt or dust. You can build your life on Jesus.

Jesus, you are my firm foundation, and I will build my life on you.

. . . .

What's one way you need Jesus to be your foundation today?

Day 56

YOU ADD LIGHT WHEREVER YOU ARE

Let your light shine before others. (Matthew 5:16)

One evening as I sat at my desk and tried to write encouraging words, my thoughts kept being interrupted by news headlines: violence, disease, tragedy, corruption, poverty. Feeling completely overwhelmed, I finally paused and asked God, "How do I get rid of the darkness in our world? It seems impossible to even make a difference."

Have you felt or asked the same?

In an instant it seemed I heard the whisper of an answer in my heart: *The only way to get rid of darkness is to add more light.* Hope flickered back into being within me. We can all add more light wherever we are, for whoever God places in front of us, because we all have the Light of the World within us.

Simply ask God this: "How do you want me to add more light to my world today?" It might be by loving your family, doing excellent work at your job, serving in a small way, smiling at someone who's having a hard day. It only takes a spark to start setting your world ablaze. Don't let cynicism convince you nothing can change. Don't tell yourself, "The little bit I have to offer can't make a difference." Let me assure you, with Jesus it can.

You are here at this time in history for a purpose, and no one can take your place. Be who you are, give what you can, do what only you can do. Let's drive out the darkness together.

God, show me how to add light wherever I am today.

· · · ·

How have you seen God bring light into a dark situation?

GOD HELPS YOU DWELL IN PEACE

The LORD gives his people strength.
The LORD blesses them with peace. (Psalm 29:11 NLT)

The biblical word for peace is *shalom*; and while it's difficult to translate into our language, it essentially means wholeness and well-being.

The story of Scripture starts with Adam and Eve in the garden, a place of complete peace. It ends in heaven, also a place of well-being and wholeness. It seems God is intent on seeing his people thrive, whatever it takes.

This doesn't mean we'll experience shalom fully in this world. But there's something comforting in knowing that God is always working to bring us closer to it until we're home forever.

We will go *through* hardship and suffering in this life. But peace is the place God has for us to dwell.

If we're in a season where life is happy, then that means we embrace it without fear or apology. We receive the gifts God is bestowing on us. We celebrate and savor every moment. We let the joy we feel now be a small preview of what we'll one day experience forever.

If we're in a season where life is hard and stressful, then that means we let shalom be our hope. No matter how broken we feel now, we can trust one day we'll be whole and that all will be well.

For so long I thought peace was the absence of something. I know now it's the presence of someone. A God who loves us. A God who is for us. A God who is making all things new, including me and you.

God, you don't just give me peace; you are my peace.

· · · ·

How do you need shalom in your life today?

YOU'RE INVITED TO REST

Let's go off by ourselves to a quiet place and rest awhile. (Mark 6:31 NLT)

For years I operated on this principle: I'll rest when *the work* is done. But I slowly came to realize the work is never done. And as a result, I was never resting. It took a brush with serious burnout to convince me I had to change my thinking. I needed to learn to say, "I'll rest when I'm done." In other words, when I become weary or depleted it's my sacred duty to stop for a bit.

Jesus illustrated this when he invited his disciples to rest in Mark 6:31. Those words might lead us to believe they had helped everyone they could and done all that was possible. But the opposite was actually true. The same verse continues, "He said this because there were so many people coming and going that Jesus and his apostles didn't even have time to eat."

Choosing to say "I'm done for now" is not weakness. It's wisdom. It's also essential to staying strong and finishing well. The work will be there tomorrow. The real question is, if we refuse to rest, will we be?

Thankfully, Jesus still extends the same invitation he did to the disciples: "Let's go off by ourselves to a quiet place and rest awhile." We can trust he will use those times to fill us up and then send us out again to serve even more powerfully than before.

Here's the secret I've finally discovered: sometimes the most important, productive thing we can do is nothing at all.

God, thank you for your invitation to rest.
Please give me the courage to receive it.

. . . .

What keeps you from resting when you need to do so?

YOU'RE MADE FOR INTIMACY

A new command I give you: Love one another. (John 13:34)

Two friends and I stand under a lovely early evening sky. We've just come from a gathering of women, the kind that is both wonderful and vulnerable at the same time. "That was intimidating," one of us says. Then I say something that has never occurred to me before: "I think the cure for intimidation is intimacy."

We first need intimacy with Jesus because he is the one whose voice tells us who we really are, who we're created to be, and what is true of us no matter how we feel in any given moment. He says we are loved and chosen, wonderfully made and part of his plan.

Then we need intimacy with others—safe places where we can say to each other, "I don't have it all together." We are all more alike than different. We are all broken and beloved daughters in need of a Savior.

And we need intimacy with our own hearts too. Because when we don't take time to discover who we are, we feel a lot of pressure to be someone else.

Next time I feel insecure I'm going to pause and ask myself, "How can I choose intimacy instead of intimidation right now?" That conversation on a spring evening with my friends felt like a start to something freeing and new. So in case you've ever felt intimidated too, I wanted to pass it along to you.

God, thank you that you call us to do life together,
that you give us the courage to choose connection.

· · · ·

What helps you overcome feeling intimidated?

GOD IS STEADFAST

My dear brothers and sisters, be steadfast, immovable. (1 Corinthians 15:58 CSB)

In the center of my childhood backyard was a tetherball set, a tall white pole with a rope attached to it that had a ball on the end. My brother and I would take turns hitting that ball as hard as we could and watching the rope wind around the pole—spin, spin, spin.

I thought of that pole recently on a hard day. As I prayed about a particular scenario in my life, I kept picturing the tetherball set. The memory felt a bit faded around the edges but somehow seemed important. Surprisingly, the word *steadfast* kept coming to mind. I looked up the Hebrew meaning and learned that to be steadfast is to be "firmly fixed." Huh, just like the tetherball pole.

Sometimes the most courageous, loving thing we can do is to hold steady. It's the position of trusting God when it feels like everything in our lives is changing without our consent. Is this easy? Absolutely not. Choosing to be steadfast requires grit and perseverance, bravery and great strength. It's far easier to just do something, *anything*, because at least then we feel as if we have some control.

I don't know what happened to my old tetherball set. But today I'm grateful for the unexpected memory of it. Next time I'm tempted to jump into the chaos around me, I'll picture that rusty, banged-up, resilient pole. I'll pray for the courage to be a little more like it, a little more like Jesus—strong, faithful, steadfast.

God, I'm so glad you are always steadfast— help me to hold steady even in chaos too.

· · · ·

What's a situation in your life where God is calling you to be steadfast?

GOD SEES YOU TODAY

For the eyes of the LORD range throughout the earth to strengthen those whose hearts are fully committed to him. (2 Chronicles 16:9)

The sun slips behind the spring trees exploding green. The birds declare love and war from the tips of branches. My dog stares down a squirrel, daring it to take one more step along the fence. The firepit is just beginning to crackle to life, sparks of gold and orange scattering into ashes.

I lean back into the chair, one that rocks, and find a rhythm that matches my thoughts. I feel small today. Like one of the sparrows scurrying across the yard. Back and forth. Back and forth. It's hard to see what all the fuss is about.

Then I remember that just as I see that sparrow, I'm seen too. By a God who made me. Knows me. Calls my name above the treetops and within my heart. Yes, I'm small.

But in God's eyes, size doesn't equal significance.

The one who spun the stars onto the floor of the sky like dancers in evening gowns does not consider me of little importance. The one who watches seeds sleep beneath the earth and then unfold into glory has a different point of view.

I matter to him.

You do too.

We are not unseen.

Not ever.

I let the night fall around me like a curtain, watch the fire drift away in slivers of smoke. I am invisible, hidden, small. And at the same time fully seen, known, given significance beyond what I can even grasp. This is the beautiful paradox we live in each day.

God, thank you for seeing me where I am and as I am today.

· · · ·

How have you sensed God watching over you?

YOU CAN FIGHT BACK

Fight the good fight for the true faith. (1 Timothy 6:12 NLT)

We all hear harsh lies inside sometimes. The accusations toward our souls aren't proof of our inadequacy; they're proof that we have an adversary. We use the phrase *beating ourselves up*, but the enemy is not ourselves. When we think the problem is us, we become harsh toward our own hearts. Our primary battle isn't against any person—including ourselves.

My husband and I recently watched a TV show in which the hero faces a powerful opponent. At one point the hero becomes weary and takes punch after punch. With tears in my eyes, I said over and over, "Fight back. Please fight back."

It's the same feeling I get when I look at my sisters in Christ. It's the same one I get when I think about how I let my own soul be treated. And it makes me want to shout: ENOUGH. It's time to *fight back*. It's time to guard our hearts. It's time to protect our minds. It's time to stop taking the punches and instead take the victory in Jesus's name.

Here's the truth about us today no matter what we may hear: We are overcomers. We are more than conquerors. We are stronger than we know, braver than we feel, and loved more than we can even imagine.

God, when I am under attack, help me fight back.
You are mighty, and you are on my side.

. . . .

What's a lie you've battled and the truth that can defeat it?

GOD IS AN OPPORTUNIST

Stay alert! Watch out for your great enemy, the devil. He prowls around like a roaring lion, looking for someone to devour. (1 Peter 5:8 NLT)

The enemy of our heart is an opportunist. We need to know this so we can be on guard, so we can fight for our own hearts and each other rather than against.

But God is an opportunist too. When things get tough in our lives, he looks for a chance to do even more good to and for us—to unite, bring hope, whisper truth. We need to know this so we can look for what he wants to offer our hearts, the treasures hidden in the darkness, the unexpected spoils of war.

Years ago my mom had heart surgery. As I paced the halls of a hospital for three weeks, it sometimes seemed the enemy wanted to devour our family's peace. But, even more, I could sense the presence of Jesus, the Lion of Judah (Rev. 5:5) walking with me, roaring for our family, giving us what we needed most in that hard place.

We are humans on a broken, spinning earth. We are warriors disguised in tennis shoes and yoga pants. We bleed and cry and drink bitter cups of hospital coffee. We are small and yet part of a bigger, wilder story than we can even imagine, one that's been unfolding since the beginning of time.

Today the enemy of our hearts is working in our lives.

Today the God of all eternity is working in our lives.

I don't think I have to tell you which one has already won.

God, you are more powerful than anything, and you are working in my life today.

. . . .

How have you sensed God's presence in a hard time?

GOD WANTS TO ENCOURAGE YOU

You, Lord, hear the desire of the afflicted;
you encourage them, and you listen to their cry. (Psalm 10:17)

I love how this verse says God encourages us. Have you ever thought about that? When the day seems difficult, when you're weary, when you feel like a failure . . . God is encouraging you. For so long I thought of him as standing by and shaking his head as he wondered, *Why can't you get it together?* But that's not his heart toward us at all.

To encourage literally means "to give courage," and that's what God wants to do for us on the hard days. He says to us, *I'm here. I will help you. I will give you strength to take one more step.* He looks at your life with infinite love and tenderness. And he knows how hard it is to be us sometimes. He lived in this world. He experienced pain. He died on a cross.

What if, on the days when it's hard for you to get out of bed, you imagine him reaching out to lift you up instead of being disappointed in you? What if he's cheering as you take your first step into a day that's not one you want to face? What if instead of saying "get it together," he's whispering, *Let's do this together*?

That changes everything.

And it can change us.

You are encouraged, not condemned.

God, I'm thankful for the grace and encouragement
you extend toward me.

. . . .

What's an encouraging truth God wants to say to your heart today?

YOUR WORK WILL BE WORTH IT

For who despises the day of small things? (Zechariah 4:10 CSB)

Several years ago we moved to a new home with a little pond behind it. When the weather is nice, we can hear bullfrogs. Turtles sun themselves like movie stars circled around a pool. And, one evening last spring, a pair of Canadian geese appeared like guests checking into their favorite bed and breakfast.

We watched the two of them build a nest. For twenty-eight days the female faithfully sat on it, undisturbed even by harsh wind and torrential rain. From my perspective it seemed absolutely nothing was happening. But one morning seven fuzzy yellow goslings appeared. Over the next few months, we watched them waddle, then swim, then finally take flight toward their next adventure.

The quiet persistence of that mother goose is a reminder I need. Zechariah 4:10 asks, "For who despises the day of small things?" Truthfully, sometimes I do. I don't want the waiting on the nest. I don't want the discomfort. I don't want to sit still, practice patience, believe without seeing, be faithful when it seems nothing at all is happening.

Geese can fly up to three thousand miles in a migration. Sometimes I look out my window and wonder where the little family from our pond is now. I'm glad I got to witness the start of the great distance they will go, to celebrate their days of little things. Let's pause for a moment to do the same, to be reassured that even the biggest changes and accomplishments start small.

*God, thank you for the gift of small beginnings
that grow into beautiful things.*

. . . .

What's a small beginning you can be thankful for today?

YOU'RE INVITED TO REMEMBER, MEDITATE, REFLECT

I remember the days of old;
I meditate on all you have done;
I reflect on the work of your hands. (Psalm 143:5 CSB)

Those three words—remember, meditate, reflect—offer us a way of slowing down and connecting with God during our busy lives.

To remember means to recount or be mindful. Moses told the Israelites over and over, "Remember. . . ." We can do the same by asking this simple question: "What has God brought me through in my life?"

After we've focused on what's happened, we can go deeper by meditating, which simply means thinking about something in an intentional way. It's not just recalling specific events but considering who's behind them. We can ask ourselves, "Where have I seen God's hand in my life?"

Once we recognize God's hand in our lives, we can reflect on what he has done for us. As David often showed through his psalms, this leads to gratitude, praise, and spiritual growth. We can ask, "What am I grateful for, and what have I learned that will help me grow?"

We live in a world that tells us we must always keep moving. But sometimes what we need most is to pause for a few moments. Sometimes we go forward by looking back. Sometimes we make progress by being still. Sometimes silence is where we finally discover what our hearts really need to hear.

Let's offer our hurried hearts the gift of a few moments to remember, meditate, and reflect.

God, I'm pausing now to remember, meditate, and reflect.

. . . .

How do you want to remember, meditate, and reflect today?

YOUR GOALS CAN BE SMALLER

If you are faithful in little things, you will be faithful in large ones.
(Luke 16:10 NLT)

Where goals are concerned, I had a change of heart that came from working with coaching clients. They would tell me of some idealistic goal they had such as "I want to run a marathon in three weeks!" I would say, "I think the desire to be more active is great! Now what's the *minimum* that will make you feel like you're making progress?" The response would be something like, "I could take a walk three evenings a week."

Here's the magic of identifying a minimum: it starts to build momentum. Imagine I had two clients, one who insisted on the three-week marathon goal and the other who started with the minimum. If someone asked me which one would *actually* run a marathon one day, I'd choose the walker every single time.

For myself and my clients, I've started looking at goals differently. We come up with not one goal but three: a minimum, medium, and maximum. For example, walking three nights a week is minimum, adding one day of running is medium, and running four days a week is maximum.

Traditional systems of goal setting can feel rigid. And we all know life is not rigid. It requires us to continually adapt, shift, change, grow, slow down, speed up, juggle, try again.

God's goal for our lives isn't perfection; it's growth and connection. Every effort counts. Every step matters. Every little bit of progress can be a reason for rejoicing.

God, help me be faithful in little things today.

. . . .

What's a goal you can adjust in your life?

YOUR PERSPECTIVE IS POWERFUL

For as he thinks in his heart, so is he. (Proverbs 23:7 NKJV)

Psychologist Martin Seligman asserted that there are two distinct styles of explaining events in our lives. With the first style, pessimism, people see unfortunate events as personal, permanent, and pervasive. In other words, those with this style believe it's their fault, it will last forever, and it affects every area of their lives.[1]

With the second style, optimism, people see those same events as external, temporary, and specific. In other words, they attribute the cause to something outside themselves, and they believe that whatever happened won't last forever and is related only to this individual situation.

Here's the good news: we can change our style. We can ask ourselves the following questions:

- "What external factors contributed to this?"
- "Will this really last forever?"
- "Does this really affect every area of my life?"

Sometimes I'm still tempted to look at what happens in my life as personal, permanent, and pervasive. We all have this tendency. When our spouse leaves. When our evaluation report at work is not what we had hoped. When our teenager yells and then slams the door. When we get laid off. When our friend stops returning our calls. When we spill the milk.

We often can't control what happens to us. But we can control what we think about it. And that can make all the difference.

God, when I start to give in to negativity and self-criticism, shift me back toward grace and compassion.

. . . .

What situation can you look at in a different way today?

Day 69

GOD WILL DEFEAT THE GIANTS IN YOUR LIFE

"Don't worry about this Philistine," David told Saul. "I'll go fight him!"
(1 Samuel 17:32 NLT)

Notice how David brings a secret weapon with him that no one else has—a different perspective. Saul, the Israelites, and even Goliath see this as a human battle. But David views it as a spiritual one.

When Saul tells David he can't possibly win because he's only a boy, David replies, "The LORD . . . will rescue me" (1 Sam. 17:37 NLT).

When Goliath warns David that he's going to be defeated, David responds, "The LORD will conquer you" (v. 46 NLT).

After forty days of the Israelites believing the outcome is up to them, David declares, "This is the LORD's battle" (v. 47 NLT).

We can use the same phrases that David did.

When anxiety tells us "You can't handle this," we can reply, "The Lord will rescue me."

When anxiety warns we're going to be defeated, we can respond, "The Lord will conquer the giants in my life."

When anxiety tempts us to believe it's all up to us, we can declare, "This is the Lord's battle."

With only a sling and small stones, David took down a giant. What seemed impossible from an earthly viewpoint became reality when approached with an eternal perspective. Like David, we can look beyond our human limitations to what only God can do.

God, you will rescue me. You will conquer the giants in my life.
This is your battle.

. . . .

What giant do you need God to give victory over in your life?

YOU'RE CALLED TO LOVE

Just as I have loved you, you should love each other. (John 13:34 NLT)

Before he went home to Jesus, my Grandpa Hollie celebrated his ninetieth birthday with a party. I had the privilege of being there and serving punch. That put me in a position to do a lot of listening.

On and on the stories went of how my grandpa had spent his life loving well, in little and big ways. I nodded my head in agreement because I'd experienced the same. For over fifteen years, my grandpa took me out on breakfast dates to ask me how I was doing and encourage me in my faith.

Grandpa Hollie never went to Hollywood. He wasn't the CEO of a big corporation or a high-position politician. He was a regular guy in a small town who simply said yes when God asked to use him.

It turns out that doing so blessed those around him; it's also probably one of the reasons he lived so long. Research has shown that those who have strong relationships and serve others tend to live healthier, more joyful lives.[1]

What I've seen through my grandpa's life is that true service isn't about grand gestures; it's about a series of small choices. Most of them unseen. Many times we won't know their impact this side of heaven. All of which add up to a lifetime of resilience and loving well.

God, show me who I can love today, and help me reach out when I need encouragement too.

. . . .

Who can you give love to today, and who do you need to receive it from?

GOD WANTS TO FREE YOU FROM INSECURITY

I lift up my eyes to the mountains—
where does my help come from?
My help comes from the LORD. (Psalm 121:1–2)

I wake to a tap-tap against glass, stumble bleary-eyed into the kitchen, and ask my husband, "What's that sound?" He gestures to the small pane above our front door and says, "Robin."

"This is crazy behavior," I say to the bird. I do some research and discover my feathered friend thinks its reflection is an enemy. While there's not another bird who's actually a threat, there is a different kind of danger for this robin because it neglects important things like nest building.

But maybe the robin's behavior isn't as strange as it seems. Instead it starts to feel familiar. Because at the root of all that wasted time and energy is simply this: false insecurity.

Confession: I peck my share of windows too. Maybe I tap-tap my computer keyboard to check social media one more time because I don't want to miss out on anything. I let worry-filled thoughts pace back and forth in my mind. Sometimes I even stare at my own reflection like it's an enemy. You too?

There's only one way to change this behavior in birds: get them to stop looking at themselves. It's the only way our hearts can be free too.

I finally persuaded the robin to move on from its imaginary battle. Maybe it's time for us to do the same. Because here's what I'm learning is real: We are loved. We are safe. When we feel insecure, we can look to the God who cares for us and he will always help.

God, help me to focus on your love for me.

. . . .

What helps you look to God instead of focusing on insecurity?

JESUS IS YOUR COUNSELOR

He will be called Wonderful Counselor. (Isaiah 9:6)

D r. Henry Cloud, a psychologist and author, describes how one of his professors told the class he was going to reveal the one factor that research had proven truly helps clients.

> I sat eagerly, waiting to find out the secret of helping people. Here, at last, I would learn that esoteric kernel of wisdom that I had been seeking all of this time. The professor looked at us and said, "It's the relationship. What actually brings about change in people, and the cure, is the relationship between the psychologist and the client," he explained.[1]

The same is true in our relationship with Jesus, our Wonderful Counselor. As a counselor, my role was to help provide certain things for the clients who stepped through my door: A safe place. A listening ear. An encouraging presence. Truth spoken in love. Hope for the future.

I think these reflect so much of what Jesus offers us too. But Jesus goes far beyond this as well. Because he is not an ordinary human counselor; he is *the* Wonderful Counselor. The word *wonderful* in this verse is actually much more powerful than the way we use it today. In the original language, it means to cause great wonder, to be beyond understanding.

Our Wonderful Counselor knows more than we can even comprehend.

He loves us more than we can imagine.

He is always inviting us to simply come and connect with him.

God, I'm so glad you are my counselor.
Please give me your wisdom, encouragement, and care.

. . . .

How has Jesus been a counselor to you?

Day 73

WE NEED WHAT
YOU HAVE TO OFFER

*For the LORD is good, and his faithful love endures forever;
his faithfulness, through all generations. (Psalm 100:5 CSB)*

Years ago I attended a tea party with my grandmother, daughter, and granddaughter in the fellowship hall of a small-town church about an hour from my home. This was where my parents had their wedding reception, my grandparents had their fiftieth anniversary party, and my great-grandparents held hands in the pews. I thought of how we need each generation and the gifts they bring.

If you're in the senior crowd, we need the perspective and resilience you've gained from many life experiences. You know what it is to overcome obstacles, make it through challenges, and see God's hand in history. We long for your encouragement and hard-won wisdom.

To those of us in the middle, let's not miss the divine hidden among the mundane and ordinary. We can touch a life whether we're holding a microphone or warming up mac-and-cheese in the microwave. We can show up where we are, as we are, steadily and faithfully. We can remember that what's visible isn't more valuable.

To those younger, it's never too early for God to use you. You don't have to wait to feel ready. We need your optimism and energy, your fresh outlook on the future, and your daring. If you received something yesterday—even five minutes ago—then you have something to give to someone else.

We all have something to offer. We all have something to receive. Now, more than ever, we are better together.

God, thank you that you are at work in and through each generation.

. . . .

What are you thankful for about someone in a different generation?

YOU CAN RUN TO GOD

Rescue me from my enemies, Lord;
I run to you to hide me. (Psalm 143:9 NLT)

When we're afraid, our natural tendency is to hide. We physically or emotionally retreat to where it feels safer. I've done this by literally diving under the covers in my bedroom. Or I've hidden my heart by putting on a smiling face when I felt broken inside.

God knows of this tendency we have as humans, and he doesn't tell us not to hide. We aren't in trouble for this instinct. What God does want to change is where and how we hide. God himself wants to be our hiding place.

I used to think I had to get rid of my fears before I came to God. But years ago a counselor asked me to make a list of my fears. When I looked at the words I wrote, I wanted to run from my fears. Instead, perhaps fully for the first time, I realized I can run to God with them. I got on my knees and told him what scares me most. "I prayed to the Lord, and he answered me. He freed me from all my fears" (Ps. 34:4 NLT).

Yes, I will face fears again in this life, but that moment felt like a breakthrough. Because I know now whatever I'm facing, I can come to God with it. He is our strength and security. He gives us courage and makes us brave. His love and truth are bigger and stronger than anything we fear.

God, you are the place I can run to and hide in when fear chases me.

· · · ·

How do you need to run to God and hide in him today?

GOD HELPS YOU HANDLE YOUR BROKEN PLACES

So prepare your minds for action and exercise self-control. (1 Peter 1:13 NLT)

Mark and I walk across a new foundation we recently watched being poured. He points to straight lines in the concrete that run from one end to the other, both horizontally and vertically, creating a pattern of large squares. "These are control joints," he tells me.

Then he points to a small crack running up the side of the foundation. It leads directly to one of the control joints and disappears into it. "There will always be cracks," he says. "You just have to give them somewhere to go." I think of the brokenness I'm walking through in this season, how cracks seemed to appear in the foundation of my life with no warning. Just yesterday I sat in my counselor's office and processed more hurt, sought more healing.

"My counselor is a control joint," I tell Mark. He nods in agreement. I add, "So are exercise, time with supportive friends, naps, journaling, and prayer." I start picturing all of these laid over my life like the squares in the concrete. I've always thought of self-control as simply restraint, but perhaps it's also part of how we handle the broken parts of our lives.

We all need "control joints" in our lives—people, places, and rhythms where the cracks in our souls can go. Brokenness is inevitable; being intentional about how we handle it is optional.

God, show me what control joints you've given me to handle the brokenness in my life.

. . . .

What are the control joints that help with brokenness in your life?

GOD WON'T HURRY
YOUR HEART

Return to your rest, my soul. (Psalm 116:7)

I stare out the window into the backyard. From my breakfast table, I can see a robin fluffing out her feathers. The trees reach up to the sky with new leaves that wave good morning. A chubby squirrel gathers a few acorns to save for later. As I look, I realize the pace beyond my windows is so different from the one within them. We, as humans, are tempted to hurry. And yet it seems God is intent on slowing us down.

He gives us a Sabbath, and we work through the weekend.

He gives us three meals a day to let us slow down, and we pick fast food.

He gives us eight hours of sleep a night, and we try to squeak by on far less.

We hurry when we're afraid that we'll be late, miss out on something, or disappoint someone. God doesn't need to hurry because he has all the time in eternity. This is good news for us, friends. It means . . .

God will not rush your healing.

And God will not rush your growth.

God is okay with where you are right now. He's not tapping his toe impatiently. He's not looking at his watch with a sigh. He's not trying to get you out the door a few minutes sooner. The God who loves you is willing to give you the time you need. All of time belongs to him, and he is generous with it. He gives it freely to fluffy birds and budding trees and chubby squirrels.

And he'll give it to your heart—as much as you need.

God, thank you for giving me time, space, and rest.

. . . .

What does your hurried heart need most today?

GOD WILL CARE FOR YOU

Elijah said to her, "Don't be afraid! Go ahead and do just what you've said." (1 Kings 17:13 NLT)

The prophet Elijah asks a widow for water and bread. She responds, "I swear by the LORD your God that I don't have a single piece of bread in the house. And I have only a handful of flour left in the jar and a little cooking oil in the bottom of the jug. I was just gathering a few sticks to cook this last meal, and then my son and I will die" (1 Kings 17:12 NLT).

Elijah tells her to do what she has said but first to make him a little bread. Then he adds the impossible: "For this is what the LORD, the God of Israel, says: There will always be flour and olive oil left in your containers until the time when the LORD sends rain and the crops grow again!" (v. 14 NLT).

Her fear tells her this is foolish. But she does as Elijah tells her. And "there was always enough flour and olive oil left in the containers, just as the LORD had promised" (v. 16 NLT).

What will we choose? When we dare to trust, we can discover our own version of this story. Yours might sound like this: "There was always enough courage and strength left in her heart, just as the Lord had promised."

Fear is an emotion of scarcity. It whispers that there's not enough, that we can't survive this, that we've been abandoned to fate. But we serve a God of abundance. With him, there is always more grace, more love, more of whatever we need in any moment.

God, thank you for being the source of what my heart needs today.

. . . .

What is anxiety telling you that you don't have enough of today?

Day 78

GOD WILL GIVE YOU
THE DESIRES OF YOUR HEART

Take delight in the LORD,
and he will give you your heart's desires.
Commit everything you do to the LORD.
Trust him, and he will help you. (Psalm 37:4–5 NLT)

On the surface, these verses can sound like "delight in God and he'll do what you want." But the opposite is true. When we delight in God, our hearts are in sync with what *he* wants.

Every morning I pray, "God, align my mind with yours. Align my heart with yours. Align my eyes, ears, mouth, hands, and feet with yours." When I shared this with my friend, she said, "Then you can trust that what you choose to do will align with what God wants."

Yes, God gives us boundaries through clear commands in his Word (no murdering anyone today), and we're encouraged to get godly advice. But God's will isn't a tightrope; it's an invitation to walk with someone we love for a lifetime.

I'm adding a new line to my prayer each morning: "God, give me the courage to trust myself today because I trust in you." I want more holy risking and less anxious retreating, more mistakes that help me learn and less missed opportunities, more pushing forward and less being paralyzed by fear.

God, align my mind with yours. Align my heart with yours.
Align my eyes, ears, mouth, hands, and feet with yours. Give me the
courage to trust myself today because I trust in you.

. . . .

What piece of advice would you give someone else
based on what God has taught you?

YOU CAN TELL GOD
THE HAPPY AND HARD

I trust in your unfailing love. (Psalm 13:5)

We tend to think in terms of all or nothing. So we insist that life is great when we're breaking apart inside. Because to do otherwise would be to discount all of God's goodness in our lives, right? Not so. We always live with both brokenness and blessings. Challenges and victories. Sorrow and joy. They're all mixed up together.

God understands both.

So what do we do? We embrace the paradox. We bring our sorrows as well as our joys to God. We say, "Thank you for this job. Please help me because it's wearing me out." We pray, "Thank you for this child. Please give me strength because it's hard being a mom today." We declare, "Thank you for the blessings in my life. Please grant the desire of my heart that's still unfulfilled."

What does it tell God when we do that? It says that we trust him. Like the psalmist says in Psalm 13, "I trust in your unfailing love." In other words, "No matter what my circumstances are, I believe that you love me. And I will choose to recognize your love in both the hard and happy parts of my life. I know I'm safe with you, and I can bring everything about my experience on this earth to you."

God is leaning toward you right now and he's asking, "How are you, really?"

He truly wants to know.

And it's okay to tell him.

All of it.

God, I praise and thank you for how good you are to me. I'm also struggling with some things, so I'm coming to you to share those too.

. . . .

What's one happy thing and one hard thing in your life today?

YOU CAN FIGHT THE LIES

Our struggle is not against flesh and blood, but against the rulers, against the authorities, against the powers of this dark world and against the spiritual forces of evil in the heavenly realms. (Ephesians 6:12)

You're not doing enough.
    You're letting people down.
When are you going to get it together?

When the lies come, we can defeat them with what God says instead. We aren't fighting alone. God is with us, for us, and on our side. He is even more committed to our victory than we are.

You're not doing enough. Truth: I only have to do what Jesus wants me to today, and he will enable me to do so. "I can do all this through him who gives me strength" (Phil. 4:13).

You're letting people down. Truth: I'm not perfect, so sometimes I will let people down. What matters is being obedient to God. "If pleasing people were my goal, I would not be Christ's servant" (Gal. 1:10 NLT).

When are you going to get it together? Truth: I'm human, and as long as I'm on earth, I'll still be in progress. But God is growing me each day. "He who began a good work in you will carry it on to completion until the day of Christ Jesus" (Phil. 1:6).

We don't have to believe the enemy. We're not weaklings. We're warriors. So let's stand firm. Raise the sword of truth. Never surrender our joy. It's time to fight like women who belong to the God who can never be defeated—which means we can't be either.

God, may your love always be louder than the lies. I will live in the truth.

. . . .

What's a truth you're using to fight lies today?

Day 81

YOUR PRACTICE
CAN BE IMPERFECT

Based on his promise, we wait for new heavens and a new earth.
(2 Peter 3:13 CSB)

I'm standing at our kitchen counter with a sliver of my attempt at pie crust in my hand. I voice my concerns about it to my husband. He lays a hand on my shoulder and gently says, "It's all practice." I want to do my very best. There's nothing wrong with this desire in general, but sometimes it steals my joy. Maybe you can relate?

If so, then let's whisper to both our hearts today, "It's all practice." Life *is* a dress rehearsal when we believe eternity is where the real show begins. The apostle Peter said, "Based on his promise, we wait for new heavens and a new earth" (2 Pet. 3:13 CSB).

There's a myth that says all we're going to do in heaven is sit around on clouds and sing. But Scripture says we're heading for heaven and *a new earth*. God hasn't ever given up on his original vision. What exactly our eternal lives will be like is a mystery. But it seems we can assume they'll involve what humankind did before the fall—love, holy work, enjoying God's creation, and bringing him glory.

Sometimes it feels I don't have enough time to make things perfect, including myself. I so easily forget my time isn't limited; I have all of eternity. And I'm not the one who makes things perfect. Only God does, and one day he will. Right now it really is all just practice.

I've heard in heaven there will be feasts too. Who knows, maybe I'll bring an apple pie.

God, help me to remember that it's all just practice today.

. . . .

What are you practicing in your life right now?

GOD WILL BE YOUR GUIDE

For this God is our God for ever and ever;
he will be our guide even to the end. (Psalm 48:14)

Life is a series of decisions. A job offer presents itself, but we're not sure it's the right fit. We could move to another city, but we also like where we are right now. Someone shares an opportunity with us, and we're curious but also cautious.

We might sometimes think, *I need a guide*. In other words, we need someone to help us know what to do and where to go. Thankfully, God is ready and able to direct us. Here are just a few examples:

In your unfailing love you will lead
the people you have redeemed.
In your strength you will guide them
to your holy dwelling. (Exod. 15:13)

He guides me along the right paths
for his name's sake. (Ps. 23:3)

The LORD will guide you always;
He will satisfy your needs in a sun-scorched land. (Isa. 58:11)

We won't suddenly know every step or all the answers. But we can trust that somehow, someway we're going to end up where we need to be. Yes, there may be distractions and detours. We might wander off and get ourselves lost for a bit. But someone is always going to bring us back and make sure we reach the destination.

Having God as our guide changes our role. Instead of carrying the burden of figuring everything out, our job becomes to trust and faithfully follow.

God, thank you for being so wise, loving, and faithful.
You have promised to be with me every step of the way.

. . . .

How do you need God to be your guide today?

GOD WILL HELP WHEN YOU'RE OVERWHELMED

I cry to you for help when my heart is overwhelmed. (Psalm 61:2 NLT)

Imagine a moment when you become overwhelmed. Your brain freezes. Your emotions rise. You hear an inner voice say, *This is all just too much.* We become overwhelmed when the requirements of our lives (real or perceived) feel greater than our personal resources. Feeling overwhelmed is a reality we all will face at some point. So let's talk about what's going on and what will help.

- If we've taken *on* too much: *What can I eliminate, delegate, or minimize today?* For example, order takeout instead of cooking dinner.
- If we've taken *in* too much: *What boundaries or limitations do I need to set today?* This often means turning something off—the TV, app notifications, the bedside light—so we can go to sleep earlier.
- If we're going too fast: *What's one way I can slow down today?* Ironically, this may mean *adding* one more thing to our day like a walk, bath, nap, or anything else that has a different pace.

Try different things as you answer these questions. Over time, you'll discover what works best for you. Having times when you become overwhelmed is part of being human, but you can learn to manage them. And you don't have to do it alone. Pause today and recognize that being overwhelmed doesn't mean you're weak. *It means you have given absolutely everything you've got.* Now it's time to give yourself what you need too.

God, I'm so grateful that I, like the psalmist, can cry out to you when I'm overwhelmed.

. . . .

What helps when you feel overwhelmed?

OUR WORST TENDENCIES
ARE NOT OUR DESTINIES

Anyone who belongs to Christ has become a new person. (2 Corinthians 5:17 NLT)

I have a tendency to be anxious. It runs like a red thread through the fabric of my life. It's been sewn in through genetics and experiences, my temperament and various temptations. It's almost always present in some form or another.

On my worst days I can believe this lie: I am an anxious woman, and I will never change. (You can fill in your own lie: I am _____, and I will never change.) Maybe you've been told this by a parent or spouse, the bully on the middle school playground, a boss at work, or a preacher at church.

But whatever lie we've heard isn't true. Because of Jesus our worst tendency is not our destiny.

This is the truth: I am a beloved, strong, cherished daughter of God who struggles with anxiety.

Will I likely struggle with anxiety in some form until I am home with Jesus? Yes. But here's the distinction we all need to make: your worst tendency may be your biggest battle, but it's not the basis of your identity.

What did you think of when you filled in the blank above? You are not whatever tendency came to mind either. You too are a beloved, strong, cherished daughter of God.

So let's not define ourselves by our weaknesses but by who loves us. Let's not see ourselves in light of our worst moments but through the eyes of grace. Let's not label our hearts with lies but instead lean into the truth of what Jesus did for us on the cross.

God, thank you that my worst tendencies are never my identity or destiny.

. . . .

How have you defined yourself in a way that isn't true?

JESUS CARES ABOUT YOUR TEARS

"Woman," Jesus said to her, "why are you crying?" (John 20:15 CSB)

One morning as we made our way down the trail through our neighborhood, I decided to speak the lies my heart had been hearing out loud to Mark. Tears streamed down my face and, unsure of what to do, I ran. I kept going until I heard a familiar voice speak one word with love: *Holley*.

In that moment I felt a bit like Mary Magdalene outside the tomb of Jesus after she's discovered it's empty. A man, whom she thinks is the gardener, asks, "Woman, why are you crying?" (This is the same question my poor husband probably wanted to ask when he caught up to me.) Mary doesn't realize who has come for her. Then Jesus speaks one word, her name: "Mary." She knows, right then and there, exactly who she is and who Jesus is too.

The miracle of the resurrection is that, yes, Jesus overcame sin and death. But it's also that he never stops coming for us. He never stops finding us in our moments of hurt and weakness. He never stops asking, "Woman, why are you crying?"

The voice that's louder, stronger, and truer than the lies our hearts hear is the voice of Jesus. He knows us by name. He calls us to himself. He meets us in the places where it seems all is lost and brings us back to life again too. Wherever we are today, whatever we're struggling with, Jesus is with us.

God, you are the one who came for me and who still comes for me in my hardest moments.

. . . .

What's the last thing that made you cry, and how was God with you in it?

GOD WILL SATISFY YOUR SOUL THIRST

He leads me beside quiet waters. (Psalm 23:2)

I've lived through seasons when everything has been rush-rush, hurry-hurry, stress-stress, until my soul has felt parched. Psalm 23 gives us a beautiful metaphor about what sheep need to quench their thirst. A modern-day sheep rancher says, "Sheep prefer to drink still water as opposed to water from a moving stream."[1] It seems it's easier for humans and sheep to receive what they need when there's not a rush.

We may think we have to settle for a quick sip, that God's priority is for us to cover as much ground as we can in as little time as we can. But his true invitation is for us to slow down, drink deep, and take all the time we need. Three times throughout Scripture God gives us this offer.

This is the miracle and mystery: God is pointing us not to an external source but to *himself*. He is "the LORD, the fountain of living water" (Jer. 17:13 CSB) and "when he said 'living water,' he was speaking of the Spirit" (John 7:39 NLT).

We hear, "Go faster, do more, get to the finish line." What a relief to know we serve a God who instead simply says, "Anytime you're thirsty, anytime you need to receive, slow down and come to me."

God, help me remember that when my heart is weary and my soul is thirsty, I can come to you.

. . . .

What is your soul thirsty for right now?

GOD SOOTHES YOUR SOUL

I have calmed and quieted myself,
like a weaned child who no longer cries for its mother's milk.
Yes, like a weaned child is my soul within me. (Psalm 131:2 NLT)

In the Old Testament, God instructed Jews to make three pilgrimages to Jerusalem each year—in spring for Passover, in summer for Shavuot, and in the fall for Sukkot. David had these travelers in mind when he wrote Psalm 131, and it starts with this dedication: "A song for pilgrims ascending to Jerusalem."

Imagine the scene: men walking on dusty roads, children playing tag as they weave in and out of the crowd, mothers with babies swaddled to their chests. It's this last image David brings to mind with the words, "I have calmed and quieted myself, like a weaned child." It's a picture of contentment, not want; endearment, not distress; satisfaction, not seeking more.

A weaned child no longer connects with her mother from a place of need. It's not just about what she wants; it's about relationship. For the pilgrims, this meant journeying to Jerusalem not to get something, like a favor from God or a prayer answered, but to experience God's presence in new yet familiar ways. For us, this can mean embracing spiritual practices like gratitude, praise, and reflection that aren't need-based but are simply about being with God.

Like a mother with her baby on a pilgrimage, God will be carrying you and caring for you every step of the way.

God, thank you for carrying me every step of my journey.
My soul is safe with you.

. . . .

What helps you calm and quiet yourself?

YOU HAVE A FOREVER FRIEND

I have called you friends. (John 15:15)

Our lives are like paths, and sometimes we walk parallel to each other. When that happens, we tend to think we'll stay side by side as friends forever. Then we come to an unexpected fork in the road, and God asks us to take steps in different directions. And over time, we discover we're not as close.

Confession: I hate it when that happens.

My natural tendency is going back to the past. Or abandoning the road God has for me so I can get on the one he's chosen for my friend. Or running ahead to where our paths might cross again. But here's the trouble with those choices: I would be following my heart instead of following Jesus.

Here's the hard reality I'm learning to embrace: some friends are with us for a reason (a specific goal/purpose from God); some friends are with us for a season (a particular time in his plan). Very few will walk beside us for a lifetime.

That doesn't mean we're a failure at friendship or we've done something wrong. It simply means God has a unique path for each of us. Yes, sometimes friendships drift through neglect or self-destruct because of unresolved conflict. But I've found more often we have just completed the part of the journey God intended for us to share. And that's okay.

The only person we must walk with for a lifetime is Jesus. As we do, we can trust he'll bring friends alongside us for a reason, a season, or a lifetime in the ways and times that are truly best.

God, thank you for being my heart's most faithful friend.

· · · ·

How has Jesus been a friend to you?

YOUR HEART IS IN A NEEDED SEASON

For everything there is a season. (Ecclesiastes 3:1 NLT)

Spring is just coming fully to the trees behind my house. Branches are becoming homes. I watch squirrels and birds build nests with leaves, twigs, and enthusiastic effort.

We welcome spring with open arms—it's a time of hope and joy after a long, dark winter. A reprieve before the stretched-out, hot summer. If we could, many of us would choose spring outside all year long.

But that's not how the seasons work. The trees need the intense sunshine of summer. They need time to let go in the fall. They need time to be quiet and grow deeper roots in winter. All are part of the rhythm that keeps them living and growing.

I tend to always want it to be spring inside me too. I love the dreaming and the doing, the wildflower adventures. I resist the stillness and the in-between seasons. But lately God is whispering to me that it can't always be spring. All of the seasons have their place and value. All have gifts to offer. All are necessary.

Especially when I find myself in winter, I wonder if I'm as valuable to God. What am I giving? What am I producing?

But God sees what I can't—the growth going on beneath the surface. The silence. The preparing my heart needs so that when spring comes, I will be able to grow, to give, to bear fruit again.

If you're in spring, grow. If you're in summer, take care of yourself so you don't burn out. If you're in fall, let go. If you're in winter, rest. Every season has a purpose.

God, help me embrace the season I'm in right now.

. . . .

What season are you in today?

YOU'RE MORE THAN YOU THINK YOU ARE

Looking intently at Simon, Jesus said, "Your name is Simon, son of John—but you will be called Cephas" (which means "Peter"). (John 1:42 NLT)

I love that Jesus starts with how Simon has likely always seen himself, but then doesn't stop there. Jesus goes beyond the human and gives not just a new name but a new identity. *Cephas* and *Peter* both mean "Rock."

I wonder if Peter had ever thought of himself in this way. Over the next few chapters, he shows himself to be volatile, unsteady, impulsive—so much more like the waves he has fished on than a firm foundation. But Jesus calls out something in Peter and he grows into it, becomes it. He does the same in us.

How would you define yourself today? Mama, wife, friend, sister, coworker. Introvert, extrovert. Southern, Northern, Australian. Or maybe the words are not so kind: failure, addict, broken, insecure, unworthy. Whatever the description might be, Jesus has more to add: beloved, chosen, accepted, forgiven, free, more than a conqueror.

Like Peter, it's okay if we can't yet feel, see, or even fully understand what God says is true of us. What matters is that we trust our human identity is not our ultimate destiny. So when the world around us tries to tell us who we are this week, let's pause and listen for the only voice that gets the final say.

We are loved. We are chosen. We are part of God's plan today.

God, thank you for seeing more in me than I can see in myself. Help me to continue becoming all you created me to be.

· · · ·

How would you define yourself today?

YOU CAN TRY AGAIN

May the Lord direct your hearts into God's love and Christ's perseverance.
(2 Thessalonians 3:5)

We can picture courage like a mighty warrior, sword raised high. But I've found courage is often more like a scrappy kid with skinned knees and dirt under her fingernails who just won't quit.

None of us get it right the first time. Most of us don't get it right the tenth. Maybe not even the hundredth. This isn't being a failure; it's being human.

We believe we have to win every time, but what matters is that we don't give up. We think God is calling the flawless, but instead he's calling the faithful. We strive for perfection, yet what makes life magic is growth and connection.

I'm thinking about all of this because I had a setback last week in an area where I'd made progress. Can anyone else relate?

Years ago this kind of mistake would have defeated me. But I've slowly learned setbacks aren't the real threat. No, the real danger is that my setbacks could lead me to set down my hope, my goals, my belief that tomorrow can be better.

I don't want to do that today. So I'm choosing courage, the scrappy kind with skinned knees and dirt under her fingernails who just won't quit. I'm going to try again. You too? Here are four steps to trying again:

1. Acknowledge that things didn't go the way you hoped.
2. Recognize any lies you're believing ("I'm a failure").
3. Replace those lies with truth ("I just haven't figured it out yet").
4. Ask God for help and try again.

God, thank you for turning my setbacks into stepping stones.

. . . .

What do you want to try again today?

YOUR WORDS CAN BE HEALING

Pleasant words are a honeycomb:
sweet to the taste and health to the body. (Proverbs 16:24 CSB)

Both in the ancient world and today, honey is primarily considered *a healing agent in wound care*. Isn't that beautiful?

First, honey has antibacterial properties. It helps keep the yuck out during the healing process. When our hearts are wounded, we always battle lies. Kind words from those with the truth help protect us.

Honey also has anti-inflammatory qualities. It prevents what's already bad from getting worse. Kind words can keep us from sliding into destructive patterns of thinking or reacting.

Honey is soothing as well. Sometimes on a hard day we just need some tenderness and compassion in our lives. There have been many times when words have given me strength, renewed faith, and courage.

When others share with us, we can treat them the way we want to be treated when we're hurting. We can resist the urge to rub salt in their wounds with criticism or clichés. We can hold back our human opinions and extend divine grace. We can intentionally be considerate and ask God for wisdom as we offer gentle comfort, encouragement, and support.

We all have the opportunity to make a difference in the life of whoever is right in front of us today. All we have to do is open our hearts and ears, then our mouths. Our words are a sweeter and more mysterious force than we can ever fully know this side of heaven. Let's never underestimate their God-given power to heal.

God, make my words sweet and healing like honey today.

. . . .

Who in your life needs healing words?

GOD DELIGHTS IN YOU

The LORD was my support.
He brought me out into a spacious place;
he rescued me because he delighted in me. (Psalm 18:18–19 CSB)

What assumptions have your circumstances led you to make about how God feels about you? Are those really true?

The enemy would love to persuade you that God is against you. He would love for you to become convinced that you don't have God's support. He would love to make you believe that you've fallen beyond God's ability to hold you up.

Will you pause for a moment and reject those lies? We live in a fallen, broken world, and we all face difficulties. That doesn't mean we're being punished. Jesus lived an absolutely perfect life, and yet he was still "a man of suffering, and familiar with pain" (Isa. 53:3). None of us gets to go through life without hard times. That doesn't say anything about you except this: you're human.

God knows that as humans we're weak and frail. He knows we need help. He wants to offer that to us. Yet it's up to us to receive it. And if we think he's mad at us, then that's a lot harder to do. Instead of thinking God is disappointed with us, let's say with the psalmist, "He rescued me because he delighted in me."

God, thank you so much for supporting and rescuing me. Help me to
believe you delight in me and your love for me is secure forever.

· · · ·

What makes it hard to believe God delights in you,
and what helps you believe it's true?

Day 94

YOU ARE STILL GROWING

All people are like grass,
and all their glory is like the flowers of the field. (1 Peter 1:24)

I stood in the curtain section of TJ Maxx saying these words over and over to myself: *You're learning to decorate your house. You're learning to decorate your house.*

Doesn't that sound silly? But it was much better than what I said over and over last time: *You can't decorate your house. What's the matter with you?*

I share this example because it's amazing how small a crack shame needs to slip through into our lives. God doesn't judge us that way. I used to read 1 Peter 1:24 as simply meaning life is brief. But I'm seeing it with new eyes lately. And I think what God is also reminding us of here is that grass is growing, flowers are growing, WE are growing.

Which means he knows that from our first breath to our last, we are in process. And that applies to everything from picking out curtains to becoming who he's created us to be.

And you know what? God's okay with that. He already knows us better than we know ourselves. If he's okay with it, then we can be too. He doesn't ask us for perfection. Just growth. Every day, a little bit at a time, all the way until we're home with him.

You are not who you were yesterday.
You are not who you will be tomorrow.
You're growing, the beautiful process of becoming.

God, thank you that you are growing me into
more of who you created me to be each day.

. . . .

How is God growing you, even in small or seemingly silly ways?

YOU DON'T HAVE TO UNDERSTAND

Jesus answered him, "What I'm doing you don't realize now, but after-ward you will understand." (John 13:7 CSB)

Jesus speaks these words to Peter. It's their Last Supper, the one in the upper room. The cross is coming. I imagine the disciples are confused and uncertain. So when Jesus begins to wash their feet, it's just one more thing that doesn't make sense. Peter protests, and John 13:7 is Jesus's response.

What I love about this verse is that Jesus doesn't try to explain. He doesn't correct or rebuke. He doesn't sigh in frustration. He isn't the parent using the cliché, "Because I said so, that's why." Jesus gives us a beautiful gift: permission to not understand.

When I look at the world around us, there's so much I don't comprehend. When I look at my own life, the same is true. What God is up to so often remains a mystery. It's okay not to know, not to have all the answers. Yet there's hope in these words as well—"but afterward you will understand."

Someday we *will* understand. All the blanks will be filled in at last. All the tears will be wiped away. All the injustices will be made right. This doesn't mean we don't grieve now, that we don't get frustrated or even angry. Jesus knows what it's like to live in this world. What it does mean is we can be sure that whatever trial we're facing, whatever questions we're wrestling with, whatever unknown wakes us up at night, it will not last forever.

Even when we don't understand, we can trust God's heart; we can put our whole lives in his hands.

God, even when I don't understand, I choose to trust you.

. . . .

What's something you don't understand but want
to trust God with today?

YOUR WORDS ARE POWERFUL

I want their hearts to be encouraged and joined together in love.
(Colossians 2:2 CSB)

I sit alone and pray about how I've become afraid of words—of what they can do. And it seems in the dark I sense a whisper: *Daughter, words can defend and protect too*. It's right there in our armor: "The sword of the Spirit, which is the word of God" (Eph. 6:17).

So how do we wield this sword? Let's put our words firmly on the side of the kingdom and use them to protect, never to harm. I'm raising my sword and pledging my allegiance to you and to the one who loves us. Will you join me?

A Commitment of Words

We commit to using our words to defend and heal, not to harm.

We will not gossip.

We will not belittle.

We will guard our sisters by always speaking the best about them, encouraging them into all God would have them to be, and offering grace instead of condemnation.

We will be loyal and loving, remembering that even if we disagree, we still fight on the same side—never against each other.

We will use our words to build up and not tear down, to bring hope and not hurt.

We offer our words as powerful weapons to fight for each other on the side of all that is good, right, and true.

Words matter and make a difference. The choice of how we will use them is ours to make. So let's choose to wield our words in ways that change the world.

God, help me to protect, defend, and encourage others with what I say.

· · · ·

When has someone spoken encouraging words to you?

YOU HAVE THE GIFT
OF GRACE TODAY

The grace of our Lord Jesus Christ be with you all. (2 Thessalonians 3:18 CSB)

*A*mazing grace! How sweet the sound that saved a wretch like me!
For a long time I only understood half of what grace really means. Yes, grace saved us once. But it also *keeps* saving us. I don't mean the latter in the sense of salvation—once we belong to Jesus we are his forever and always. I mean that grace continually rescues us and fills in the gaps where we fall short in our daily lives.

Every single morning we wake up with a vision of who we want to be and what we want to do. Every single night we fall asleep knowing we didn't completely fulfill that vision. *And that's okay.* God already knew that would be true the moment we opened our eyes. He knows it will be true tomorrow and every day until we're home with him and his work in us is complete.

What can trip us up, wear us out, and leave us discouraged is not acknowledging that reality. It's when we say, "Jesus saved me by his grace but the rest is up to me." No, Jesus saved us by his grace, and he'll sustain us with it in every breath, every heartache, every failure. Grace is not a one-time event—it is an ongoing experience. It is not just waiting for us in a church, it is with us every step of our broken, beautiful journey. Wherever you are, whatever you're going through, this same grace is yours too.

God, today I will give you my best.
And I will let your grace cover the rest.

. . . .

What are you grateful for about God's grace today?

YOU'RE AN ENCOURAGER

If your gift is to encourage others, be encouraging. (Romans 12:8 NLT)

A popular commercial featured people saying things like, "Tell me I'm loved. Tell me I'm going to be okay. Tell me I'm beautiful." We connect with these phrases and could add our own. Life knocks the wind out of all of us at times, and we need to be encouraged.

The word *encouragement* appears far more times in the New Testament than in the Old. It's a spiritual gift. But even those who may not specifically have that particular gift are still called to encourage. Encouragement comes from two sources—God and each other. And unlike simple compliments or kind words, encouragement is rooted in truth. It brings us back to what's real. It reminds our hearts that what we see or experience right now is not the full story. There is more to life and more to us than meets the eye.

Encouragement literally means to help give someone courage. It helps us get back up, face our day with joy, and fulfill the purpose God has for us. It's more than a simple pat on the back or a feel-good pep talk. It's fuel for our faith that provides what we need to move forward even on the most difficult of days.

You are an encourager, called by God and commissioned to strengthen the hearts of people. You have all you need to make a difference in the lives of whoever you meet today.

God, show me how I can be an encourager today to whoever you place in my life.

. . . .

Who can you encourage today?

YOUR OPPOSITION MIGHT BE AN OPPORTUNITY

I will stay on ... because a great door for effective work has opened to me, and there are many who oppose me. (1 Corinthians 16:8–9)

The apostle Paul was looking at opposition as affirmation and confirmation. He was where he needed to be, doing what he needed to do. It was not a reason to give up or feel like a failure, to think he must have misheard God or was doing it wrong. Just the opposite: he decided this meant he should carry on.

We will all get to the place where we face "opposition" in God's will for our lives. In that moment the most natural, human thing in the world to say is, "I'm walking away. I've clearly messed this up." But perhaps Jesus is whispering, *Stay ... a great door for effective work has opened to you, and there are many who oppose you.*

Sometimes what looks like opposition turns out to be an opportunity. It's an indication that it's time to press in, press on, and refuse to give up. It's a message that says we are fighting a worthwhile battle. It's proof that we are making a difference.

If we find ourselves in the middle of blood and sweat and tears today, then we can remember this doesn't mean we're failing; it means we're fighting. The enemy of our hearts knows the only way he can beat us is if he can convince us to retreat, to forfeit. If we stand firm, we can't lose. We'll never be defeated. We won't be overcome.

Here's the crazy secret the apostle Paul knew: with God, we've already won.

God, show me how to turn opposition into opportunity today.

. . . .

When have you overcome opposition?

YOU DON'T HAVE TO FEAR THE FUTURE

*She is clothed with strength and dignity;
she can laugh at the days to come. (Proverbs 31:25)*

The Proverbs 31 woman has a life full of verbs. She brings, selects, works, gets up, provides, considers, plants, sees, holds, grasps, extends, makes, sells, supplies, speaks, watches, and fears the Lord. While her virtues are often praised, it's clear that all of them are more than simply beliefs. She's a woman of action. When you are always taking the next step of obedience, fear of the future diminishes.

Many times when God says to his people, "Do not fear," it is followed by some kind of specific instruction. He's reassuring them and then showing them what they will need to do to replace that fear with faith.

In the life of the Proverbs 31 woman, we see this in two specific ways: strength and dignity. She is "clothed with strength and dignity"; therefore, she doesn't fear the future.

Strength conveys that she's willing to do whatever it takes to see God's purposes for her life fulfilled. She doesn't just talk the talk, she walks the walk.

Dignity describes her character—how she conducts herself as she takes action.

Doing what you need to do right now and becoming who God wants you to be a little more each day are two of the best ways to face the future without fear.

We can join her as women who are confident our future is in God's hands. And that means we can focus on what he has for our hands to do right here and now.

*God, clothe me with strength and dignity so that I can laugh
without fear of the future.*

. . . .

What helps you face the future without fear?

GOD CREATED FUN TOO

So I recommend having fun, because there is nothing better for people in this world than to eat, drink, and enjoy life. That way they will experience some happiness along with all the hard work God gives them under the sun. (Ecclesiastes 8:15 NLT)

Ecclesiastes 8:15 seems a bit scandalous to me. Did God create us to have fun? But then I think of slick otters playing in a river, the surprising satisfaction of blowing a bubble with chewing gum, and the sound of a baby's first chuckle.

I recently finished a sweet book called *When Mischief Came to Town* about a ten-year-old girl, Inge Maria, who comes to live with her stern and unsmiling grandmother. Inge Maria reminds her grandma and the whole town how to be happy again.

Toward the end of the story, the grandmother says, "We are told to be mature and behave, and for some silly reason, we believe this means that we can no longer have fun. We forget how to laugh, how to yell, how to run, and worst of all, how to delight in each other's company. I think we . . . have failed to notice that the same Lord God who gave us the strength to work and the wrinkles to frown also gave us the legs to dance and the voices to sing!"[1]

Yes, let's live intentionally and be in awe of this splendid universe God made. But let's also dare to revel in God's many gifts to us as his children.

God, help me to live not only purposefully but also simply and to have fun and enjoy your good gifts with the faith of a child.

. . . .

What's a gift from God that brings you delight and fun?

GOD IS GREATER
THAN ALL YOUR FEARS

The fear of the LORD is the beginning of wisdom,
and knowledge of the Holy One is understanding. (Proverbs 9:10)

When we hear the word *fear*, it can sound strange to us because we don't often use it in a similar way today.

Author and pastor Chuck Swindoll explains, "The fear of the Lord refers to our viewing him with the respect he deserves."[1]

As a king himself, Solomon understood this kind of fear because it's what he wanted from those he ruled. Proverbs 24:21 says, "Fear the LORD and the king." So fear like this is about *authority*. Who will we listen to and obey?

Some of us have been taught a distorted view of God. We've been told he's not a benevolent king but a vindictive dictator. He rules not through love but through punishment. He's waiting with a lightning bolt in hand so he can show us who's in charge. But the God we serve leads through mercy, not manipulation. He humbled himself and dwelled among us. He laid down his life on our behalf. He is good, wise, and kind. We can trust him.

William D. Eisenhower says, "As I walk with the Lord, I discover that God poses an ominous threat to my ego, but not to me. He rescues me from my delusions, so he may reveal the truth that sets me free. . . . Fear of the Lord is the beginning of wisdom, but love from the Lord is its completion."[2]

God, I fear you and approach you with awe, respect, humility, and trust.

. . . .

What does fearing God mean to you?

GOD IS YOUR GOOD SHEPHERD

> *Your rod and your staff*
> *protect and comfort me. (Psalm 23:4 NLT)*

The shepherd's rod and staff have two different purposes. The rod provides protection from *external* threats. W. Phillip Keller, author of *A Shepherd Looks at Psalm 23*, says, "The shepherd's rod is an instrument of protection both for himself and his sheep when they are in danger. It is used both as a defense and a deterrent against anything that would attack."[1]

The shepherd's staff provides protection from *internal* threats. Sheep are likely to get themselves into trouble, and so are we. Keller explains, "Being stubborn creatures, sheep often get into the most ridiculous and preposterous dilemmas. I have seen my own sheep, greedy for one more mouthful of green grass, climb down steep cliffs where they slipped and fell into the sea. Only my long shepherd's staff could lift them out of the water back onto solid ground again."[2]

The staff is used not for punishment but to draw the sheep back toward the shepherd. When we've strayed, intentionally or not, the heart of the Good Shepherd is to rescue us and restore our relationship with him. We may feel the staff of God pulling our hearts toward his through his Word, caring friends, and other gentle but compelling ways.

Our Good Shepherd is with us. He will protect us with his rod, pursue us with his staff, and guide us to the other side.

God, you are my Good Shepherd, and I'm so grateful to be in your care.

. . . .

How have you seen God use his rod and staff in your life?

GOD'S PLANS MIGHT BE DIFFERENT FROM YOURS

But the angel said to her, "Do not be afraid, Mary; you have found favor with God. You will conceive and give birth to a son, and you are to call him Jesus. He will be great and will be called the Son of the Most High. The Lord God will give him the throne of his father David, and he will reign over Jacob's descendants forever; his kingdom will never end." (Luke 1:30–33)

Those words from Luke 1 keep echoing in my mind. I've heard them since I was a child. But this time I thought of something new, the dreams that might have been born in Mary's heart that day that didn't come true in the way she might have imagined.

I don't know what was going through Mary's mind as Jesus's life unfolded and she eventually watched him be crucified, but I can imagine what may have filled her heart at times: confusion, questioning, wondering if she heard God wrong. Have you ever felt that way? Maybe you even do today?

What got her through? I imagine Mary kept praying that same prayer she did when the angel first spoke to her: "I am the Lord's servant. May your word to me be fulfilled" (v. 38).

Here's the hope Mary gives us: just because what God has said to us doesn't look the way we pictured doesn't mean it's not real. Jesus is great. He does have a throne. He is reigning over a kingdom that will never end. It didn't happen the way Mary probably expected, but it did happen exactly as God planned.

God, help me to trust you even when things don't turn out the way I expect.

. . . .

When has an answered prayer looked different than you imagined?

GOD WANTS TO SETTLE YOU

The LORD will have compassion on Jacob;
once again he will choose Israel
and will settle them in their own land. (Isaiah 14:1)

"I'm afraid to settle." Have you ever said these words? I have. Years ago they pushed me toward burnout and exhaustion, insecurity and comparison, an endless search for more.

Then it seemed Jesus began whispering something to me that I never expected: *Settle.* At first I thought I must be mishearing. I'd read the story about God's people leaving Egypt and crossing the promised land. Wasn't I to bravely go? But I'd missed the ending point of the story: God's plan had always been to bring his people to a place where they could settle. In other words, a place where they could dwell and thrive.

We get confused about the difference between *settling* and *being settled*. Settling is when we know what God wants us to do or where he wants us to go—and we flat-out refuse. We intentionally and persistently make-do with less than he has for us.

But being settled, which is a gift from God, is embracing the place where he has us right now. It's choosing to look at our everyday lives and say, "This is good. This is enough." It's not that we don't grow but that we don't strive. We don't make choices from a place of fear.

When we choose contentment, gratitude, and peace, we're not settling. Our hearts are being settled by a God who loves us and wants the very best for us.

God, you are the one who gives me a place in life to settle
that is holy and good.

. . . .

Where is God inviting you to settle today?

YOU'RE NOT UNDER THE LAW

You no longer live under the requirements of the law. Instead, you live under the freedom of God's grace. (Romans 6:14 NLT)

I scroll through my social media accounts one evening just to see how many "shoulds" I can find at one time—whether directly stated or implied. I should follow a diet, declutter my home, do a weekly date night.

Years ago I learned to identify legalism by recognizing this formula: "You must _____, or _____ will happen." You must read your Bible every single morning, or God will be mad at you. You must show up at church every time the doors are open, or your life won't be blessed. It's a language of guilt and fear, not love and grace. It took me a long time to get free from it. But lately I find myself surrounded by it again—it's just that this time I'm on social media, not in church.

You should use this color scheme in your home, or no one will want to spend time there. You should do this exact exercise program, or you will never be healthy and happy. You should never watch television, or you'll become a lonely recluse.

It doesn't matter if it's religious legalism or secular legalism. When we give in to this message, no matter the source, we place ourselves under law instead of grace.

Yes, we can make progress, learn, and grow. But if what we thought would improve our lives has become an obstacle to our peace and joy, then it's time to let it go. True transformation comes not from working *on* ourselves but from giving ourselves fully to the God working *in* us.

God, you have freed me from shoulds and invited me into a life of joy.

. . . .

What shoulds have you placed on yourself?

WHAT YOUR HEART NEEDS WHEN YOU MESS UP

God's kindness is intended to lead you to repentance. (Romans 2:4)

I sit across from a friend who knows me well. We've walked together for more than a decade. My eyes are tear-filled as I look at her and say, "I messed up." I tell her of how I have failed in an area that has been an off-and-on battle in my life for years. We all have one, don't we? I call it our "signature struggle."

My friend leans in and puts both arms around my shoulders. She says, so gently, "Don't let the shame win. Don't give the enemy that victory." She wisely understands that what the enemy is really after is not simply to make us sin—the cross means we're already forgiven. It's to make us abandon our identity as God's beloved children.

The enemy of our hearts would always rather have us embrace shame and guilt instead of grace. Because grace is what transforms us, what brings us out of hiding, what gives us the courage to keep trying.

Later that day when the shame tries to slink in again, I close my eyes and picture my friend sitting next to me. Then I imagine that it's Jesus instead. Because isn't that how he loves us?

If you, like me, have given in to a signature struggle recently, then let me put my arms around your shoulders right now too. Let me whisper again to both of us what my friend reminded me is true: We are still loved. Who we are in Christ hasn't changed. We will rise. We will fight again. Grace always wins in the end.

God, thank you for your endless grace and victory over my struggles.

. . . .

What is your signature struggle?

Day 108

YOU PRAY AND WORK

He sought his God and worked wholeheartedly. And so he prospered.
(2 Chronicles 31:21)

I'll just pray about it."

"I'm going to make this happen no matter what."

Those statements reflect common mindsets in our culture and even the church. In the first, change is all up to God. We just sit back and wait. In the second, change is all up to us. We move ahead by our own effort without much regard for what God might have in mind.

I love 2 Chronicles 31:21 because it represents a beautiful hybrid of both. The backstory: Hezekiah was king in Israel at a time when the nation had drifted far away from God. A lot of change was needed spiritually as well as practically in the lives of the people. Hezekiah approached this situation by first seeking God with his heart and then doing whatever God commanded with his hands. He combined faith with works.

Throughout Scripture, we're encouraged to do the same. When we say we'll simply "pray about it" without following up with actual work, it may seem spiritual. But if we peel that back a bit, it can also be a way of avoiding risk or fear. In the other scenario, we may choose to simply apply our own efforts because we don't want to give up control. We fear that if we ask God what he wants us to do, we might not like the answer.

You have the beautiful gift of free will. You can choose to partner with God as you make changes in your life. And what's even more amazing is that he's ready and willing to partner with you.

God, help me to seek you and work wholeheartedly.

. . . .

What can you pray about and work toward today?

GOD MAY LEAD YOU
THE ROUNDABOUT WAY

So God led them in a roundabout way. (Exodus 13:18 NLT)

Exodus 13:18 is a crazy little jewel of a verse in a passage about the Israelites leaving Egypt to go to the promised land. It comes before they goofed up and God said they had to wander around for forty years. This is a different situation where God intentionally led them the roundabout way.

Although this is confusing and strange and unexpected, it also gives me hope. Because in my mind the will of God always looks like a thin, straight line. Then life invariably does not. So I start thinking I must have taken a detour somewhere or I would already be there. Have you ever felt that way?

I imagine some things in your life may not have turned out the way you planned. There might have been a bit of chaos. Something unexpected. A few twists and turns. If so, let's take heart. This doesn't automatically mean that we're not in the will of God. Sometimes he just leads his people the roundabout way.

Why? Because he knows us better than we know ourselves. Because his ways are not like ours. Because we think in terms of minutes, but he grasps all of eternity. Because we barely see a foot in front of us, but he knows the whole story, the whole winding way that is going to get us where he wants us to go.

God sometimes takes the scenic route. Life is like a race, but it's also like a road trip. It's about so much more than getting there.

God, I trust you to guide me, even if you take me the roundabout way.

. . . .

Where is God leading you in your life right now?

YOU DON'T NEED TO
HAVE IT ALL TOGETHER

If the whole body were an eye, where would the sense of hearing be?
If the whole body were an ear, where would the sense of smell be?
(1 Corinthians 12:17)

A friend of mine and I recently talked about how we both felt guilty for not being more like each other. I lamented to her, "I wish I could cook like you and make my house cozy like yours!" She also saw some qualities and skills in me she'd like to have.

Next time we chatted, we both laughed and shook our heads at our silly comparison game. But it reminded us that it's easy to lose sight of God's heart and his unique purpose for each of us.

As women, it seems we often compare ourselves to one another. If someone is gifted in different ways than we are, we feel inadequate and wish we could change. But God has a completely different plan. He places each of us within the body of Christ with a specific role to fulfill.

We may think, "They don't need me. Sally is so much more creative. Alison is so much better with kids. Hannah is a much better speaker." Meanwhile, other women are probably thinking the same about us! When someone excels where we struggle, it doesn't mean we need to change or withdraw. It simply means she may have a different role in the body than we do.

None of us need to have it all together. We just need to remember we're all better together. We need you just as you are, and no one can take your place.

God, thank you for creating me just as I am and
creating others with amazing gifts too.

. . . .

What's one strength or gift God has given you?

YOU HAVE A GOOD SHEPHERD

The LORD is my shepherd, I lack nothing. (Psalm 23:1)

In Psalm 23, the shepherd has the sheep lie down in "green pastures" (v. 2). What does a green pasture mean to a sheep? It means its needs are going to be met. The sheep is not worrying about going hungry. God wants us to live that way too. And not just when it comes to our physical needs but also those in our hearts as well. He says, "Lie down, daughter. I'm going to take care of your needs. You can stop striving. Rest."

He also leads us to "quiet waters" (v. 2). As we've already talked about, sheep need water that's quiet in order to be able to quench their thirst. They don't want to drink from raging rivers or stand on shores with crashing waves. We also need still places to be refreshed. Our schedules may feel like a tsunami is coming toward us, yet our Shepherd says that he has "quiet waters" for us to drink from instead.

You have a Good Shepherd. He doesn't want to drive you so hard that you fall down from exhaustion. He doesn't want to force you to go through life without nourishment and refreshment. Shepherds understand sheep. Yours already knows where you are and what you've been through, and it brings him joy to care for you.

God, I'm so grateful I belong to a good and faithful Shepherd like you. Thank you for watching over me and caring for all my needs.

· · · ·

What do you need from your Good Shepherd today?

YOU CAN LOVE LIKE JESUS

"What do you want me to do for you?" (Matthew 20:32 NLT)

I love that in so many of the encounters Jesus had with people on this earth he asked, "What do you want me to do for you?" The One who knows everything, who can do anything, still chose to listen and respond. He could have skipped this part and simply solved the problem. But Jesus understood that what mattered most was not the solution but the soul in front of him.

What people want most isn't for us to solve their problems but to stay with them in their pain. It's tempting to offer solutions, advice, or reassurance that all will be well. It's harder to not react but respond, to sit in the sadness or anger of the people we love, to be a safe space where they can feel whatever they need to so they can begin to heal.

I've worked as a counselor and life coach, engaged with thousands of people as a writer, and spent decades on this earth full of brokenhearted people. In all of that, I've found this one simple question to be the most helpful when someone in my life is hurting: How can I love you well right now?

This question means we're asking rather than assuming, focusing on the other person instead of our own feelings, discovering what they truly want rather than what we think they need. No matter what the person says, even if their answer is entirely different from what ours would be, we listen with love and grace, and then do what we can to love them like Jesus.

God, help me love like Jesus today.

. . . .

Who can you love like Jesus today?

YOU CAN LEAN ON JESUS

The Lord is good to those who depend on him. (Lamentations 3:25 NLT)

Lord," I whispered, "I don't understand why I'm so worn out if I'm doing what you want. What lie am I believing?" In that moment it felt as if the Holy Spirit shined a flashlight on my heart, and I could finally see this sinister sentence hiding in a dark corner: *It all depends on me.*

It all depends on me to make people like me.

It all depends on me to get the work done.

It all depends on me to be a "good Christian."

If that's true, then "try harder" is the only reasonable response. But I serve the scandalously gracious Savior who said, "Come to me." So I paused and asked him, "What's the truth my heart needs in order to be set free?" And suddenly I realized, it doesn't all depend on me; *I only need to depend on Jesus.*

I forgot my role is obedience; God's job is results. Believing is all that's asked of us today. "This is the work of God—that you believe in the one he has sent" (John 6:29 CSB).

Jesus didn't die on the cross and come back to life so we could try hard.

He did it so we could live loved.

God, you release me from the burden of living like it all depends on me and invite me to lean on you instead. Help me to receive that gift of grace today.

. . . .

What's one way you can depend on Jesus instead of carrying everything yourself today?

YOU CAN LET GO OF EXPECTATIONS

Be silent before the LORD and wait expectantly for him. (Psalm 37:7 CSB)

In my early twenties, I went to counseling for the first time. I was struggling with anxiety and depression. I don't remember everything my counselor said, but one vivid image remains in my mind.

My counselor pulled out a yellow notepad and drew a horizontal line across it. Then she drew a series of vertical lines reaching toward it but never quite getting there. She tapped the horizontal line and said, "These are your expectations." Then she pointed toward the vertical lines and added, "This is reality." Her point? Until I lowered my expectations, especially of myself, I would continue to battle anxiety and depression. At that time in my life, my expectation was perfection. And, as you know, real life never quite gets there either.

Instead of wearing myself out with expectations, I can live *expectantly*. What's the difference? Expectations are of our own making; living expectantly means opening ourselves to what God will do.

Isn't faith really the ultimate example of living expectantly? The Jewish people expectantly watched for a Messiah. Mary and Joseph expectantly waited for their son to come. The wise men expectantly followed the star.

I don't know what the world will be like when you're reading this, but I know there will still be expectations and the opportunity to live instead with expectancy. This is my simple prayer for this season and whatever one you're in today. *God, give me the courage to let go of expectations and live expectantly.* Will you pray this with me?

*God, I will say it again—give me the courage
to let go of expectations and live expectantly.*

. . . .

What's an expectation you need to let go of
that's weighing you down?

YOU CAN RELEASE YOUR WORRIES

Who of you by worrying can add a single hour to your life? (Luke 12:25)

Who of us by worrying can make the prodigal come home, the marriage be restored, the meeting go well, the weight come off, the lights come on, the kids stay safe, the wrong be undone, the project turn out right?

One day into a place of fear there comes a God-whisper for my heart: *Your worry cannot change the world, only I can.* This doesn't feel like a rebuke; it feels like a relief. Jesus, in all his gentleness and kindness, his extravagant mercy and care, has taken the boulder from my hands and said, "It doesn't depend on you." As I picture this, I see the scars on his own palms, hear his voice on the cross saying, "It is finished."

Isn't that what we really want to know? That someone is taking care of it, of them, of the situation, the circumstance, the thing that causes us to make our pillow soggy with salty tears. This is what God says he will do. He will look out for our tender hearts and glass lives.

What frees our hearts isn't worry; it's worship. In other words, taking all the hard things to the One who cares for us. Choosing to trust and let go. Believing through the blood, sweat, and tears he will mysteriously work it all together for good.

Here's what we can rest in today: the only One who has ever been able to bear the weight of the world on his shoulders is still strong and loving enough to carry all that concerns us too.

God, I give all my worries and concerns to you.

. . . .

What is a worry you need God to replace with worship today?

YOU ARE FREE FROM JUDGMENT

There is no judgment against anyone who believes in him. (John 3:18 NLT)

Our daughter runs half marathons, and we wait for her at the finish line. Watching each runner come in always brings tears to my eyes. Because no matter how weary they are, the reaction is the same. We cheer, and then inevitably someone they love finds them, embraces them, and says something like "Well done!" I have never heard a runner criticized at the finish line.

When we get to heaven, it will be a joyful homecoming. It will not be about the mistakes we made but about the wonder that we made it through this life. We crossed the finish line, and the great cloud of witnesses can cheer. We'll see Jesus face-to-face at last.

On the cross when he took God's wrath for us, when he died for our sins, Jesus said, "It is finished!" (John 19:30). There is no eternal PS to that statement. There's not an "oops, I forgot that one really terrible thing you did." We are right with God today. We are right with God tomorrow. We are right with God for all eternity.

The story that will be told when we get to heaven won't be one of judgment; it will be one of victory. It won't be about everything we've done wrong; it will be about all Jesus has done for us. It won't be about guilt and what we lack; it will be about grace and love far beyond what we can even imagine.

God, thank you that because I've trusted in Jesus as my Savior, I can be absolutely at peace about standing before you one day.

. . . .

What are you looking forward to in heaven?

GOD CAN HANDLE YOUR FEAR

Do not fear; I will help you. (Isaiah 41:13)

I've studied a lot about how our brains work. We actually can't help it when our nervous system triggers our fight-or-flight response. It's automatic and always involves fear. So how do we reconcile what God seems to tell us to *do* with how he's created us to *feel*?

As I looked closer at what God says, I finally found my answer. Verses that say "Do not be afraid" are almost always spoken to or for someone who is *already* afraid.

Israelite armies about to go into battle (Deut. 20:1–4).

Mary being startled by an unexpected angel (Luke 1:30).

The apostle Paul facing a serious storm (Acts 27:23–26).

In other words, when God says, "Do not be afraid," it is most often offered as a reassurance, not issued as a command. He's not saying, "Don't ever feel fear." He's saying, "Here's why you don't have to *stay* afraid."

"Do not fear, for I am with you." (Isa. 41:10)

"Do not fear; I will help you." (Isa. 41:13)

"Do not fear . . . I have called you by your name; you are mine." (Isa. 43:1 CSB)

It's the kind of language a loving parent would use to comfort a child who's afraid of the dark. A compassionate mom or dad knows their little one is going to be okay, but they give words that soothe hearts and calm minds anyway. And most beautiful of all, their love defeats the fear.

God, thank you that my fear is not a surprise to you. You are always willing to encourage me and help me be brave.

. . . .

What's a truth that helps you be brave?

GOD SPEAKS TO YOU
IN THE STORM

Then the LORD spoke to Job out of the storm. (Job 38:1)

Job thinks of all he has lost—his children, his possessions, and even his health. What will he do now? He sits for many days with his friends and processes all he's endured, including his questions, confusion, and frustration. His expressions of emotion include sorrow, rage, despair, and a desire for his life to end.

Finally, the Lord speaks to Job "out of the storm." He asks Job a series of questions like, "Where were you when I laid the earth's foundations?" (38:4). In the end, Job says, "My ears had heard of you but now my eyes have seen you" (42:5). What Job needs most isn't answers to his questions but rather an assurance that God is real and is still in control despite all that had happened.

Job discovers a truth many of us never experience: *whatever we're feeling, God can take it.* We tend to tiptoe around God as if he's a weak old man we shouldn't upset. Or we see him as a heavenly avenger just waiting to send yet another lightning bolt our way. But he loves us unconditionally and is strong enough to handle anything we share with him.

If you have only been sharing with God what you think he wants to hear, then perhaps it's your turn to give God the opportunity to speak to you in the storm too.

God, give me the courage to bring all I feel to you,
trusting you can take it.

. . . .

What are you sometimes afraid to share with God?

GOD IS WITH YOU NOW

God said to Moses, "I AM WHO I AM. This is what you are to say to the Israelites: 'I AM has sent me to you.'" (Exodus 3:14)

When God appeared in a burning bush, he didn't say to Moses, "Tell them 'I was' sent me to you" or "Tell them 'I will be' sent me to you." No, instead he insisted, "Tell them 'I AM' sent me to you."

Sometimes when I look back at the past with regret or toward tomorrow with fear, it can be disturbing because I can't seem to find God in those places. And I think all the while he might be saying, "I was there when you were. And I will be there when you arrive at that place tomorrow. But right now I'm right here."

This is true all through the New Testament too. When our hearts are hungry, Jesus says, "*I am* the bread of life" (John 6:35).

When darkness comes to our lives, he says, "*I am* the light of the world" (8:12).

When we feel like we've lost our way, he says, "*I am* the good shepherd" (10:11).

Whatever you need right now, Jesus is saying, "I am . . ." He's not only present; he's actively providing in this very second. Whatever year, month, or moment it may be, our God is with us. The burning bush is inside us. And wherever we are standing right now is holy ground.

God, it's so comforting to know you are here with me
and you promise to provide my every need.

. . . .

What do you need from God right now in this moment?

Day 120

YOU CAN BE KIND TO YOURSELF

Put on compassion, kindness, humility, gentleness, and patience, bearing with one another and forgiving one another. . . . Above all, put on love. (Colossians 3:12–14 CSB)

The list of attributes in Colossians 3 makes me nod as I think about how I want to treat others. But there's one person in my life for whom this list proves to be truly challenging. We're also to love *ourselves* as we love each other.

I recently had a conversation with two extraordinary women. Neither is perfect, of course, but when I think of their lives, I see strength, beauty, and enduring faithfulness to Jesus. Yet all three of us confessed one of our biggest battles is being our own worst critic.

I've had similar talks with many other women, and I'm ready to declare *enough is enough*. Let's see what Paul's list might look like for us then.

We show compassion when we talk to ourselves like we would a hurting friend.

We live with kindness when we remove something from our endless to-do list so we can rest.

We embrace humility when we stop trying to be perfect and accept being human.

We discover gentleness when we fire our inner critic and listen to grace.

We practice patience when we refuse to beat ourselves up for mistakes.

We bear with who we are when we intentionally say "yes!" to who God made us.

We forgive when we stop dishing out punishment for our perceived failures.

In other words, *we put on love when we treat ourselves the way we do others.* Let's dare to put on love for each other and ourselves today.

God, help me to put on love in beautiful ways that reflect your heart today.

. . . .

What's one way you can put on love today?

SHOW UP ANYWAY

Be on your guard; stand firm in the faith; be courageous; be strong.
(1 Corinthians 16:13)

One evening at a women's event, a speaker shares and then it's time for discussion questions. The first one: *What makes you feel brave?*

The women at my table have inspiring answers. Mine feels uncertain to me. Alone in my room later that evening, I realize why: *I never feel brave.*

I know what it is to *be* brave. But in those times, what I feel first is still fear. The pounding of my heart and the quickening of my breath. The spinning of the earth beneath my feet and the sense that I may be full-out crazy to go through with what I'm about to do. As I think about this, I realize maybe I've misunderstood what brave feels like. I thought it was a roar and a lunge. But maybe it is a whisper and a trembling step. I thought it was loud and bold. Perhaps it is quiet and almost invisible. I thought it meant the absence of all insecurity. Yet I'm wondering now if it's just faith dancing the two-step with doubt.

This lets me breathe a sigh of relief because it means I don't have to wait to be filled with confidence before I can do anything. I can just show up anyway. If that's so, then I have more courage than I thought.

If I could answer that question about being brave again, I'd say, "I'm not sure what makes me brave, but I know *who* does."

God, even when I'm afraid, I can show up and be brave
because I belong to you.

* * * *

What's a time you felt afraid and did something brave anyway?

YOU ARE ALREADY RISING

Victory comes from you, O LORD. (Psalm 3:8 NLT)

A re you going through a hard season where you've been hurt by life? Some mornings you struggle just to get out of bed, do the next thing, keep pushing forward. Sometimes it seems like it would be easier to give up. But you keep pressing in, pressing on, refusing to surrender to the discouragement or fear.

You didn't choose this and you don't deserve it. But we live in a shattered world where things (and people) are not as they were meant to be. Hear the whisper of this to your heart today: *Not everything that happens is your fault or responsibility.*

You keep going back over the details and asking, "How could I have made this turn out differently?" But the reality is that sometimes things happen that we can't control. Sometimes people make choices we never saw coming. Sometimes the gap between what we hoped for and the reality we find ourselves in is as vast as the Grand Canyon.

You did not break this and you cannot fix it. You can only surrender to what is and choose how you show up in each moment. You can remember you are loved. You can believe you are worthy of a better tomorrow. You can whisper, "Jesus, help" as often as needed.

You may feel down some days, but you are not going to be taken down by this. One morning at a time, you are already rising.

God, thank you that when life gets me down, you help me rise up.

. . . .

What helps you rise even on hard days?

YOU ARE A WORSHIPER
AND A WARRIOR

We do not know what to do, but our eyes are on you. (2 Chronicles 20:12)

Jehoshaphat spoke these words as a vast army was approaching.

We think we must know what to do, but all we really need to know is who God is. Because that's what makes the difference. That's what matters on the hard days. That's what brings the victory.

After this declaration, Jehoshaphat did something we won't find in any tactical guide. He put the worshipers in front of the army. He led not with generals but the choir members.

Truth is a powerful weapon. And the truest thing of all is who God is. His character is a fortress and battering ram, an all-out assault against evil. This means worship is absolutely undefeatable.

Perhaps too the worshipers needed to go first as an act of war against fear. This battle didn't look easily won. The Israelites were outnumbered, weary, and seemingly ready to be overrun.

So if we are unsure about what to do today, if the enemy is coming and the battle is raging and maybe we have even been wounded—let us stand our ground and raise our voices. Let us speak the truth about who God is and what he has done. How big he is. How much he loves us. How he has always held the universe and our little part of it in his hands.

We cannot lose with him. We cannot be overcome.

Jehoshaphat won his battle. We will too.

To be a worshiper is to be a warrior.

God, I praise you because you are powerful, wise, and kind.
You will bring me victory.

. . . .

What victory can you praise God for today?

GOD ALONE KNOWS
YOUR FUTURE

You can make many plans,
but the LORD's purpose will prevail. (Proverbs 19:21 NLT)

As king, Solomon spent much of his time making decisions. Life is even more complex now, and researchers estimate we make about thirty-five thousand decisions a day.[1]

We run imaginary scenarios through our minds. For example, "If I (choose this option), then (this will happen)." Our brains often naturally picture the worst-case scenario, even if it's highly unlikely to happen.

God alone actually knows the future. That's why Proverbs 19:21 is so reassuring. It means that when we seek God, no matter what we choose, he will still accomplish his purpose in our lives.

I have this verse on a canvas print in my office to remind me of this truth. I'm often tempted to believe the lie that unless I get everything exactly right, then everything will go completely wrong. That's a lot of pressure. I'm learning to trust instead that even in my imperfection, in my limitations, in the little that I know, God is able to get me where he wants me to go. He's able to redeem, redirect, and work all things together for my good—and yours too. It's not up to us to get every detail of every decision perfect; our role is simply to depend on him and keep taking one small step after another.

God, give me the courage to trust you and to keep moving forward
one step at a time, believing your purposes in my life will prevail.

. . . .

What plans do you want to entrust to God today?

YOU ARE MOTHERING

Villagers in Israel would not fight;
they held back until I, Deborah, arose,
until I arose, a mother in Israel. (Judges 5:7)

Deborah, a judge in ancient Israel, also served as a mighty warrior who helped win a significant victory on God's behalf. Scripture gives no indication that Deborah had children of her own. Yet she clearly sees herself as a strong, fierce mother. Because of her courage and obedience, "the land had peace for forty years" (Judg. 5:31).

Perhaps you've never married and wonder if you're disqualified from mothering. Maybe you have children but feel like you're "not really a mother" compared to others. You might be an empty nester who believes your work as a mom has ended. Whatever your circumstances, I want to gently challenge you to believe this: *you are a mother.*

God may have you mother your department at work, a group of teenagers at church, or the children in your neighborhood. He might have you mentor individuals who never got what they needed from their own moms. He could have you give birth to a project, idea, or dream that wouldn't make it into this world without you.

How God calls each of us to mother looks different, but we all have this in common: we are a powerful force God wants to use to change the world. Never underestimate what God can do through the heart and hands of a woman. We are influencers. We are nurturers. We are fighters. We are Deborahs. *We are mothers.*

God, thank you for making me a woman and a mother.
Show me who or what I can nurture in this season of my life.

. . . .

How are you mothering, even if you don't have physical children?

GOD IS CALLING YOU

Don't be afraid of the people, for I will be with you and will protect you. I, the LORD, have spoken! (Jeremiah 1:8 NLT)

God calls Jeremiah to be a prophet. Rather than replying with enthusiasm, Jeremiah protests, "O Sovereign LORD . . . I can't speak for you! I'm too young!" (Jer. 1:6 NLT). We're all tempted to believe we're "too" something.

Too young. Too old.

Too quiet. Too loud.

Too much. Too little.

God addresses the real cause for Jeremiah's pause: "Don't be afraid of the people" (v. 8 NLT). When we say we're "too" something, usually we're worried about what people will think of us. Considering how others will view us is a natural and healthy part of being human. God created us to consider what people think of us; he just doesn't want us to be controlled by it. What he said to Jeremiah is true for us too: "I will be with you and will protect you" (v. 8 NLT).

Jeremiah cared about the messages God entrusted to him and the people he served as a prophet for the next forty years. The phrase "do not be afraid" appears several more times in his writing. Through Jeremiah, we see that "do not be afraid" isn't a condemning command; it's a soul-comforting challenge to move past our fear and into obedience because God is always with and for us.

Jeremiah felt the fear and obeyed anyway.

Let's choose to do the same today.

God, give me the courage to listen to your voice, believe you can use me, and trust your plan for my future.

. . . .

How do you sometimes finish this sentence: "I'm too . . . "?

YOU'RE NOT STAYING DOWN

He lifted me out of the slimy pit,
out of the mud and mire;
he set my feet on a rock
and gave me a firm place to stand. (Psalm 40:2)

"How are you doing this week?" I ask, and she replies, "Feeling a little low." It's interesting how we use the word *low* to describe challenging times in our lives. When life brings hard times, it's difficult to look up and stand tall.

Yet in Psalm 40:2 and in other Scriptures, being "low" is a place where God can work, and it's always meant to be temporary.

"In his love and mercy he redeemed them; he lifted them up" (Isa. 63:9).

"Humble yourself before the Lord, and he will lift you up" (James 4:10).

I'm not talking about plastering a smile on your face and pretending everything is okay when it's not. That's not helpful either. I actually mean the opposite—that it's time to get really honest about how hard things are as well as the help you need.

We will all have times when life knocks us down. That's simply part of being human. Yet God doesn't want us to stay there forever.

So what do you do if you find yourself in that place? You do whatever it takes: ask God for help, reach out to friends, see a doctor, join a support group, take care of yourself. You're worth it. And you're not alone.

Through his gentleness, love, and patient timing, God wants to lift you up and give you a new, stronger place to stand.

God, when life lets me down, thank you for being
the one who always lifts me up.

. . . .

How do you need God to lift you up today?

GOD IS WITH YOU IN THE STORM

You are a refuge from the storm. (Isaiah 25:4 NLT)

For many years my life was mostly sunny. I could grin and bear it through the few showers that came along. But then came The Storm—the type that makes The Weather Channel flash maps covered with red and send warnings about taking shelter immediately.

Like the rain that streamed down in my world, something opened in my heart and hurt poured out from a place I had kept locked for years. Then I waited. I listened for the rebukes. I watched for the disapproving stares. I stiffened my soul for the hard hand of God. But instead of those things I encountered the last thing I ever expected to find.

Love.

I felt it in the kindness of friends and family. I heard it in comforting words. I discovered it deep within my heart as God whispered, *I'm here with you.* I also realized I wasn't the only one who was wet. People began to open up to me. Everyone I knew had some type of rain in their lives. We were one great, big, beautiful soggy mess . . . and God loved us all.

So if you're still muttering under your breath, "I'm dry, really, I'm dry," then I invite you to admit that there's a storm in your life. It's okay to not be okay. When we embrace that grace, we're finally free to discover that God's love is waiting for us in the center of the storm.

God, thank you that I don't have to be okay right now,
but I can also trust that because of you I will be one day.

. . . .

How has God been there for you in a storm?

YOU CAN FIND HOPE
IN YOUR DARK MOMENTS

Count it all joy when you fall into various trials. (James 1:2 NKJV)

I shake my head a bit at the words in James 1:2 and think, *I'm not so sure I want to do that right now.* I pray, "God, can you please help me understand what this means? I know you're compassionate and you're not telling me to just fake my joy."

As I continued to pray and considered the passage more, I realized that when we count something it means we're intentionally recognizing the worth in it. When we count something as joy, we're saying there's not only worth there but maybe even something good.

Years ago I went through several losses and felt utterly discouraged. One day I prayed, "Lord, I feel like I'm in a deep, dark cave right now." Of course, I didn't hear an audible response, but he did impress on my heart, *You may be in a cave but you have a choice: you can sit in the dark or you can diamond-mine your difficulties.* I became determined to gain everything I could from that time.

"Counting it all joy" isn't a one-time thing. It's more of a process and a promise. It's something we'll be learning to do until we step into heaven where all the darkness is finally gone. Until then, we can know that with our God nothing is ever worthless. It all counts even more than we can see right now. And that hope can light the way to treasures we never imagined we could find in our hard times.

God, show me how to count it all joy. Thank you for your tenderness and compassion toward me too.

. . . .

What's something valuable that has come from
a hard time in your life?

YOU CAN SURRENDER

O LORD, I give my life to you. (Psalm 25:1 NLT)

I *surrender all . . .*
The words are familiar. I know what it is to sing this hymn in a church with a white-painted steeple, bricks as sturdy as a daddy's shoulders, and a red carpet right down the aisle. I sang it first as a girl, when surrendering might bring to mind giving up things like toys, the doll with the blond braided hair, or the most coveted swing at recess.

But today I hear them in a sanctuary wide and modern, with a screen up front, fancy graphics scrolling across, and not a single choir robe in sight at the moment. I'm all grown up now, and I'm singing these words from a new perspective. I find, to my surprise, that what I'm most reluctant to surrender is *control.*

Will I trust God to defend me, care for me, bring victory in my life? Will I believe he is able to and, even more, that he wants to? I have sometimes said, in essence, "I will trust you after I have done all I can." This is hard and heavy. Instead I can say, "I will trust you because *you* can do all things."

I surrender all . . .

I whisper it under my breath as the song ends, a closing prayer.

I imagine I will say it again in other ways, other places, over a lifetime. Because this is the song of our lives as the Jesus people.

We surrender all . . .

And he gives all—everything our weary hearts really need—in return.

God, I surrender all to you. I give you full control,
trusting you will take care of me.

. . . .

What do you want to surrender to God today?

YOU CAN START SMALL

The LORD rejoices to see the work begin. (Zechariah 4:10 NLT)

The sun is just starting to rise outside my window. I'm walking on my tread-mill and wishing for coffee. I'm in a challenging season and want to talk with God about it.

I tell God I feel weary and wounded, that I'm struggling to move forward. I share the deep confusion I feel about what's next. I ask for help.

I don't instantly receive a magical cure for what ails my heart. But it is a beginning to my day being better than it was before, to breathing in new grace. And I'm finding so often that's what I need—to simply get started.

Say the first word of a prayer.

Take the first step on a walk.

Make the first decision to get out of bed and try again.

Because without firsts, nothing else comes after. I can get caught up in grand plans, big dreams, and idealized visions of what could be. But even the longest, most glorious adventure starts with a single step. Even the most profound, soul-stirring conversation begins with one word.

Maybe the work he's calling you to is an impossible project.

Maybe it's a person who's struggling right now.

Maybe, like it is for me, it's embracing the process of healing.

Whatever your work is, God is not asking you to get it all done today. He is inviting you to simply get started—one moment, one prayer, one step with him. He will meet you where you are; he will get you where you need to go.

God, help me to take the next small step of obedience today.

. . . .

What's one small step you can take today?

YOU CAN MAKE FRIENDS WITH FRUSTRATION

So let's not get tired of doing what is good. At just the right time we will reap a harvest of blessing if we don't give up. (Galatians 6:9 NLT)

I once heard a podcast guest trained in neuroscience give advice to graduates. He said, "Get comfortable, and even appreciate feeling frustrated and confused."[1]

This seemed like odd advice, but he went on to explain that confusion and frustration are the emotions we experience when the brain is rewiring itself. When we persevere, we will eventually experience an aha moment when we start to really grasp whatever it is that we're trying to learn or do.

The apostle Paul said, "Suffering produces perseverance; perseverance, character; and character, hope" (Rom. 5:3–4). I've always thought of this in terms of external physical suffering, but I think it applies to the pain of personal growth too.

When we have a confusing or frustrating day—when we don't make as much progress as we'd hoped, when we feel inadequate for what we're trying to do, when we can't quite seem to understand, when nothing really goes as planned—we can see it as a sign not of failure but of moving forward. In those moments, it's tempting to criticize ourselves or give up. Instead, we can recognize that we are doing hard work.

We are living with courage.

We are choosing to grow.

We are doing so much better than we know.

God, I want to learn, grow, and move forward with you for a lifetime.

. . . .

What's a time when you experienced confusion and frustration that eventually led to learning and growth?

YOU HAVE PERMISSION TO REST

You see me when I travel
and when I rest at home.
You know everything I do. (Psalm 139:3 NLT)

If you're tired today, that's okay. Being tired means you've worked hard, given much, loved deeply. To need rest isn't weakness; it's proof you've offered your all.

In the moments when you need rest, welcome yourself with gentleness the way you would a warrior returning from battle. Put an invisible hand on your shoulder and tell yourself, "Well done, that wasn't easy." Ask yourself what you need.

You only require rest when you've worked hard in some way. Maybe it was with your heart, doing the work of loving or healing. It might have been with your head, doing the work of creating or solving. Perhaps it was with your hands, serving or supporting.

It's easy to say, "I should be able to do more" or "I should be able to keep going." But rest is a rhythm we all need. Work hard, rest, repeat. Having limitations is not a sin; it's a reality of being human.

You serve a Savior who took a nap on a boat, who sat down by a well because he was weary, who retreated to quiet places to pray. God wrapped in skin rested. God creating the world in the beginning rested. To rest is not to fail; it is to follow the example of the One whose image you're created in.

Rest doesn't begin by stopping what you're doing; it begins by daring to believe what's true. Take a deep breath, then say to your soul, "I am already loved. I am already enough. I have nothing to prove." Then, dear warrior, let yourself rest today.

God, give me the courage to embrace your gift of rest today.

. . . .

What's one way you can rest today?

GOD'S LOVE IS BETTER
THAN A FAIRY TALE

As a bridegroom rejoices over his bride,
so will your God rejoice over you. (Isaiah 62:5)

The prince falls in love with Cinderella. He searches the kingdom for her and slides the glass slipper on her foot like an engagement ring. We all know how the story ends: "And they lived happily ever after."

We also know that's not how real-life stories usually go. Fast-forward a year later and the prince is upset because Cinderella has spent too much money on this season's glass slippers at her favorite store. And she's locked herself in her bedroom to cry into her pillow about the unemotional man she married.

We view marriage with a lot of expectations. Even if we marry someone wonderful, those expectations aren't going to be met. We want the fairy tale—the happily ever after with a perfect husband.

And here's the thing: there's nothing wrong with that desire. It's just that we misplace it sometimes. You do have a perfect husband. His name is Jesus, and one day you'll be in heaven with him for your happily-ever-after story.

No human relationship can completely fulfill your need for love. When the men we love fall short, it's a signal to our souls to turn to Jesus instead. Over and over, Scripture describes God's people as a bride.

This is what's truer than a fairy tale: we're loved beyond what we can even imagine. Whether we are single or married, whatever may have happened in our romantic relationships, even if we feel alone sometimes, we are the beloved bride of the perfect husband. And there's still a happily ever after in our future.

God, thank you for being the true love my heart longs to find.

. . . .

How has God been a husband to you?

YOU'RE NOT GIVING UP

Let perseverance finish its work so that you may be mature and complete, not lacking anything. (James 1:4)

God loves messy people. The wild ones. The kind we might pass by. David the murderer and adulterer. Peter the fisherman with rough edges. Rahab the lady of the night who found the light.

It doesn't make any sense to us. We would pick the ones who have it all together. The ones who didn't cause such a scene. The ones who played by the rules.

So what do the people God chooses have in common? They don't quit. The mistakes they make are astounding. The baggage they carry could fill a huge truck. The stunts they pull would get most of us fired. But they never stop. They fall down and get back up. They say the wrong thing and then repent. They fail and stubbornly press forward anyway.

I imagine you're the same way. You never quit pursuing Jesus. You never quit saying yes when he asks you to do something crazy. You never quit letting him teach you through your mistakes. You never quit giving it one more try, even when you're scared silly.

That is what brings God joy. Not when you're perfect on the outside. Not when you have a tidy existence. Not when you get it right the first time. Nope, God loves it when you will stop at nothing to have more of him in your life.

God, sometimes it seems easier to give up than keep moving forward. When I'm tempted to quit, give me what I need to carry on. I will persevere with you.

. . . .

What helps you keep going when you want to give up?

NEW EVERY MORNING

His compassions never fail. They are new every morning. (Lamentations 3:22–23)

Lamentations says God's compassions are new every morning. I've always thought of this in literal terms, that we wake up to another round of grace every day. I wonder if those words mean more than that as well. Whenever we make it through a stressful moment in life, isn't it a new morning too?

A few years ago, Mark and I went on another trip to the beach. I'm not an early riser, but we climbed out of bed and quickly made coffee. Then we walked toward the shore, the sand still cool beneath our feet. We were joined by many others—silver-haired seniors in straw hats, parents holding the hands of their children, the occasional dog leaping into the surf. All different ages, colors, sizes, stories. What we all seemed to have in common was a draw toward the sunrise.

I think this is a picture of humanity, of how we live in this world. No matter how hard this world gets, we keep finding our way through the dark. We keep moving toward the light. We keep believing that what looks like an ending could really be a beginning.

We choose to fix our eyes on the horizon of the future, look for the first light breaking through the clouds, believe in what we can't yet fully see. Oh, of course we'll still experience tears, anger, and disappointment sometimes. That's part of being human too. But we never give up hope.

A new morning is always coming. The sun will rise again, and so will we.

God, thank you for the gift of new starts and unending hope.
No matter what comes, the morning will too.

· · · ·

What's a "morning" you've experienced in your life?

GOD HAS HEART WORK
JUST FOR YOU

Pay careful attention to your own work. (Galatians 6:4 NLT)

I've fixated on a particular problem for months, looked at it from every angle, broken it apart and put it back together. But I can't find peace. I feel weary, so tired of worrying, exhausted from carrying the weight. I pause and pray, *God, give me the wisdom to know what work is mine to do today. I release everything and everyone else to you.*

I feel a shift within my soul as soon as I finish. I thought I wanted a solution, but what I really needed was to surrender. Stop fighting what I can't change. Start focusing on my own life instead of what I can't fix. Release responsibility for other people, and return to what God has asked of me.

The funny thing? The second I said "amen," the person I'd been struggling with sent me a text message. I'd been holding on so tight and when I finally let go, it seemed to unlock something in a way beyond what my human mind is able to comprehend.

I've had to pray that same little prayer over and over again. I've said it at least five times this morning. I might say it a hundred times before I go to sleep tonight. And that's okay. Surrender is often a process, not an event.

If you're worn out from trying to control something or someone, I'm inviting you to say this prayer with me too.

Today let's do our work and let God do his.

God, give me the wisdom to know what work is mine to do today. I release everything and everyone else to you.

. . . .

What work is yours today, and what do you need to release?

YOU'RE RUNNING
WITH PERSEVERANCE

*Let us run with perseverance the race marked out for us, fixing our
eyes on Jesus. (Hebrews 12:1–2)*

We can so quickly shift from focusing on "the race marked out *for us*" to comparing ourselves with someone else. God invites us to fix our eyes not on those around us but on the Savior who has gone before us. If we're focusing on a path besides our own, let's make sure it's the one that led to the cross. Because that changes everything.

Instead of what we don't have, it reminds us of all we've received.

Instead of how we don't measure up, it reminds us of the limitless grace that's ours.

Instead of self-pity, it gives us a reason to lift our hands and hearts in praise.

The path to the cross enables us to not grow weary and lose heart. It helps us keep pursuing God's best for us and protects us from distraction. It also reminds us that the journey we're on is not about competition but completion. These days when I try to be like someone else, I go back to a phrase someone shared with me long ago: not my race, not my pace.

I so easily forget this truth: when I choose someone else's path, I also choose their destination. What God has for someone else may look good, but only his will for my life is truly best. I don't want to miss out on what God has prepared for me—even if sometimes I'm a little slower and less graceful getting there.

*God, thank you for the path you have prepared for me
and the Savior who has gone before me.*

. . . .

What helps you fix your eyes on Jesus and stay focused
on the path he has for you?

YOU ARE ACCEPTED

Do not reject me or forsake me,
  God my Savior.
Though my father and mother forsake me,
  the LORD will receive me. (Psalm 27:9–10)

You may struggle with believing the lie that if you're weak or broken, you're not acceptable. Surely you'll be rejected. Yet the truth is none of us are perfect. We're all messy. We're all in process. We're all still trying to figure life out.

So what can give us the courage to move past this lie and back into love? Psalm 27:9–10 gives us the reassurance we need. God says, "No matter what other people do, I will not reject you. I will always receive you. I will never leave you." Sometimes people will say the wrong thing. Sometimes they won't be there for you. Sometimes they'll let you down. And we can handle that when we know that God won't ever do any of those things to us. That truth frees us up to love and be loved by people.

God wants to use other people in our lives to bring us comfort, joy, friendship, wisdom, or whatever else we might need. In order for that to happen, we have to be willing to open our hearts and receive. Love is always risky. There's simply no way around that reality. Having confidence in God's perfect care makes us brave enough to reach out. Even if we don't get the response we want, we can trust God will always give us the love we need.

God, I'm so grateful that you will never reject me
and you will always receive me.

. . . .

How does knowing God accepts you change
the way you see yourself?

YOU ARE MADE
FOR A PURPOSE

Yet for us there is only one God, the Father, from whom are all things, and we exist for Him; and one Lord, Jesus Christ, by whom are all things, and we exist through Him. (1 Corinthians 8:6 NASB)

We can find ourselves asking, "Why am I really here?" Is there more than the Monday morning commute, the Saturday sleep-in, the working and the doing? This life can feel big, and we struggle to find our place in it. It can feel small, and we wonder if we matter.

Let's dare to ask not "Why am I here?" but "Who am I here for?" The first inquiry seems to hang in the air unanswered, but the response to the latter is at the tips of our fingers on holy pages: we exist for God.

We try to find a purpose for our being. But the reality is we are not only made for a purpose; we are made for a person. We are made for the star-scatterer, the water-walker, the man-sculptor who brought us forth from dust. We are made for the One who still holds all the world in his hands.

And we exist through Jesus, the One who made it possible for us to make our way home to this grand God, who laid down his life that we might find ours. We live by the Spirit too, the greatest mystery. Our everyday life doesn't depend on you and me. We are empowered, equipped, strengthened, and comforted. We are never, ever alone.

We are his. He is ours. This is enough reason to exist for a lifetime . . . and eternity.

God, you are my purpose.

. . . .

What's one way you can live your purpose today?

GOD IS BIGGER THAN ANY NEWS HEADLINE

Don't be afraid, for I am with you.
Don't be discouraged, for I am your God.
I will strengthen you and help you.
I will hold you up with my victorious right hand. (Isaiah 41:10 NLT)

We live in a time much like Isaiah's in which political division and social injustice abound. It's easy to think a leader, political party, or new law is the solution. But Isaiah reminds us of the one sure thing in our lives—*God himself.*

"Don't be afraid, for I am with you." God's presence is pervasive and permanent. He is with us every moment, in whatever circumstances we face. He has promised to never leave or forsake us.

"Don't be discouraged, for I am your God." Human leaders will fail us. Politicians will make promises they won't keep. God is the only authority who is completely trustworthy, who will never disillusion us or let us down.

"I will strengthen you and help you." We don't have to rely on our own power or handle everything by ourselves. God will give us what we need to persevere and keep pursuing his will, one day at a time.

"I will hold you up with my victorious right hand." God's right hand symbolizes his strength, authority, and blessing. When we're weary of all that's going on in the world, God will support and sustain us. The battle is his, and with him we can't be defeated.

God is not done with history. He's not done with your story either.

God, sometimes all that's going on in our world feels scary and overwhelming. You are my hope, and I choose to trust in you.

. . . .

Which of the four phrases in Isaiah 41:10
did you most need to hear today?

YOU'RE PART OF
THE BODY OF CHRIST

*God has arranged each one of the parts in the body just as he wanted.
And if they were all the same part, where would the body be? As it
is, there are many parts, but one body. (1 Corinthians 12:18–20 CSB)*

Scholars describe Corinth as an important city of Greece both commercially
and politically. That means Christians who worshiped there likely differed
in everything from economic status to nationalities.

Today the kinds of variances we get stuck on tend to also include personali-
ties or preferences. We have thoughts like, *Everyone is so outgoing and I'm more
of a listener, so I don't belong*. Or the reverse, *These women are so quiet and gentle,
but I can't stop talking*. But Paul's encouragement still remains true for us now.
Are you content to let those around you share their stories while you offer the
support of your presence? Then you're probably an ear. And if you're the one
who seems to find the nearest microphone (or you don't even need one), then
you're probably a mouth.

That's the way God created the body of Christ to be. It's his beautiful plan for
us to need, help, and serve each other. Yet instead of embracing that, we often
let our insecurity or pride convince us that we need to go find a whole church
full of ears or mouths. But what if when we discover we're the only one like us
it doesn't mean we don't belong? What if it just means we've found where we're
needed most? In Jesus, it's our differences that can really make the difference.

*God, thank you for placing me in a body of Christ
where differences make us better.*

. . . .

What part of the body of Christ do you think you are?

GOD IS YOUR ABBA

And because we are his children, God has sent the Spirit of his Son into our hearts, prompting us to call out, "Abba, Father." (Galatians 4:6 NLT)

My husband's phone rings, and as he answers, I overhear a single word: *Dad*. Our daughter is calling. Paul tells us, "God has sent the Spirit of his Son into our hearts, prompting us to call out, 'Abba, Father.'" It's beautiful to me that this verse doesn't simply say "Father." The word *Father* indicates a position, but *Abba* reveals so much more.

Easton's Bible Dictionary says Abba "is a term expressing warm affection and . . . confidence."[1] The same entry also notes, "It has no perfect equivalent in our language." I nod at this because it's so true. There's no perfect equivalent to the kind of dad that God is to us. Even the best ones will let us down because they are imperfect humans, and so are we.

But our hearts can always know we have an Abba who is inviting us to come to him, to call on him when we're in need or afraid or overflowing with joy. Not with hesitation, uncertainty, or fear but with wide-open arms and even exclamation points. Because we really are his beloved children, adopted into his family forever.

God, it's such a gift to know that you look on me with affection and desire to be a true father to me in the ways my heart longs for most.

. . . .

What's one way you need God to be a father to you today?

GOD IS YOUR SECURITY

It is God who ... keeps my way secure. (Psalm 18:32)

Our culture is obsessed with safety. Sometimes we transfer that same approach to our prayer lives too. Yes, safety and protection are one aspect of what we can ask God to give us. But when I search the Scriptures, what God really promises isn't safety but true security no matter what happens. He often asks his followers to take outrageous risks that cost them everything and lead them far away from the comfort zones of their lives.

Yes, we can pray for protection for ourselves and those we love. Yet two caveats need to come along with those prayers. First, the recognition that the greatest threats are not physical but spiritual. And second, our desire for safety ultimately has to yield to God's greater plan. We are not to ask for safety above all else. It can become an idol that keeps us from fulfilling God's purpose for our lives.

When prayers for safety and protection appear in the Bible, it's usually because the person is doing something dangerous for God. Yes, we ask for safety. We pray for protection. And then we yield to the one whose ways are far beyond our understanding. We go with God where he asks, and we cheer on those in our lives when they do too.

We know there's more to life than just playing it safe; we live courageously by faith.

God, I ask for safety and protection today but also for the courage to take holy risks when you ask me to do so.

. . . .

When has God asked you to take a step of faith
that didn't feel totally safe?

GOD WILL GET YOU THROUGH

When you go through deep waters,
I will be with you.
When you go through rivers of difficulty,
you will not drown.
When you walk through the fire of oppression,
you will not be burned up;
the flames will not consume you. (Isaiah 43:2 NLT)

When you go through deep waters . . ." Noah and the ark, safe in the flood until dry land appeared again.

"When you go through rivers of difficulty . . ." The people of Israel finally crossing the Jordan into the promised land after the wilderness.

"When you walk through the fire of oppression . . ." Shadrach, Meshach, and Abednego exiting the furnace unscathed.

God is still writing stories of his faithfulness—showing up in our everyday, anxious lives, reminding us that he is with and for us. Getting through doesn't mean getting what we want. It means having what we need in each moment regardless of the results.

The diagnosis might not instantly disappear, but he will get you through it.

The prodigal might not return tomorrow, but he will get you through it.

The challenges at work might not resolve in one meeting, but he will get you through it.

We are not alone in our deep waters. We are not forsaken in our rivers of difficulty. We are not abandoned to the flames. No, we are God's people, and we press on, refusing to give up, remembering we are loved in every circumstance. He will get you through.

God, I trust you will get me through whatever I face.

. . . .

What is God helping you get through now?

YOUR GRIEF CAN TURN TO JOY

You turned my wailing into dancing;
you removed my sackcloth and clothed me with joy,
that my heart may sing your praises and not be silent.
LORD my God, I will praise you forever. (Psalm 30:11–12)

When someone mourned in ancient Israel, they put on sackcloth to show the world that they had experienced loss. Sackcloth was a coarse cloth similar to burlap. It rubbed against the skin and showed the world, "Life is rough right now."

The psalmist says God "removed my sackcloth and clothed me with joy" (Ps. 30:11). God wants to exchange our pain for joy. He wants to give us something better for our hearts to wear. Does that happen all at once? No, because grief is one way he has created for us to process life. Grief can feel like a negative emotion, but while painful it can also be a positive one because it moves us forward over time. Grief covers our hearts for a season until we're ready for joy again.

Our role is to be sensitive to ourselves and each other so that we can understand the timing for our wardrobe switch. If we try to make ourselves stop hurting before we've finished healing, then we go through life with hearts that are bare and vulnerable. It takes time to be ready for joy again, and we need to be patient. Give yourself permission to hurt. It's okay. And you can have hope even in those times because you know that you will one day be clothed with joy again.

God, thank you for helping me heal and gently replacing
my grief with joy. You take such good care of my heart.

. . . .

How have you seen God turn grief into joy in
your own life or someone else's story?

YOU DON'T HAVE TO MAKE EVERYONE HAPPY

When Jesus realized that they were about to come and take him by force to make him king, he withdrew again to the mountain by himself. (John 6:15 CSB)

Jesus multiplies five barley loaves and two fish into enough to feed a crowd of five thousand—with leftovers. But I'd never really noticed verse 15 in John 6 that follows this famous story.

Even after being miraculously fed, the people still want *more*. Why settle for one free lunch when you can have a king who could make that happen every day? It's a quick switch from God's plan to man's agenda. And Jesus is having none of it.

Let's pause and take this in. Jesus had the chance to become the most popular person in Israel. All he had to do was keep producing. People would come, they'd be impressed, and everyone would be happy. And wouldn't that help the spread of the gospel? But becoming a fish and loaves factory wasn't why Jesus was sent. He had his eyes fixed on the cross, the tomb, and eternal life with us.

Jesus didn't do everything he could. He didn't even do all that others wanted. He simply did what God asked. No more, no less. He understood that while people thought another free meal would fill them, what they really needed was a Savior who could satisfy their soul hunger.

We will have requests to do many *good* things. Instead of just giving people what they want, we can follow the example of Jesus and ask God to provide what they truly need.

God, give me the wisdom to do not what people want but what's truly needed.

. . . .

What is one thing God is inviting you to do today?

YOU DON'T NEED
TO FEEL READY

My grace is sufficient for you. (2 Corinthians 12:9)

A young man and his mentor sat next to me in a coffee shop talking about faith. Apparently they've been meeting awhile, because the young man asked, "When am I going to be ready to help someone else?"

The mentor paused and then answered, "I think you're asking the wrong question. Because as long as you ask 'Am I ready?' you'll always be able to find a reason you're not. A flaw. A struggle. Something you think you need to learn more about. The better question to ask is 'Have I received something?' If so, then you have something to share. When is the best time to start passing it on? Yesterday."

Here is a secret of faith I'm learning: we never feel qualified; we never feel like professionals; we never feel like we've got it together enough to really make a difference. And maybe this is a good thing. Because the only folks who seem to have believed otherwise were the Pharisees.

God is not looking for perfect examples. He's looking for ordinary people who will love each other. He's calling the messy, the broken, and the incomplete. This is good news for all of us. It means Jesus will give to us and then he'll give through us. We're simply asked to be willing and brave enough to do it as we are and not as we'd like to be.

God, thank you that I don't have to be perfect to be used by you;
I only need to be willing.

. . . .

What's one way you can help or encourage someone
even if you don't feel fully ready?

IT'S OKAY IF YOU DON'T FIGURE IT OUT TODAY

Just as you cannot understand the path of the wind or the mystery of a tiny baby growing in its mother's womb, so you cannot understand the activity of God, who does all things. (Ecclesiastes 11:5 NLT)

Sometimes when we want answers, what we're really looking for is a way to calm our anxiety. If we knew the plan and what would happen, then we could relax. We could feel more in control. Things would be better if we could just KNOW.

But I'm finding so much of life is mystery and waiting. It's uncertainty and change. It's guessing and detours. What we need to know isn't what's going to happen; it's what will still be true no matter what does.

The question we're asking isn't really "What's next?" It's "Am I going to be okay?" The answer is yes; we're going to be okay. Perhaps not today. Maybe not tomorrow. But someday.

Our circumstances aren't our identity, and our struggles aren't our destiny. We are loved where we are right now. We will be loved wherever we end up tomorrow. We are part of a bigger plan than we can understand. We are not lost or forgotten, behind or ahead, early or late. We are on the confusing and glorious journey of being humans who are walking to our eternal home.

Let's surrender to the not knowing.

Let's rest in the certainty of God's love.

It's okay if you don't figure it out today.

God, so much of what you do is a mystery, but your love for me today is a certainty.

. . . .

What unknown are you trusting God with today?

JESUS IS A FRIEND TO YOU

You are my friends if you do what I command. (John 15:14 NLT)

True friends say, "Talk to me. Tell me what's really going on in your world." They listen without judging or leaving. They look for the best in us, like miners panning for gold. They speak the eternal reality when all that's temporary—emotions, circumstances, opinions—are telling an entirely different story. They sit by us and stay by us and pray for us when we can't do these things for ourselves.

When I consider what friendship really means, I think it comes down to this one thing: true friends are *for* us no matter what. They are not crossing their arms and saying, "I knew she couldn't do it." They are not passing the gossip along with the potato salad at the Sunday picnic. They are not wondering when we'll get over it but instead how they can walk with us through it.

When I think of Jesus being a friend to us in these ways, it changes everything.

We are his friends too. This means I want to be sure I'm not doing all the talking. I want to understand what Jesus is passionate about, what causes him pain, what brings him joy. I want to know all the parts of his heart.

It's easy to think of Jesus as powerful, mighty, and holy. It's simpler for me to bend my knee than to dare to bend his ear about my daily, ordinary struggles. But we are his friends. We can go to him with anything and everything. We can trust he'll be there to love, encourage, and support us.

God, it's still a stunning realization to know I can call you friend.
Thank you for wanting to be part of my life in
an intimate, personal way.

. . . .

How has Jesus been a good friend to you?

YOU ARE SO LOVED

For as high as the heavens are above the earth,
so great is his love for those who fear him. (Psalm 103:11)

We ask, sometimes without even realizing it, "Am I truly loved?" The answer is *yes*. That truth comes to us straight from the heart of God.

I recall realizing this in a new way as I stood on the beach in the dark, staring at the sky spread endlessly above me. I thought of the words in Psalm 103:11. I watched two shooting stars streak across the expanse, and I thought about how our lives are so much like that. We're here for a moment, we get a chance to shine, and we're gone. Knowing this didn't fill me with sadness. Instead it filled me with comfort.

I sighed with relief and let the pressure roll off my shoulders. I'm not God, and it's not my role to keep the universe running. Instead I'm a living paradox—small and yet called to big purposes, broken and yet showing God's glory, weak and yet growing stronger every day.

When we remember who God is, we regain perspective. As much as it feels like it on some days, the world is not on our shoulders; it's in God's hands. And we are too. He loves us in ways far beyond what we can even comprehend, as high as the stars, as endless as the sky. All we have to do is receive that love and respond to it. When we look to him, we see who we truly are: imperfect people who are infinitely, perfectly loved.

God, I'm so grateful your love for me is as high
as the heavens above the earth.

. . . .

What helps you feel God's love?

YOU ARE COURAGEOUS

Jesus immediately said to them: "Take courage! It is I. Don't be afraid."
(Matthew 14:27)

There's a fine line between courageous and crazy. Flipping through TV shows one night, I watched a teenage boy climb on top of his buddy's car and decide to "surf" down the highway. Crazy.

Then I landed on a story about another teenage boy. This one wore a military uniform. He told of going back for his buddies when they had been injured in battle. Courageous.

What's the difference between crazy and courageous? I believe that courage always requires a worthwhile reason. It's a determination to take right action in the face of fear.

Being courageous is not an emotion or an option. It's an invitation from God. Over and over in Scripture, God tells his people to be courageous. I love what he often does next—he follows the command with a compelling "because."

Because I am with you.

Because I have promised.

Because I will do this through you.

God knows that courage isn't easy. No human can face danger and not feel fear. We're simply not created that way. Most of the time that survival system serves us well. And yet for all of us, there are moments when God wants to override that system and asks us to lean in and listen harder to his voice than to the fear yelling at us to stop. Because courage changes the world. It breaks through what is and leads into what's to come. And we become different people in the process too.

God, I pray that you would give me courage when I need it today.

. . . .

When have you done something that took courage
even though you were afraid?

JESUS IS COMING FOR YOU

Come, Lord! The grace of the Lord Jesus be with you. (1 Corinthians 16:22–23)

I woke up long before the sun rose one morning. With a heavy heart, I thought of a friend going through a hard time. One word kept coming to mind: *Maranatha*. I knew it originated in Scripture but couldn't recall where it appeared or even what it meant. When I started researching, I found that *Maranatha* is translated "Come, Lord!"

Early Christians greeted each other with Maranatha. It's a one-word prayer. And, yes, the ultimate desire behind it is for Jesus to come back and take us home. But it means much more than that too.

I said "Maranatha" over and over as I prayed for my friend.

Come, Lord, into the middle of these hard circumstances.

Come, Lord, with your power and peace.

Come, Lord, with your comfort and strength.

Yes, God is always with us, but I've had moments—and I imagine you've had them too—when he feels *especially* present.

When our world falls apart, plans crumble, and our hope flutters like a tattered flag, God has not left us. He's a God not of distance but devotion, not of neglect but infinite nearness, not of apathy but affection so great he gave everything for us.

I don't know how my friend's story will unfold in the next few months, but I'm certain she won't face it alone. Whatever you're going through, that's true for you too.

Come, Lord, into whatever the future holds.

. . . .

What's a hard moment in your life when you sensed
God's presence and care?

GOD SPEAKS ON YOUR BEHALF

In the shelter of your presence you hide them
  from all human intrigues;
you keep them safe in your dwelling
  from accusing tongues. (Psalm 31:20)

The saying "Sticks and stones can break my bones but words will never hurt me" did not come from the pages of Scripture. The God who spoke the world into being knows that words can have an impact.

That's exactly why he promises to keep our hearts safe—no matter what anyone says. He hides us from the nosy questions, the gossip, the misunderstandings. And where he hides us is truly beautiful: *in his presence.*

Imagine a little girl running to her mama for comfort after being teased at school. As she buries her face against her mother's chest, the taunts fade away and all she can hear is the heartbeat of love.

Now imagine the bullies coming toward them and that mama raising a hand that declares, "Stop right there. You're not messing with my girl. Don't you say another word."

That's what Jesus does when the accuser of our hearts comes at us. He speaks on our behalf. No matter what anyone may say, Jesus is talking truth about you today. "Who then is the one who condemns? No one. Christ Jesus . . . is at the right hand of God and is also interceding for us" (Rom. 8:34).

Jesus says you are loved (1 John 4:16–18). You are accepted (Rom. 15:7). You are chosen (1 Pet. 2:9). You are *his.*

What he says about you is the ultimate truth. And he always gets the final word.

God, please protect me from words that could hurt me
and replace them with your truth instead.

. . . .

What do you sense Jesus is saying to your heart today?

YOU LIVE WELL WHEN
YOU LOVE WELL

Love the Lord your God with all your heart, with all your soul, and with all your mind. This is the greatest and most important command. The second is like it: Love your neighbor as yourself. All the Law and the Prophets depend on these two commands. (Matthew 22:37–40 CSB)

As I read Matthew 22 recently, I was struck in a new way by the phrase "all the Law and the Prophets depend on these two commands." Another way of saying it might be this: *When we love we have done everything worth doing.* This is a relief. It's a gift. It's the shredder we can put all the expectations and demands through until they are tiny pieces of confetti.

I think Jesus's response to the question of what matters most is about more than morality; it's about setting our hearts free. We are prone to strive and please and live like being on this earth is a job. We are not made for this kind of pressure. We are created, instead, to simply love and be loved.

Lately instead of to-do lists, I've started making to-love lists. For example, where I would have put "Go to meeting" I write, "Love Shannon, Alex, and Claire in meeting."

Putting my day in these terms changes everything. It means what's ahead is not a series of performances but opportunities to serve. It's not about completing but connecting. These are not pass/fail endeavors but heart-to-heart encounters.

Whatever this day holds there will be love. There will be grace. There will be Jesus.

God, show me who you have placed on my to-love list today.

. . . .

Who can you love as you go about your day?

GOD GIVES YOU WISDOM

If any of you lacks wisdom, you should ask God, who gives generously to all without finding fault, and it will be given to you. (James 1:5)

In the information age, there's no shortage of answers. I could type *stress* in the search bar of my internet page right now. Thousands of results about everything from time management to massage would appear. Advice is abundant. But the wisdom our hearts truly need can be hard to find.

What exactly is wisdom? I believe it's seeing the world, and our specific situations, through God's eyes. It's having his perspective, a deeper knowledge of what's happening than we can get just from our five senses. Often it's contradictory to what look like the right answers. Instead, it's the real answer. Wisdom does more than just provide solutions; it leads to breakthroughs.

Interestingly enough, when Scripture talks about wisdom, it's most often associated with the heart, not the mind. Walking in wisdom takes faith and courage. It can't often be justified with a spreadsheet or measured with numbers. It has to be lived and experienced.

The great news is that God promises to give us the wisdom we need. All we have to do is ask and have the humility to receive the response, even if it's not what we expected. The God who knows absolutely everything is living within you. And whoever you're praying for now is known by him too. There's no problem too complex, no circumstance too confusing, no situation too overwhelming for him. He's already got the answer. Even better, he *is* the answer.

God, please give me the wisdom I need to do your will today.

· · · ·

When has God given you wisdom for a decision or situation?

YOUR DORMANT SEASONS
HAVE VALUE

Planted in the house of the LORD,
They will flourish in the courts of our God. (Psalm 92:13 AMP)

The book of Psalms compares those who love God to trees. I understood the parts of the metaphor that involved growth and bearing fruit. But I'd missed an essential element of every tree's life: dormancy. When a tree goes dormant, it releases its leaves, slows its growth, and produces no visible fruit for a time.

This seems wasteful to me. Why not have trees bear fruit all year long? Isn't dormancy optional? When I researched this question, I discovered the following:

It's possible to force a tree to evade dormancy if you keep it inside and with a stable temperature and light pattern. However, this is usually bad for the tree. It's natural for trees to go through dormancy cycles, and the lifespan of the plant is dramatically decreased if the tree isn't allowed to go dormant for a few months. Trees have winter dormancy for a reason, and it's best to just let them run their course as nature intended.[1]

It's possible to force a human to evade dormancy too, but it's hard on our souls. We become weary and depleted. The quality of the fruit in our lives suffers.

We, like the trees, have our seasons. It takes courage to slow down. It takes guts to let go. It is a brave thing to focus only on what's essential. But if God is inviting us into dormancy, we can trust it will not last forever. There will be growth again.

God, thank you that seasons change, but I am always loved the same.

. . . .

What season of life are you in right now?

YOUR SHEPHERD
WILL CARE FOR YOU

He makes me lie down in green pastures. (Psalm 23:2)

We've talked about God as our Good Shepherd; let's go even deeper. Can you relate to these words of modern shepherd Chuck Wooster?

> Sheep go out of their way to disguise when they are sick or in distress. . . . Sheep will go to great lengths to appear inconspicuous when they are in trouble. Therefore, the first place to look for a sick sheep is not right in front of you—waving its hooves up and down, trying to get your attention—but deep in the middle of your flock, trying to look invisible.[1]

Our Good Shepherd sees through our facades to the places where we're sick and hurt and broken. Psalm 23 says, "He makes me lie down in green pastures." Why would anyone need to make a sheep lie down? It turns out sheep won't lie down when they're afraid. I picture a sheep that looks a lot like me standing there saying, "I'm fine," while her knees knock and her heart pounds. Maybe what we really need is to lie down on the inside, to not be so strong all the time, to receive the care we need.

The times when we look the most put together might actually be the ones when we're falling apart. Our Good Shepherd knows this. Because he really, truly knows us.

*God, you see my heart and what I truly feel even
when it may seem like I'm fine on the outside.*

. . . .

What do you need to tell God about how you're really doing today?

GOD GIVES YOU GOOD GIFTS

God… richly gives us all we need for our enjoyment. (1 Timothy 6:17 NLT)

The sunset spreads like a multicolored quilt above the hills. Oranges, reds, yellows, and patches of turquoise show the handiwork of their maker. My husband is next to me. My tummy is full of delicious food. My eyes are feasting on beauty.

Yet in that moment I feel the wild ache that comes when we encounter what's truly good. It's as if so much is a reminder to my soul that this world is not enough.

Have you ever felt that way too? Maybe when you've seen extraordinary art, listened to astonishing music, shared a moment of intimacy with someone you love, enjoyed exquisite food, held a new baby, stood on the beach and listened to the waves.

I have this thought as I stand on the balcony watching the sun slip lower: *The Creator is better than anything he's created.* God alone can satisfy us. Everything else, even the best gifts, bring with them a longing that we can't name or explain. And it's supposed to be that way. God's gifts make us homesick for the giver.

An early evening hush falls over the landscape in front of me. Cicadas sing, trees swish, and my heart fills with praise. All of this goodness has fulfilled its purpose: it has reminded me of the One who is best of all.

I close my eyes and whisper two phrases, the only ones I seem to know how to speak into that longing: "Thank you" and "More, please."

God, thank you for every good gift in my life and how each one points to you.

· · · ·

What's a gift from God you're grateful for today?

YOU DON'T HAVE TO BE BUSY

You will be delivered by returning and resting. (Isaiah 30:15 CSB)

We have an obsession with busyness in our culture. We complain about it. We buy fancy calendars to contain it. We take vacations to escape it. And yet we also wear it like a badge of honor. Surely "busy" means we're important. We're wanted. We have places to go and people to see. And, for believers, "busy" can even mean we also must be especially spiritual.

I want to gently challenge us to think about the way our world tells us to see busyness. Perhaps it's time to consider that all the striving we think is required may not be what God truly desires. I'll confess there have been many times when a "no" would have been the wisest answer to an opportunity, but instead I said a stubborn, exhausted "yes." And those choices took a toll on my soul. So I can relate to the words God spoke in Isaiah 30:15.

God has a totally different kind of invitation for us today. He longs to bring us not into more busyness but into his very best. He wants to replace our hectic pace with heart-deep peace. He desires to free us from fear and give us true security. May we have the courage to slow down, let go, and live in grace. We do not have to prove our worth by living "busy." We only need to remember we are already beloved.

God, when the world tells me to be busy,
help me to choose what's truly best instead.

. . . .

How do you know when you're too busy?

GOD IS WHO YOU NEED TODAY

Then you will know the truth, and the truth will set you free. (John 8:32)

I grab a small white note card and thick black pen. This has become my habit. Each morning I seek out a name of God in Scripture and write it down.

The stack of cards by my bed has grown. It tells me that God is love. It reminds me that he is my defender. It whispers to me that he is the purpose-giver and peace-bringer and creator of all. No matter what this day holds, none of this will change. He is forever the same.

In my journal, I record what I'm grateful for and who I am, based on this reality. Because God is love, I am loved. Because God is my defender, I can't be defeated. Because God is my purpose-giver, I have an identity and destiny. Because he is my peace-bringer, I can walk in rest and trust. Because he is my creator, I can be confident in who he has made me.

Eventually I sit up and my feet touch the stretched and stained carpet. I don't know what this day will bring, but I know what will not change. I am God's daughter. I am beloved. I have everything I need for whatever I may face. Today I can walk in the truth of who I am and whose I am.

*God, I'm so grateful that who you are never changes,
and you are the one who tells me who I am too.*

. . . .

What's a name of God that really resonates with your heart?

GOD IS YOUR ULTIMATE CERTAINTY

*Jerusalem, once so full of people,
is now deserted. (Lamentations 1:1 NLT)*

I magine the prophet Jeremiah walking the empty streets. Gone are the signs of life and joy, the sound of singing, the laughter of children, the friendly bargaining in the market. Babylon has invaded and destroyed the once glorious city. Yet in the middle of mourning, Jeremiah offers words of hope:

> The faithful love of the LORD never ends!
>> His mercies never cease.
> Great is his faithfulness;
>> his mercies begin afresh each morning. (Lam. 3:22–23 NLT)

When we're dealing with difficult circumstances or anxiety, we need security. When everything is changing, we need to know God is unchanging. He is our certainty. Even when our whole world falls apart and all we can feel is our frantic heart racing, he is our steady, ever-present strength.

To show us this is true, God has provided things we can count on in the world around us. Each sunrise reminds us his mercies are new every morning. Each sunset tells us that even as night comes, he is still in control. Nature's rhythms soothe us. If nothing in nature was orderly or predictable, we'd experience confusion and chaos.

In a changing world, we can count on a God of sunrises and sunsets, of faithful love, of mercies that are new every morning—because that's how often we need them.

*God, it's reassuring to know your faithful love never ends
and your mercies are new every morning.*

. . . .

What's one way you see God's mercies in your life today?

YOUR SAVIOR MEETS THE STANDARD

We all fall short of God's glorious standard. Yet God, in his grace, freely makes us right in his sight. (Romans 3:23–24 NLT)

I'm holding a bar with weight on it and trying to execute a new exercise move. A coach watches me and offers feedback. Elbows up higher. Back straighter. Knees bent. Two letters, Rx, are scrawled on a whiteboard next to the standard I'm supposed to meet. There is no way. All I can do is show up and try my best every day.

Sometimes this frustrates me. But the coaches remind us that the goal isn't perfection; it's progress. Each of us is different. Each day our capacities for what we can do, how much weight we can lift, vary. The standard is there to give us a goal to move toward, but falling short of it isn't failure—it's just the reality of our humanness.

I think of this at other moments when I try hard in my life but fall short. I want to be content but struggle with worry. I want to be grateful but find myself complaining. I want to stop an unhelpful habit only to slip up again. I don't quite hit God's Rx either.

Have you ever felt the same? If so, here's the good news: Jesus met the standard for us. Now our role is simply to show up and do our best each day. The Holy Spirit is present to be our coach. When we fall short, we aren't failing; we're learning and growing. We're getting stronger every time we try.

God, thank you for sending Jesus to meet the standard for me.
Help me to keep learning and growing each day with you.

. . . .

How are you learning and growing right now?

GOD WILL HOLD YOU UP

Now to him who is able to protect you from stumbling and to make you stand in the presence of his glory. (Jude 1:24 CSB)

When my granddaughter, Eula, was learning to walk, her steps were wobbly. One day she became fascinated by a pair of rain boots. They were several sizes too big but she slid them onto her feet.

She also insisted on wearing her bright pink coat. As she tromped around in her borrowed boots, I walked behind her holding the coat's hood. When she stumbled, she didn't hit the ground because I held her up. She carried on, not realizing someone was watching out for her, making sure she didn't fall.

Walking with my granddaughter made me think of our God, who loves us. It's human to feel unsteady in hard situations. It can seem we're stumbling, that we don't have what it takes to handle whatever we're walking through. We feel insecure and out of balance. Maybe it's safer to stand still, not take chances, avoid all these feelings of inadequacy.

But fear is always a liar. We have a God who promises that even if we stumble, we will not stay down. He is with us, seeing us through, making sure we get where he's asking us to go. There is nothing too difficult for us because there is nothing too difficult for him.

If there's something overwhelming in your life, rest assured the hand of God in your life is more than enough to hold you up. He will not let you down. He will not let you go. Even when you don't feel it, he's there with you.

God, thank you for holding me up and walking with me every step.

. . . .

How is God holding you up?

YOU CAN DARE TO BE WHO YOU ARE

Love each other with genuine affection. (Romans 12:10 NLT)

I'm getting together with two friends. One I've known for years. She's already aware of my faults and quirks. But the other girl joining us is someone I don't know as well yet.

I've bought into the lie that if I can just make this new girl think I'm perfect, then surely we'll be friends. But I look at my other friend, the one who's known me forever, and know right then this isn't going to be an effective tactic. Because what we really want aren't people we can impress; we want people who will love us *anyway*.

The reality is, I'm a flawed human being. I'm not perfect today, and I won't be tomorrow, next year, or on the day I take my final breath. I'm also a person created by God with strengths, gifts, and much to offer. We all are.

What we really need from each other is not a pared-down version of ourselves that's been polished and carefully presented. We need to be true to who we are, to show up as is, because that's the only way we actually feel less alone.

Maybe this friendship will grow. But if not, that will be okay too. We don't need the whole world to love us as we are (that's impossible); we just need a few brave folks. And the best way to start finding those grace-givers is to dare to be one of them ourselves.

God, give me the courage not to prove I'm perfect but to show up as I am and grow into all you want me to be.

. . . .

What helps you dare to be who you really are?

GOD ENJOYS YOUR JOY

May they always say, "The LORD be exalted,
who delights in the well-being of his servant." (Psalm 35:27)

The first time I read Psalm 35:27, I thought my Bible might have a misprint. I'd been raised in a denomination that placed a heavy emphasis on rules, not delight. From what I could tell, God didn't seem very committed to my happiness. Yet through the years I've come to understand that my joy brings my heavenly Father joy too.

If we believe that God is a killjoy who isn't really interested in our joy or happiness, then we'll believe hard times are punishment from him. But if we know his heart is to bring what's best to his children, it changes everything. Then we can say, "God delights in my well-being, and even if things aren't okay now, I can trust him to make them better."

We will go through difficulties in this life. We will face challenges. We will have questions that don't get answered until heaven. But we can know that even in all that, God wants us to thrive. He delights in seeing us enjoy our lives. He wants what's best for us. What kind of father would he be if he didn't?

We have a faithful and kind heavenly Father who loves to find big and small ways to bring joy to his children—especially on the hard days.

God, thank you for being a loving heavenly Father who delights
in the well-being of his children.

. . . .

What's one thing that is bringing you joy today?

YOU CAN POUR OUT YOUR COMPLAINTS

I pour out my complaints before him
and tell him all my troubles. (Psalm 142:2 NLT)

The dictionary has several definitions of *complaint*, but they all really come down to this: a complaint is a statement that things are not as we would like for them to be.

We live in a fallen, broken world. We are fallen, broken people. We are going to have complaints. There's simply no way around it. It's what we do with those complaints that makes the difference. God understands that and invites us to come to him in those moments.

God wants us to be open with all of our emotions—hurt, anger, disappointment, and whatever else we may feel. He also wants us to be honest about our desires. It's the attitude behind how we express our emotions and desires that matters most to him.

When I worked as a counselor, I saw so many Christians who tried to hide their negative feelings because they were afraid of "complaining." It never worked out well. God doesn't want you to ignore or deny what's hurting you or making you angry.

You are allowed to have complaints in life. God just asks you to do so in a way that honors him, leads to healing in your heart, and helps others too. Be open with God. Be honest. Be real about where you are. Tell him what's in your heart. He's listening and he will hear you.

You don't have to hold anything back from the God who promises to hold you through every experience and emotion you have in this life.

God, I pour out my complaints before you and tell you all my troubles.

. . . .

What is a complaint you want to process with God today?

GOD CARES ABOUT IT ALL

The God of all comfort...comforts us in all our troubles. (2 Corinthians 1:3–4)

Sometimes I've been hurt or faced a loss or found fear catching me by surprise, and I've told myself, "This is too insignificant to bother God about. It's nothing compared to what other people face." I think of the news headline, the social media post, or the prayer request, and I tell myself that I'm selfish for even thinking I have a right to mourn something silly or small in my life.

But God says he will comfort us "in *all* our troubles" (2 Cor. 1:4). There is no size limit. No height requirement. No difficulty level assigned. It's unequivocal, universal, all-encompassing. The other day my daughter called and shared a hard thing. Then she said, "I'm sorry for bothering you with something so small." And I said, "If it matters to you, it matters to me."

I thought afterward, with a bit of surprise, that this must be how the heart of our God is toward us. He is not waiting for us to get over it, to snap out of it and put on a brave face. He is instead coming for us with outstretched arms to wipe the tears from our cheeks, to pull us close, to whisper love words until we are ready to take his hand again.

Yes, we need to know nothing is too big for our God to handle. But we also need to know nothing is too small for him to reach out his hands to us and hold us close.

God, it means so much to know you care about every detail of my life.

. . . .

What's something "small" you need God's comfort for today?

YOU'VE ALWAYS BEEN LOVED

"I have always loved you," says the LORD.
But you retort, "Really? How have you loved us?" (Malachi 1:2 NLT)

I have always loved you." Those are the words we want to know in our bones, on our bad days, in the moments we wake up during the thick of night. And yet we, like Israel, often answer, "Really? How have you loved us?"

God answers his people with what he has done, how he has shown his faithfulness, the ways he has fulfilled his promises—it just doesn't look like what they expected. Sometimes the ways God shows his love to us don't either.

But his love is wound through your history like a scarlet thread even in the dark moments. It is the one constant in the chaos. It cannot be lost. It cannot be won. It is yours in the blink of this life and the vastness of eternity.

So I am praying today, not for God to give us what we want, not for us to be perfect, but for us to see how loved we already are, how loved we always have been. Sometimes what is most true is the hardest to feel. Sometimes what is more certain seems the least real. This is a paradox of being human.

God knows this because he has lived on this spinning earth. He has put on our skin. He is willing to say what our hearts need to hear over and over again.

God, thank you for always loving me, even on the days
when it's hard to see or feel.

. . . .

How have you seen God's love in your life?

GOD IS THE SOURCE OF YOUR CONFIDENCE

For you have been my hope, Sovereign LORD,
my confidence since my youth. (Psalm 71:5)

"Now faith is confidence in what we hope for and assurance about what we do not see" (Heb. 11:1). If we take these words at face value, then we might assume that faith is just the more spiritual version of a wish or that it all depends on us. It's about the effort we put into believing. It's about being good enough to have what we pray for granted. This seems to me to be a recipe for disappointment and bitterness, shame and guilt. Because if we must make it happen and then it doesn't, surely it means we have done something wrong.

So when I read David's words—"You have been my hope, Sovereign LORD, my confidence since my youth" (Ps. 71:5)—it felt like finding the key to a locked door, the back entrance to the place my heart had been longing for all along. Because those words mean this: when Hebrews says, "Faith is confidence," it's not saying to trust in a particular outcome. It's telling us the only sure bet is to place our faith in God himself. It means being certain he is good no matter what. He has a plan that's bigger than we can see. He loves us more than we can imagine.

I am learning faith is not about what we want to happen; it's about who we're trusting in no matter what the future holds. God is our hope. He is our confidence. He is the answer to every question, longing, and whispered, uncertain prayer.

God, you are the one I place my trust in, who will not
let me down or let me go.

. . . .

What's one way you're trusting God today?

YOU CAN PAUSE, PRAY, REPEAT

Daniel answered, "Long live the king! My God sent his angel to shut the lions' mouths so that they would not hurt me." (Daniel 6:21–22 NLT)

The king issued a decree: pray only to him or be thrown into a den of lions. Daniel could not obey; he continued to pray to God. Throughout all that happened in his life—being taken captive, threats from rivals, even facing death in a lions' den—he also seemed to have had a supernatural steadiness.

What was his secret? Part of it appears to be his rhythm of praying three times a day. Whatever was going on in his world, regardless of what he might have been facing in his royal role, even when he experienced intense opposition, Daniel paused to pray. Like an elite athlete practicing, he trained himself to respond to anxiety-provoking situations with three steps: *pause, pray, repeat.*

Daniel chose a rhythm that fit his life—kneel and pray three times a day. What's a similar rhythm that would work for you? There's no right or wrong way to pray, just choose what is simple and sustainable for you in this season. You might start the day with a prayer of gratitude, meditate on Scripture for a few moments while you get ready in the morning, or intentionally pray at meals or before you go to sleep at night.

Daniel's life shows us that little things done consistently can make a big difference when it matters most.

*God, help me train my heart, mind, and soul
so that I'm ready for whatever comes.*

. . . .

What rhythm, like praying three times a day,
would you like to try this week?

YOU CAN GIVE THANKS

In everything give thanks; for this is the will of God in Christ Jesus for you. (1 Thessalonians 5:18 NKJV)

Do you ever feel, like me, that being thankful is a bit of a challenge? There's one little word in 1 Thessalonians 5:18 that can help. We're to give thanks *in* all circumstances, but we're never told to give thanks *for* all circumstances.

Often what we experience is difficult. Husbands leave. Diseases ravage. Funerals happen. God grieves over all of this just as we do, and we do not have to force ourselves to be thankful for any of these things. Whew. Does that make anyone else sigh with relief?

What we can choose to do is find God's goodness right there in the middle of it all. We can ask ourselves, "In spite of this, what can I be grateful for today?" It can be something small like a cup of coffee on a cold morning, a text from a friend, or just opening our eyes for another day. It's not the size of our thanks that matters; it's the heart behind it.

We also don't have to *feel* thankful. Our emotions and perspective can take time to catch up with our wills. God knows this, and we don't have to feel shame or guilt about the disconnect.

Let's be grateful. But let's also give ourselves lots of grace. This is one thing we can always say: "Thanks, God, for loving me as I am and however I feel today."

God, help me to see your hand in my life
and be thankful in all circumstances.

· · · ·

What's one way you can be thankful in a hard situation today?

GOD LIFTS YOUR HEAD

Why, my soul, are you downcast?
Why so disturbed within me?
Put your hope in God,
for I will yet praise him,
my Savior and my God. (Psalm 42:5)

This morning I became curious about how Psalm 42 ends. I felt surprised to find it closes by repeating *exactly* the same words as in verse 5. I'd expected a bow tied neatly around a truth, a declaration that all was now well, an upbeat and catchy phrase.

But no, the psalmist still has the same questions, stresses, and struggles. This is comforting to me because it reminds me all over again that God isn't expecting me to get over anything. He isn't requiring me to find the perfect cliché that will make my hurt go away. He isn't uncomfortable with the in-between, the places where we are not yet healed.

Another psalm I love says, "But you, LORD, are a shield around me, my glory, the One who lifts my head high" (3:3).

When we are downcast, we don't have to lift ourselves up; *God will do it*. He is so much more tender with us than we are with ourselves. He will give us time and space, all we need. He doesn't snap up our head like a general rebuking a soldier but rather lifts up our head like a father does a child with tears streaming down her cheeks. That is why we can say with the psalmist, "I will put my hope in God," even in our worst moments, our hardest times.

God, you are so patient with me. You lift my head not by force
but with great gentleness and care.

· · · ·

What's a phrase you tend to say to yourself that isn't grace-filled
(for example, "Get over it"), and what could you say instead?

Day 174

YOU ARE COVERED BY LOVE

Love covers over a multitude of sins. (1 Peter 4:8)

I take my seat and nervously eye the blank canvas in front of me. I'm here for a guided painting party. Then someone says, "The good news is you can paint over any canvas."

These words make me recall the reassurance offered in 1 Peter 4:8: "Love covers over a multitude of sins." In other words, love can paint over any canvas.

Yes, even that choice we made that feels like it could never be forgiven.

Yes, the secret that sometimes wakes us up in the middle of the night.

Yes, those mistakes that accuse us from the quiet, dark corners of our hearts.

The enemy would like to tell us, "You don't get a second chance." But the scandalously gracious Savior we serve says, "I died to give you as many chances as you need."

If we believe that we must never mess up, we'll be paralyzed with fear. We'll stare at the blank canvas of our lives without ever even taking hold of the brush God wants to place in our hands. Yes, we'll keep it all nice, neat, and clean. But there will be no beauty. There will be no boldness. There will be no inexplicable glory among the mess.

I learned a few painting tricks and tips that day. But what I learned even more is this: art isn't about perfection; it's about being brave enough to try. Life is too. Every day is a blank canvas. So let's grab our brushes, pick our colors, and begin . . . again.

God, I receive your extraordinary love and mercy.
I will walk in freedom and grace.

. . . .

Where do you need grace in your life today?

YOU'RE HEADING TOWARD HOPE

We know that suffering produces perseverance; perseverance, character; and character, hope. (Romans 5:3–4)

When I first read those words in Romans 5, I wondered if my Bible had a typo. Wasn't hope supposed to be at the beginning of the list? That's certainly where I wanted it to be. I didn't like the idea of going through suffering, perseverance, and character to get to hope.

My thoughts reflect our culture today. We view hope as an emotion rather than an outcome of choices we make. We also think hope should be automatic. Then when we don't find it right away, we despair. But this passage makes it clear that hope is a process.

The first step in that process is suffering. Loss is a part of life. We'll all endure hardship and heartache on this side of heaven. When we suffer, we have two choices: press on or give up.

If we choose discipline and perseverance, then this pattern gradually becomes part of who we are—our character. Character doesn't change based on circumstances or who is watching at the moment.

Character eventually results in hope. This kind of hope is not a vague feeling or wish. Instead it's a deep knowledge that you and God can get through anything together. That's the heart of hope: choosing to walk with God through the valleys of life and finding that he will never leave you—and that you will never leave him either.

Take heart, friend, you are doing better than you know. Jesus is with you, and hope is on its way.

God, give me the strength to persevere, the courage to have character, so that I will have the hope I need for the future.

· · · ·

How is God building perseverance, character, and hope in your life?

YOU'RE DOING BETTER THAN YOU KNOW

I press on toward the goal to win the prize for which God has called me heavenward in Christ Jesus. (Philippians 3:14)

The hill on my run taunts me and tries to steal my breath. But what really makes me want to quit are the accusations inside: *You're going so slow. This must be your worst run ever.*

I used to listen to that voice. Until I discovered something: every time I heard it, I ended up with a time that was my personal best.

In the moments when we want to give up, when we feel weak and exhausted, when we think we can't do it . . . we're actually getting stronger.

We're not tired because we're failing; we're tired because we're fighting.

We're not weary because we're weak; we're weary because we're winning the battle to go to the next level in our lives.

This is the scandalous secret: when we want to quit, it really means we're making progress.

Let's not allow the enemy of our hearts to convince us to stop because we think we're not doing well enough. Instead, let's recognize the effort and the pain for what they are—signs of growth.

Yes, sometimes the hurt means we are injured and need to rest. But often it simply means we are breaking through what has held us back and pushing with all our might toward what God has for us.

The place between what is comfortable and what seems like it will surely kill us is often where we become all we're created to be.

God, you are the one who will see me through all the way to the finish line.

. . . .

What's one step of faith, love, or courage you can take today?

IT'S OKAY IF YOU NEED HELP

They couldn't bring him to Jesus because of the crowd, so they dug a hole through the roof above his head. Then they lowered the man on his mat, right down in front of Jesus. (Mark 2:4 NLT)

I text a lie that my heart is hearing to a friend. Then I simply ask, "What is the truth? I can't come up with it right now." She writes back and tells me what I already know deep inside but can't quite manage to find in the moment. I read her words over and over, then get up with new strength to face the day.

Most of us know the story of the man lowered through a roof by his friends so that he could be laid at the feet of Jesus and find healing. What I think many of us don't realize is that there are days when it's our hearts, not our bodies, that need the same thing. We think if we can just muster up enough faith, then we should be able to get there ourselves. But that's not the way it works.

We're made to share life with each other. We're made to say, "I need you. Please help me." Those aren't words of weakness—they're the strongest words we can say. Because it's easy to try to figure things out on our own. It's much harder to say, "Please carry my heart to Jesus today."

When you really need help and you ask for it, you're not becoming a burden. You're offering an opportunity for someone to be part of a blessing.

God, give me the courage to ask for help when I need it.

. . . .

What do you need from someone else today?

Day 178

YOU HAVE AN ENCOURAGER

As soon as I pray, you answer me;
you encourage me by giving me strength. (Psalm 138:3 NLT)

*E*ncouragement means to give support, confidence, or hope to someone. Without it we begin to feel dry, our insides dusty and silent.

I found myself in such a place just yesterday. I began to pray, "Lord, will you please send someone to encourage me?" Hours later I got a voice message on my phone. A dear friend said, "God put you on my heart, and I felt like I was supposed to tell you . . ." (Disclaimer: there have been many other times I've prayed for encouragement, and the response has not been this direct or clear.)

God is our encourager. Jesus is our encourager. The Holy Spirit is our encourager. This is a mysterious and beautiful reality to me. To think that the one who spoke the world into being would also speak into my life. To dare to believe that the one who gave his life for me also breathes life into my tired bones still. To understand that the one who counts every hair on my head also addresses every care in my heart.

When we wonder, *How is God encouraging me today?* I think we can look several places. First, his Word is one long love letter of encouragement. Also, God encourages us through each other like my friend did. We can even encourage ourselves as David did: "David encouraged himself in the LORD his God" (1 Sam. 30:6 KJV). Wherever our encouragement comes from, the ultimate source is the one who loves us.

God, help me see your hand and heart in every word
and act that builds me up and gives me strength.

. . . .

How has God encouraged you lately?

GOD WILL HELP YOU STRESS LESS

I tell you not to worry about everyday life. (Matthew 6:25 NLT)

I scatter flour across parchment paper like snow in preparation for placing a pie crust on it.

As I work, I remember what the baking class instructor kept saying to us: "It's only pie." She said this when her students first walked in wide-eyed and slightly terrified, as if we were going to learn to dismantle nuclear bombs rather than bake. She repeated it when someone added a bit too much flour or too little salt. She declared it when we folded our pie crusts, wrapped them, and got ready to carry them home where we would complete our creations alone (gasp!).

Jesus said, "I tell you not to worry about everyday life—whether you have enough food and drink, or enough clothes to wear. Isn't life more than food, and your body more than clothing?" (Matt. 6:25 NLT). In other words, *it's only pie*.

I tell myself to remember that phrase, to tuck it into my heart like leftovers into the refrigerator. I want to bring it out again when I find myself anxious or concerned about something small and inconsequential.

After decades on this earth, I'm still learning to make pie. And I'm still learning to make peace with the little complications and annoyances of everyday life. But I will practice. I will be patient with myself. I will enjoy the good things that eventually come from the process.

God, thank you that I don't have to worry about the little things because you are a big God who loves me.

. . . .

Is there something you need to say "it's only pie"
about in your life today?

YOUR GOD IS STEADFAST

My dear brothers and sisters, be steadfast, immovable. (1 Corinthians 15:58 CSB)

The apostle Paul wrote these words to the church in Corinth, which was surrounded by chaos. Sometimes the most courageous, loving thing we can do is to hold steady.

This is true when someone we love is battling an addiction, and we must set boundaries instead of enabling. It's what we can do when a workplace is caught up in a swirl of stress and frustration even if it would be easier to give in to the griping and gossip. It's the position we can take when it feels like everything in our lives is changing without our consent.

Is this easy? Absolutely not. Will the people around us always understand? Not likely. Choosing to be steadfast requires grit and perseverance, bravery and great strength. It's far easier to just do something, *anything*, because at least then we feel as if we have some control. But realizing that all we can really control is our own actions and choices can be a step toward freedom.

And thankfully, we don't have to stand firm by ourselves. We're called to steadfastness because it reflects the heart and character of God.

> But this I call to mind,
>   and therefore I have hope:
> The steadfast love of the LORD never ceases. (Lam. 3:21–22 ESV)

Next time I'm tempted to give in to the chaos around me, I'll pray for the courage to be a little more steady, a little more like the God we can rely on to be steadfast forever.

*God, thank you for your steadfast love that
I can count on no matter what.*

· · · ·

What's one way you've seen God's steadfast love in your life?

YOU DON'T HAVE TO TRY SO HARD

It was not by their sword that they won the land,
nor did their arm bring them victory;
it was your right hand, your arm,
and the light of your face, for you loved them. (Psalm 44:3)

E ven the best things in our lives can become "swords" like the psalmist describes. Then it becomes tempting to rely on our own strength (our "arm") to achieve that victory for our lives. We think if we just do enough, then things have to get better. It can start to feel as if everything is depending on us. Those swords we thought would be so helpful can suddenly seem like a lot to keep holding up.

When we start resorting to our swords and our strength, it usually simply means this: we're afraid. We don't know what to do, so we decide the safest strategy is simply to do *more*. Doing so at least gives us a sense of control. Yet over time we realize not only are our circumstances not changing, but we're flat-out exhausted.

It's often in that moment that we're ready for God to come to our aid. That's when we need his arm, his right hand, and the light of his face. He uses his arm to beckon us to him. His hand takes the sword from ours, and he says, "You can lay that down, daughter. You don't have to fight anymore." Then he looks us in the eyes and reassures us, "I love you. I'm going to take care of you. It's time to stop trying so hard and instead trust me."

God, it's easy to try really hard—especially when I feel afraid.
Today I'm slowing down, taking a deep breath,
and coming to you for victory.

. . . .

What's one way you can try less and trust more today?

GOD WILL BRING NEW LIFE AND GROWTH

The trees will again be filled with fruit;
fig trees and grapevines will be loaded down once more.
(Joel 2:22 NLT)

The prophet Joel looks out over desolate land, where sheep struggle to find grass and the branches are bare. He writes words that portray a different time, one of life and growth. The wilderness will be green again. The trees will bear fruit. This is not the end.

Scripture has a recurring theme of barrenness followed by blessing, death followed by resurrection, loss followed by restoration. What can help us in those in-between times when life feels like it's on hold?

First, we can trust that God is still working while we're waiting. Trust is not an emotion; it's a decision we make all over again each day. If you still struggle with challenging feelings, that's okay.

It's also important to allow ourselves to grieve what we've lost. Some losses are tangible, like a job or loved one. Some are invisible, like a dream, our sense of safety, or our old "normal." When we process loss rather than deny it, we don't dismiss what's coming or doubt what God is doing—we make room for it.

We can also look for even the smallest signs of new life and growth. Maybe you laugh hard for the first time in a while, find the energy to text a friend, or sense a spark of creativity returning again.

In the best and worst of times, in celebration and sorrow, in laughter and languishing, in every season of change, who God is remains the same.

God, it's a relief to know that even in the seasons
when I feel weary, you are still working.

. . . .

What's a difficult season God has gotten you through?

GOD IS YOUR FREEDOM

In him and through faith in him we may approach God with freedom and confidence. (Ephesians 3:12)

A car carried me to the center of the city. I squirmed in the back seat, not knowing what to expect. Then someone escorted me to a small room with cinder walls. The click of a door sliding closed and the turn of a key sent chills up my spine. I felt stunned and quietly wondered, *How did I end up here?*

Looking at our uncomfortable faces, my college Bible study leader said with glee, "Today we're studying Paul, so I wanted you to know what it felt like to be in prison!"

As I stared at the bars in front of me on that chilly winter day, I thought also of the bars that surrounded parts of my heart. I couldn't touch them, but I could feel them just as surely as those keeping me in that jail cell. Each one had a different name:

Expectations

Fear

Comparison

In the following years, God set me free from much of what held me captive. He gave me the keys I needed. But I'll confess—well over a decade later, there are times I still step back into those old patterns and lock myself in again. I've learned to recognize the signs. Exhaustion. Irritability. Depression. Anxiety. Then I ask Jesus to set me free all over again. It's a lifelong process that will only be complete in heaven.

What's holding you captive today? Maybe it's an addiction. A destructive relationship. A striving to be perfect. All of our prison cells look different. But it's the same God who wants to set each of our hearts free.

God, thank you for being the one who gives me true freedom.

. . . .

What are you asking God to set you free from today?

YOUR SLIPS ARE
PART OF PROGRESS

I cried out, "I am slipping!"
but your unfailing love, O LORD, supported me.
(Psalm 94:18 NLT)

If you've ever pursued a dream or tried to change an area of your life, then you need to hear this: The closer you get to your goal, the steeper the climb gets. The steeper it gets, the more likely you are to slip. When you do, it will probably catch you off guard. You may say to yourself, "I was doing so well! What happened?" It suddenly feels like all the progress you've made isn't real, that God should give up on you, and that you might as well slide all the way back to the bottom.

Don't listen to those lies. We all fall. We all fail. We all have slip-ups and setbacks. That's simply part of being human. And that's why we need Jesus. The difference between those who reach the top of the mountain and those who don't isn't perfection—it's resilience. It's getting back up again and again. Taking one more step over and over. Refusing to quit even when your heart and tailbone and ego have been bruised.

If you have messed up this week, I want to whisper to your heart: "This doesn't have to mean you're done. And well done for trying to pursue something worthwhile. Trying and slipping is always better than doing nothing because at least you learn, at least you grow."

So stand tall again, brush the dirt off your backside if you need to, and set your sights again on where you're going. Then move forward just a little more today.

God, when I start slipping, lift me up and help me keep going.

· · · ·

When have you experienced a slip and
kept moving forward anyway?

GOD IS YOUR CARETAKER

*Look at the birds. They don't plant or harvest or store food in barns,
for your heavenly Father feeds them. And aren't you far more valuable
to him than they are? (Matthew 6:26 NLT)*

A crowd gathers to hear Jesus speak, much like a modern congregation having an outdoor service. As an antidote for worry, Jesus tells the crowd to look at the birds and how God feeds them, at the lilies and how God dresses them (Matt. 6:28–29). By doing so, yes, Jesus reminds us of God's care. But he also gives us a practical strategy to combat worry.

Be present. When we worry, we're not in the current moment. Jesus says, "Look at the birds." We can start by taking a deep breath and intentionally observing what's around us.

Practice gratitude. Jesus reminds the crowd of God's care for birds and lilies as examples of how he cares for each of us too. We can ask ourselves, "What's one way God is taking care of me right now?" Then express our thanks.

Fill the space. To stop worrying, we need to fill that space with something else. That can be a phrase we repeat like, "God cares for me." Or it might be occupying our mind in another way, like going for a walk or having a conversation with a friend.

Repeat, repeat, repeat. Worry is a natural part of being human—*everyone* worries. We can get frustrated when we do the hard work of getting out of rumination only to find the same thoughts coming back. When we start worrying again, we can repeat the first three steps.

God is taking good care of the birds and flowers today, and he promises to do the same for us too.

God, thank you for taking care of the birds, the flowers, and me.

. . . .

What's a worry you have right now?

YOU CAN EMBRACE THE WONKY

He has made everything beautiful in its time. (Ecclesiastes 3:11)

I'm sitting at a table with a palette of watercolors in front of me. The class instructor gives us a picture of a truck filled with hearts to trace and then paint. All through the process she keeps repeating one phrase, "Embrace the wonky."

By this she means make room for imperfection, let the water and the paint have their way, release expectations and welcome what is taking shape on the paper in front of us. She says one of the biggest obstacles for new painters is trying too hard.

I'm in a challenging season, and it seems this is the invitation Jesus keeps giving me. I have an image in my mind of what life should be like and how everything should turn out. When I cling to this, I'm inevitably disappointed. I only find joy, freedom, and creativity when I choose to let things *be*.

If you are in a season when your life doesn't look like you hoped it would by now, take heart. You are not producing perfection; you are creating art. Those are two entirely different things.

Producing perfection is about control. Creating art is about curiosity and letting go.

Producing perfection is about meeting expectations. Creating art is about accepting what's unexpected.

Producing perfection is only about the final product. Creating art is more about the process.

Our lives are not impersonal production lines at a factory. They are pieces of art being created with the one who loves us. He is making all things beautiful in his time.

God, help me embrace the wonky today and trust you're making everything beautiful in your time.

. . . .

What is God creating in your life right now?

IT'S OKAY IF YOU'RE CALLED TO STAY

Go into all the world and preach the Good News to everyone. (Mark 16:15 NLT)

When we think about going into all the world and making disciples, it's easy to assume we need to change our location. But when we see it as only that, we misunderstand the holy ripple effect of God's love.

We miss how the smile we offer to the cashier can later be passed along to the weary nurse who's grabbing lunch, which helps give her the strength to hold the hand of someone we'll never meet as they battle cancer.

We don't know how the kind word we speak to a friend will give her the courage she needs when she goes on the business trip to another continent and has a chance to answer the unexpected question, "What's so different about you?"

We will probably never see—this side of heaven—how being obedient in the here and now can wondrously go on and on through generations to someday make a difference in the then and there.

So if you're in a season where what God is whispering to your heart is not *go* but *stay*, know that it doesn't mean your reach is any less. It's not any less spiritual. It's not any less filled with potential and purpose.

We serve a God who is not boxed in by time, circumstance, or geography. He is everywhere, all the time, with everyone. The best place to start sharing his love is the ordinary, sacred ground right beneath our feet.

God, show me how I can share your love wherever you have me today.

· · · ·

Where has God placed you in this season of your life?

Day 188

GOD IS WORKING ON YOUR BEHALF

Many, Lord my God,
are the wonders you have done,
the things you planned for us. (Psalm 40:5)

We're human and it's natural for us to want to *see* to believe. We can wish prayer were more like talking to a genie in a bottle. Say a few words and *poof*—the answer appears. But often when it seems we need proof of God's love the most, it can be hardest to find.

So what's God doing in those times? He's busy working on our behalf. He's promised to work all things together for good, and we can rest in that even when we don't see the results yet.

While God is working, we can tell him what we need. "Do not be anxious about anything, but in every situation, by prayer and petition, with thanksgiving, present your requests to God" (Phil. 4:6). This isn't about filling God in, because he already knows. Instead it's about filling us with peace.

Then we can choose to actively wait on God. "But those who hope in the Lord will renew their strength. They will soar on wings like eagles; they will run and not grow weary, they will walk and not be faint" (Isa. 40:31).

And when God finally does show us what he's been up to, we show our gratitude. We can tell him, "Thank you for planning all this for me. Thank you for working behind the scenes. Thank you for bringing this together in your perfect timing."

God, sometimes it's hard to wait to see what you're doing in my life.
Please fill me with peace and show me what to do in this season.

. . . .

What has God already done in your life?
What are you waiting for him to do?

GOD IS ALL-SUFFICIENT

It is not that we are competent in ourselves to claim anything as coming from ourselves, but our adequacy is from God. (2 Corinthians 3:5 CSB)

God," I pray, "I need you to remind me of what's true right now." At the heart of what I'm struggling against is this: a belief that everything depends on me. I must not let anyone down.

I need to remember this: *God is all-sufficient*. This means that because he lives in us, we have everything we need to fulfill his purpose for our lives. And the really miraculous part is that he will do it. The beginning, the middle, and the end do not depend on us. They all depend on him.

God isn't saying, "Do as much as you can, as quickly as you can, however you can." Instead, he has specific assignments for us during our time on earth. They are not the same as the ones he has for the woman we admire, the friend we respect, or the leader we want to emulate. They are original and only for us. What we're to do not only begins with God; it is finished by him too.

What's our part in all of this? We can focus on, as Jesus said, remaining close to him. We can abide, love, and obey rather than hurry, hustle, and prove our value. We can rest, receive, and trust that our worth doesn't come from our works. We can release our striving and instead embrace what God has for us, believing it is enough and even beautiful in his eyes.

> *God, you are enough for all that's in front of me.*
> *I trust you and believe you will see me through.*
>
> . . . .
>
> How has God helped you trade hustling for trusting?

YOUR HAPPINESS CAN BE AN ACT OF WORSHIP

May the righteous be glad
and rejoice before God;
may they be happy and joyful. (Psalm 68:3)

In some Christian circles there's a myth that goes like this: happiness is worldly, therefore anything that makes you happy must be wrong.

Yet as I've dug deeper into what happiness really means, I've come to believe this instead: happiness can be an act of worship. I believe God wants authenticity, and grief is also a sacred emotion that can honor him. But it turns out being happy can also be part of living a worshipful life.

To say that God doesn't ever want us to be happy is like saying parents don't want their children to be happy. No parent wants a life of misery and suffering for their kid. Yes, parents understand their children won't always be happy. They'll have hard days and go through challenges. Sometimes they won't get what they want for their greater good. But at the heart of every parent is a deep hope for their child's well-being. How could God want any less for us and still be loving?

Maybe somewhere deep inside you've believed the lie I did—that you're not allowed to be happy. If so, let me whisper what's true: "You don't have to be happy, and there will be many days when you aren't, but you are most certainly allowed to be happy." Even more than that, God desires your well-being, and part of that is your happiness.

God, thank you for the gift of happiness and
all the ways you bring it to my life.

. . . .

What makes you happy?

YOU REALLY ARE FORGIVEN

Once again you will have compassion on us.
You will trample our sins under your feet
and throw them into the depths of the ocean! (Micah 7:19 NLT)

God doesn't just toss our sins into the ocean like a piece of driftwood that could come back with the next wave. Micah tells us our sins are thrown into the depths.

The deepest part of the ocean is the Mariana Trench, which is about thirty-six thousand feet (that's over six miles). If we were to visit this place without taking a light with us, it would be impossible to see. We'd find ourselves in inky black. In other words, when God says he has hurled our sins into the depths of the sea, it means they can no longer be seen. Not ever.

Also, in the deep sea there is great pressure that holds all within it in place. Once there, an object is not going to come back to the surface. When God says our sins are gone, he means it. They are not about to emerge from some hidden place to suddenly appear before us again.

And there is no plant life or growth in the deep. If we want healing and restoration, we will not find it by trying to dive back down to the level of our sins. We can let them stay where God has put them and let go forever because we're forgiven.

Our sins are gone forever to the depths, cast there by a God whose love is as unrelenting as the waves against the shore.

God, thank you that I am fully forgiven, that my sins
are gone forever because of you.

. . . .

What has God forgiven you for that you're glad is gone forever?

JESUS IS TRUTH

Jesus answered, "I am the way and the truth and the life." (John 14:6)

When Jesus tells us he is truth, it doesn't mean he is going to tell us everything we've done wrong. He is not recounting our character flaws. He is not reminding us of why we don't measure up. Instead, he is always "speaking the truth in love" as he calls us to do (Eph. 4:15). He is saying, "I love you. I see you. I care what's going on in your heart and life. I know who you really are. This is what you need to know so that you can be whole."

I think sometimes we get confused about truth. We read about "the sword of the Spirit, which is the word of God" (6:17), and we think this means we are to go around swinging that sword at each other. But truth is a way to love others the way Jesus loves us. To protect each other's hearts. To say, "I see a threat in your life, and I am willing to put myself on the line on your behalf." This is what Jesus did on a cross and when he came forth from an empty tomb. This is what we can dare to do for each other. Truth is not meant to be a weapon; it's intended to be a source of healing.

Truth is more than facts or opinions. Truth is a person who loves us. He wants to speak to our hearts today.

> *God, you are the only one who is fully truth and fully love.*
> *Help me remember that and model it for others.*
>
> . . . .
>
> What truth is Jesus speaking to your heart today?

GOD WILL NEVER LEAVE YOU

God has said, "Never will I leave you; never will I forsake you." (Hebrews 13:5)

A dear friend became unexpectedly distant. I asked God, "Will you promise me that this person I care so much for won't leave me?" I only heard silence in response. It seemed I finally sensed this from him: *I can't promise you that this person won't leave you. But I promise that I won't.*

I thought then of what Jesus went through on this earth. A dear friend betrayed him to be crucified. Another denied him multiple times. He knew what it felt like to be abandoned, forsaken, and disappointed by those closest to him. The hard reality of the world is this: even the best of us are capable of letting down those we love.

I also believe that because we are created for relationship, God will put people into our lives for each season. Looking back over my life, I could see that if one friend did drift away, another came along—if I had the courage to keep letting that happen.

The difficult thing about sharing this earth with one another is that we are all bulls in a china shop crashing into each other's hearts. The beautiful thing is that our God is a mender, ever-present to make us whole again. He will never leave or forsake us. This is what we can rely on, what we can forever trust.

God, you are with me and for me in every moment.
Give me the courage to keep loving despite the risks.

· · · ·

Who in your life needs to be reminded of your love for them today?

GOD IS YOUR GURU

They crush people with unbearable religious demands and never lift a finger to ease the burden. (Matthew 23:4 NLT)

The Pharisees and Sadducees were the self-appointed experts of their time. Their rigid rules added pressure in almost every area of life.

While it sounds like this would never happen in our modern world, things we hear at church or on social media can still weigh us down. When an "expert" shares anything that makes us feel heavy or burdened, we need to ask ourselves:

- When I listen to this person, does my heart feel heavier or lighter?
- Are the words *should* or *have to* used?
- Do I experience guilt and shame when I try to live this way?
- Are those who fail labeled (loser, failure, weak), or is there encouragement and support?

Unlike the Pharisees and Sadducees, Jesus says, "I am gentle and humble in heart, and you will find rest for your souls. For my yoke is easy and my burden is light" (Matt. 11:29–30). Instead of striving, he invites us to rest. Instead of being perfect, he offers us freedom and forgiveness. Instead of making life about performance, he brings us into perfect love.

Learning from others can be helpful, and we live in a time with an extraordinary amount of information. That is a gift, but we also need to be aware of when it starts being a source of anxiety and guilt.

We don't need another guru; we already have a God who loves us and promises to give us everything we need today.

God, when I place "shoulds" on my shoulders, help me choose the lightness and freedom you offer instead.

. . . .

What's a "should" you've taken on from someone else?

GOD IS YOUR DWELLING PLACE

Lord, you have been our dwelling place
throughout all generations. (Psalm 90:1)

At the end of a year full of travel for work, I found myself exhausted. I just couldn't carry on anymore. In his mercy, it felt like God gathered me up in his arms and carried me back to where I belonged.

Before this season in my life, I hadn't really grasped what God meant when he said, "I will be your dwelling place." But I slowly came to understand that these words mean he will be the place where we can put down roots, make a homestead like a pioneer, and claim the land as ours forever. No one will be able to kick us out or run us off or encroach on what's ours.

It turns out our heart-home is not one with walls and ceilings and a bathroom. It's God himself, our maker and caretaker and the one who knows us best of all. When we center ourselves in him, when we plant ourselves right in the middle of his will, then we are always safe and where we belong. We can remain or go. We can move or be still. We can venture or nest.

This is what I needed to know when I was a wanderer. It's the truth I am holding on to here and now, the one I'll take with me if I get on another plane. Home is not a place; home is a person. And he is with us always. His love is the place we can stay wherever we go.

God, you are my security and my identity.
You are the home of my heart.

. . . .

How is God a safe place for your heart?

YES, GOD DELIGHTS IN YOU

*The very hairs on your head are all numbered. So don't be afraid;
you are more valuable to God than a whole flock of sparrows. (Luke
12:7 NLT)*

Yesterday I refilled the bird feeder, and now it's surrounded by a flock of sparrows. I feed these birds not because I must. No one compels me to haul home fifty-pound bags of sunflower seeds. I do so simply because these birds delight me.

This helps me refocus on how the God who takes care of sparrows also feels the same way about us. I go searching in Scripture for reminders of this:

> He led me to a place of safety;
> he rescued me because he delights in me. (Ps. 18:19 NLT)

> The LORD directs the steps of the godly.
> He delights in every detail of their lives. (37:23 NLT)

> For the LORD delights in his people. (149:4 NLT)

As I watch these birds, I begin to understand this kind of delight in a deeper way. There is something about their innate *birdness* that I love. It's nothing impressive, really. They just eat and fly, build nests in the spring, hop around the yard, and occasionally do unspeakable things to the patio furniture.

Thinking of the sparrows is both a challenge and a comfort to me on this day. It makes me want to have the courage not to try so hard; it gives me the reassurance that I don't have to.

I watch the birds. A tenderhearted God watches me. He watches you too.

---

*God, help me to simply be who you've created me to be
and to believe doing so brings delight to you.*

. . . .

What does nature show you about who God is and who you are?

GOD GIVES YOU TRUTH
FOR TEMPTATION

Jesus was led by the Spirit into the wilderness to be tempted there by the devil. (Matthew 4:1 NLT)

Before the start of his public ministry, Jesus faces a private showdown with the enemy. After fasting in the wilderness for forty days, the devil appears and tries to lead him astray.

First, the enemy says, "Tell these stones to become loaves of bread" (Matt. 4:3 NLT). Lie: You have to *prove who you are by what you can do.* Jesus responds, "People do not live by bread alone, but by every word that comes from the mouth of God" (v. 4 NLT). Truth: *God will take care of me, and he alone gets the final say in my life.*

Next, the devil takes Jesus to the highest point of the temple and tells him to jump off because God will protect him. Lie: *You are completely in control of your personal safety.* Jesus sees the bigger picture: "You must not test the LORD your God" (v. 7 NLT). Truth: *I'm not in complete control of my personal safety (or the safety of those I love), but God does promise me true security no matter what happens.*

Finally, the devil promises to give Jesus worldly gains and glory if he'll do one thing—worship him. Lie: *Satisfaction in life comes from what we can see and obtain.* Jesus says, "You must worship the LORD your God and serve only him" (v. 10 NLT). Truth: *Satisfaction comes from aligning with our true purpose and serving and worshiping the God who created us.*

Even Jesus was tempted to believe lies. He understands what it's like, and he'll empower us to live in the truth.

God, show me the lies I've believed; set me free with your truth.

. . . .

What's a lie you're tempted to believe?

YOU DON'T HAVE TO LISTEN TO THE LIES

But encourage one another daily, as long as it is called "Today," so that none of you may be hardened by sin's deceitfulness. (Hebrews 3:13)

One of my friends says, "I've struggled with believing the lie that I'm not smart enough." Another friend replies, "You're one of the smartest people I know!" A light bulb comes on as I realize suddenly that the enemy is lying to us in areas related to our giftings.

I imagine he does the same with you. Because I think the purpose of the lie is to hold us back from who we're made to be and what we're called to do. These attacks are startling, but we need to acknowledge they're a normal part of life as a believer, soldier, and fighter. And they will be until we're in heaven.

That is reason to say, "You know what? I am a warrior! I have fought hard, and I'm going to *keep* fighting hard."

So if we are in a battle today or tomorrow or a decade from now and we hear lies, let's not allow the enemy to shame us or make us feel guilty.

Instead, let's block those arrows and say, "No, in Jesus's name, I'm a warrior and I'm going to resist until the day I go home."

At times we will need our sisters to lock shields with us too and say, "I'm going to take those arrows for a while. I'm going to stand in the gap for you." There is no shame in that either. In the kingdom of God, there is no such thing as an army of one.

We are stronger and braver together.

God, help me to recognize the lies and replace them with truth.

. . . .

What's a lie you're tempted to listen to today?

GOD TELLS YOU WHO YOU ARE

But Jesus would not entrust himself to them, for he knew all people.
(John 2:24)

*T*ell me who I am.
Isn't this the whisper of our hearts as women? The friends, the men, the crowd. They will tell us if we are okay. If we are worthy. If we are enough.

Jesus is the only human to walk this spinning planet and not say, "Tell me who I am." He didn't look to others to define his identity or determine his worth.

Of course we're going to care what others think. We're going to desire acceptance and want to fit in. This is the way we're created to connect. We can simply say, "But God gets the final word."

Tell me who I am.

God says we are beloved and chosen, cherished and gifted, divinely created wonders. When someone says, "You'll never amount to anything," his Word says, "The LORD will work out his plans for my life" (Ps. 138:8 NLT). When someone tells us, "You don't look the right way," he whispers, "[You are] fearfully and wonderfully made" (139:14). When someone implies, "You aren't wanted," he declares, "I have called you by name; you are mine" (Isa. 43:1 NLT).

He is the one who gives us our identity. The one who sets us free from condemnation and comparison, hustling to be liked and trying to be perfect. The one who is right there with us every time we feel tempted to listen to the lies. May his love always be louder than any other voice.

God, tell us who we are.

> *God, on the days when it's hard to remember what's true,*
> *remind me of who I am in you.*
>
> . . . .
>
> Who does God say you are today?

GOD WILL HELP YOU DO WHAT'S HARD

O Sovereign Lord! You made the heavens and earth by your strong hand and powerful arm. Nothing is too hard for you! (Jeremiah 32:17 NLT)

Today you will be called to do hard things. Maybe the hard thing will be getting out of bed when you'd rather hide under the covers. It might be dealing with a difficult relationship, tackling a project that feels impossible, overcoming an addiction, trying again when you've failed before, choosing to stay when you just want to go.

I don't know the details of your situation or circumstances, but I know the God who is in them with you. He is the one who spoke the world into being, who scattered the stars into place, who sculpted the first man from dust and breathed life into his lungs. He is the God who came to a manger, who hung on a cross, who defeated death and rose again. He is not a stranger to challenges, not unfamiliar with suffering. He knows what it's like to be human in a world where all is not as it should be.

He will give you the strength you need. He will give you the perseverance to take another step. He will give you the courage to face whatever is in front of you. You will never face anything alone. You will never have to rely only on your own resources. You will never be too weak because you have limitless power living within you.

Nothing is too hard for your God, which means nothing he has called you to do today will be too hard for you.

God, I trust you to give me everything I need to do all you have called me to do today.

· · · ·

What hard thing is God asking you to do today?

YOU'RE A PEACEMAKER

As iron sharpens iron, so a friend sharpens a friend. (Proverbs 27:17 NLT)

When a friend came to me a few years ago to talk about a disagreement she was having with someone in her life, I said, "Well, iron sharpens iron—that means sometimes sparks fly."

I remembered a class I took in college called Communication and Conflict. The one thing I can still recall from that entire semester is learning that the couples most likely to split up are not those who fight a lot but those who *never fight at all*. Conflict, it turns out, is necessary in a healthy relationship. At the start of a conflict, there is an "I" and an "I," but when done successfully, by the end there's a "we."

It matters that we understand the good, bad, and ugly of how conflict works, because if we don't, then we can become people who settle for peace at any price. We hear "blessed are the peacemakers" and think it's the same as "blessed are the peace*keepers*." But the two are very different.

Making peace means honest communication, grace, compassion, honesty about our wants and needs, empathy for the wants and needs of others, a willingness to be vulnerable, patience, and lots of respect. Keeping peace often means stuffing our feelings, letting ourselves be taken advantage of, letting harmful behavior continue, and building up resentment.

I'm learning to speak up when it really matters. I'm learning to let iron sharpen iron, yes, and to watch the sparks fly. I'm learning the most valuable, beautiful peace is sometimes the kind that comes after a worthwhile battle fought for the sake of love.

God, show me how to be a peacemaker, not just a peacekeeper.

· · · ·

What helps you have healthy conflict?

GOD IS YOUR SUPPLIER AND MULTIPLIER

Then he took the seven loaves and the fish, thanked God for them, and broke them into pieces. (Matthew 15:36 NLT)

Jesus asks his disciples to help him feed a hungry crowd. After witnessing miracles, the disciples respond with doubt: "Where would we get enough food here in the wilderness for such a huge crowd?" (Matt. 15:33 NLT).

I'd like to tell you I can't relate to their response at all. But when I feel exhausted and someone asks yet one more thing of me, it triggers my anxiety. All rational thought and/or faith temporarily goes out the window. I just feel panic that *it's all too much and I'm not enough*. I don't pause to reflect on all the times God has come through for me or how I don't have to rely on my own strength. I don't realize that if he's inviting me to do something, then he'll give me what I need.

Thankfully, Jesus doesn't rebuke the disciples. Instead, he asks a simple question: "How much bread do you have?" (v. 34 NLT). "Then he took the seven loaves and the fish, thanked God for them, and broke them into pieces. He gave them to the disciples, who distributed the food to the crowd" (v. 36 NLT).

In the moments when we feel "not enough," this story offers us hope and help. It reassures us that we can offer God what we have, even if it feels like very little. In his hands, there is no such thing as "small." God promises to be not only our supplier but also our multiplier.

God, you are my strength when I'm weak. You are my supplier when the needs seem like too much.

. . . .

How can you see God providing for you and through you?

GOD CATCHES YOUR TEARS

You number my wanderings;
Put my tears into Your bottle;
Are they not in Your book? (Psalm 56:8 NKJV)

A uthor and speaker Sheila Walsh stands on a stage and holds up a tiny bottle. She explains it has one singular and sacred destiny: it is a tear-catcher. A friend of hers discovered it in an antique shop in Israel. Sheila says, "I did a little research and discovered that tear bottles were common in Rome and Egypt around the time of Christ. Mourners would collect their tears as they walked toward the graveyard to bury their loved one, a tangible indication of how much that person was loved."[1]

Suddenly Psalm 56:8 shifts like a kaleidoscope, and I can see it from a new perspective. Human mourners walked and caught their *own* tears. But our wild God takes it one step further: he catches *our* tears and walks beside us in *our* sorrows. This changes everything. Because if we are carrying our own bottle of tears, then we are spilling our sadness only into emptiness. But if God is beside us, if those tears are going into his bottle, then we are releasing them into the hands of the One who can not only hold them but also transform them.

"Weeping may stay for the night, but rejoicing comes in the morning" (30:5). God can take what seems hopeless and turn it into victory. He can make beauty out of brokenness. He can redeem and restore anything.

God, thank you for treasuring my tears and transforming them into something new and beautiful.

. . . .

When was the last time you cried, and how does it feel to imagine God catching your tears?

GOD SAYS "YES" TO WHAT'S TRULY BEST

For no matter how many promises God has made, they are "Yes" in Christ. (2 Corinthians 1:20)

I curl up on the couch with hopes and dreams on my mind. Some have come true and others have not turned out the way I planned at all. I think, *I guess God said no to that one.* And it seems I hear a whisper in response within my heart: *I didn't say no ... I said "not this."* Huh.

When God promised that if you delight yourself in him then he will give you the desires of your heart, he meant it. What truly fulfills those desires may just look totally different than we first imagined. In that case, God says "yes" to the desire but "not this" to the many things we try along the journey to it. God may say not this season, not this job, not this door.

The challenge in those moments is to not close our hearts but to believe that if God says "not this" to something we hold dear to us, he's still saying yes to the desire deep within us. That takes trust and tenacity and sometimes a lot of tears. But here's the encouraging part: when we do get to what God has for us, it's better than what we dreamed for ourselves in the beginning.

And that turns all the "not this" answers along the way into one big "This was all worth it" that we can finally say.

God, thank you that behind what seems like a no from you is really a yes to your best for me.

. . . .

When has what looked like a no led you to something better?

YOU DON'T HAVE TO LISTEN TO THE CRITICS

So encourage each other and build each other up. (1 Thessalonians 5:11 NLT)

We always find what we are looking for, and critics are going to find something to criticize. Nothing this side of heaven is perfect. The casserole could use a little more sauce. The wall color would match a bit better if it were one shade lighter. The event would have been just right if only that one thing hadn't gone wrong. The book, the dream, the person could always do with a bit of tweaking.

Pursue excellence, yes. But at the end of the day, you don't answer to the critics. You answer to Christ, and what he asks for is obedience. That is success. That is enough. His way of doing things has always drawn criticism. What he calls you to do will be no exception.

Criticism is cheap. Courage is costly.

Criticism is easy. Love is hard.

Criticism is safe. Obedience is risky.

So let's be the wild ones. The women who aren't afraid to say, "I'm gonna do it anyway. And if I mess up, I'll try again." Let's be the dreamers willing to step out of the shadows and into the light, knowing that at some point it will mean exposing something we'd rather keep hidden. Let's be the stubborn and strong who refuse to give up even when progress is painful. Let's be the people who will arrive at the feet of Jesus tattered and dirty and saying, "Whew, what a ride!"

Let's not be critics. Let's be Christ followers.

God, give me courage when criticized and compassion when I'm tempted to be a critic.

. . . .

Who can you encourage today?

GOD LETS YOU DRAW NEAR

*And he said to her, "Daughter, your faith has made you well. Go in
peace. Your suffering is over." (Mark 5:34 NLT)*

The woman draws her cloak around her face, trying to hide her identity.
You shouldn't be here. You shouldn't do this. It's too late for you. Twelve years
ago, she started bleeding and never stopped. She thinks of the humiliating visits
to doctors, the last of her money being spent with no relief, the agony of her
isolation.

The crowd surges forward, and she finds herself next to Jesus. She reaches
out her hand and touches the edge of his robe.

She feels the power flow through her, the warmth of love and belonging,
healing and wholeness, restoration and all things being made right. Then Jesus
turns and asks, "Who touched my robe?" (Mark 5:30 NLT).

She has approached God in the flesh, touched him when she is unclean.
"Trembling at the realization of what had happened to her," she falls "to her
knees in front of him" and tells him what she's done (v. 33 NLT). Then she waits
for the rebuke, the harsh words, her punishment. Instead, Jesus says, "Daughter,
your faith has made you well. Go in peace. Your suffering is over" (v. 34).

Daughter. A term of endearment, acceptance, welcome, love, affection. She'd
hoped for physical healing, but this is more than she'd imagined. Her heart,
mind, and soul feel whole again too.

We can come to Jesus anytime we need to, in whatever condition we're in,
knowing his response will always be one of love, grace, and understanding.

We're not strangers in a crowd to God. We are his beloved daughters and sons.

*God, thank you for seeing my suffering and responding with care.
I'm reaching out to you today.*

· · · ·

What do you need from Jesus today?

YOU CAN BE A FRIEND

A friend loves at all times. (Proverbs 17:17)

Community is hard sometimes," my friend Stephanie admits. She shares about a woman in her life she was determined to pursue a friendship with. My friend would reach out, and the woman would respond to a certain extent, until fear kicked in and she withdrew. After months of this, the woman finally said to Stephanie, "Now I know you're my real friend because you never gave up on me."

Connecting with others in this world can be tricky. When we look at social media, it seems everyone has an abundance of "friends." But a study by *USA Today* showed the opposite is actually true. The average American has two or fewer people they can talk to about what's important to them—and that includes spouses and family members. A quarter of Americans report not having anyone at all.[1]

In the middle of our busy schedules, it's easy to push friendship to the back burner. Or life circumstances, like a move or divorce, may alter the ties we've formed with others. But friendship matters enough to keep trying—and to keep praying for those in our lives to find the friends they need as well.

Friends are one of God's most beautiful gifts to us. They help us become all he created us to be. We're not meant to go through life alone, and God will be faithful to provide others to share our journey. Like my persistent friend, he never gives up on making sure our hearts get what they need.

God, help me to be a persistent, consistent friend even when it's hard or scary to connect with others.

. . . .

Who has been a good friend to you?

Day 208

YOUR TEARS ARE LIKE SEEDS

Those who plant in tears
will harvest with shouts of joy.
They weep as they go to plant their seed,
but they sing as they return with the harvest.
(Psalm 126:5–6 NLT)

I stood next to our bird feeder and held a seed on the tip of my finger, studying it in the sunlight. The shape felt familiar but I couldn't quite place it. Then I read Psalm 126:5–6 and realized seeds are shaped remarkably like tears.

Years ago I was given a packet of seeds at a local farm. I tucked them away in my purse with the best of intentions, but I never planted them. So I never saw any growth or fruit from them in my life. I wondered if the same might be true of my tears, the ones I so valiantly resist. Perhaps crying is actually a lot more like planting, like the farmer dropping the seeds into the earth.

Maybe I resist the letting go because I know what happens next. There will be dark and dirt. There will be ugliness before loveliness. There will be little control. There will be waiting and watching. There will be the vulnerability of hope.

But it takes all these things for the becoming to happen. For the tiny seed, the little tear—so fragile—to transform itself into something strong and wild and capable of pushing through to the surface, to do whatever it takes to find the light again.

Let's take the seeds and tears from the places we hide them and watch them fall. Let's dare to believe that our tears are not really about an ending but instead, somehow, a beginning. And there is beauty coming.

God, turn my tears into new life and growth.

. . . .

How have tears been healing for you?

GOD IS WITHIN YOU

God is within her, she will not fall;
God will help her at break of day. (Psalm 46:4–5)

The headlines stream across the bottom of the television. I close my eyes and ask God, "Where is peace possible in this world?" It seems the answer comes, *Within you, because that's where I am.*

In the days of ancient Israel, a wall guarded the city of Jerusalem. It could easily seem as if that wall kept the people safe. Yet God told his people, "It's not about what's around you. It's about who is within you." They lost sight of this reality. They refused to rely on God but put their trust in their own strength. And when they did, Jerusalem fell and the people were exiled. No wall could be strong enough without God's protection.

We build walls in our lives too. We think, *If I can just save enough money for retirement, then I'll be secure.* Or, *If I can just stay in shape, then my confidence will be unshakable.* Or, *If I can have a husband and children who love me, they'll be my protection.*

We tend to focus on the external, especially in times of trouble. What God is encouraging us to do is focus on the internal and eternal instead. God has not promised you safety. But he has promised you security. Nothing can overcome you because nothing is too big for him. That means there's no breaking news that can break you.

God, I pray that you will be my ultimate security.
When I'm tempted to place my trust in something or someone else,
help me to rely on you instead.

. . . .

What do you want to entrust to God today?

YOU DON'T HAVE TO
WORK SO HARD

It is useless for you to work so hard
from early morning until late at night,
anxiously working for food to eat;
for God gives rest to his loved ones. (Psalm 127:2 NLT)

I'm sitting on the couch, laptop in front of me, typing so fast it sounds like a machine gun. I've been at my tasks for hours, barely taking a break to refill my coffee cup. My shoulders ache and so does my mind. I got to the point where I knew I should stop hours ago, but I kept going. Years ago, I often worked like this, and it took me to the brink of burnout.

Psalm 127:2 says it's useless for us to be "anxiously working." I looked up the meaning of the original phrase, and *anxiously working* basically means "work that hurts." When God spoke the world into being, sculpted a man from clay and a woman from a rib, he made work holy and good. There is work that's sacred and life-giving. But there is another kind of work too—the kind that stresses us out.

I've found the difference between the two is that one comes from a place of fear and another from love. When I work to the point of exhaustion, it's almost always because I feel I have something to prove. My best efforts happen when, instead, I believe I'm already enough and remember that success is about obedience, not outcomes.

I close my laptop and whisper a prayer. I listen to the God who invites us not to labor but to let ourselves be loved.

God, thank you for inviting me not to hustle but to hear
your voice telling me who I really am.

. . . .

How can you tell when fear is driving what you do?

RECEIVING WHAT OUR HEARTS NEED ISN'T SELFISH

Silver or gold I do not have, but what I do have I give you. (Acts 3:6)

Peter and John are going to the temple. Along the way they pass a beggar. The man wants money but what he really needs is healing. Peter says to him, "Silver or gold I do not have, but what I do have I give you."

Then in the name of Jesus, Peter lifts this man to his feet to begin a new life full of all he has never known before—running, skipping, jumping, dangling his toes into water on a hot summer day.

The words that grip me in this story come from Peter: "What I do have I give you." We can't give what we don't have. Yet at one point, Peter resisted receiving too. At the Last Supper when Jesus tried to wash his feet, Peter protested but finally relented even if he didn't yet understand.

I wonder if perhaps that day as he looked at the crippled feet of a beggar, the scene from the Last Supper flashed through his mind again. I wonder if he finally connected the dots—that receiving from Jesus is what gives us the power to give to others.

When we're weary, we often think what we need to do is just try harder. But maybe the opposite is true. Maybe what we need most is to sit down and let Jesus wash our feet.

What do you need to receive from Jesus today? Let him wash your feet, your wounds, the weariness from your heart. Let's believe. Let's receive. Let's give our Savior the joy of loving on us. And then pass it on.

God, thank you for giving to me so that I can give to others.

. . . .

What has God given you that you can share with someone else?

YOU CAN HELP SOMEONE TODAY

*Then a despised Samaritan came along, and when he saw the man,
he felt compassion for him. (Luke 10:33 NLT)*

A man travels on a road. Robbers attack. A priest passes by. Then a Levite. And finally a Samaritan (a cultural outcast). It's the Samaritan who has pity on the man. He stops and does three things that show us how we can love those who cross our path too.

First, the Samaritan bandages the man's wounds and pours oil and wine on them. For us, this means asking, "What do I have with me that I can use to help?" Your "wine and oil" might be an encouraging word, a listening ear, or even a simple act of kindness.

Next, the Samaritan places the man on his donkey and takes him to an inn. Our "donkey" is the vehicle we can use to help others. For you it might be your home that you open to others or a job that allows you to reach out. It's the "how" of the ways you help.

Lastly, the Samaritan finds an innkeeper. He tells the innkeeper to take care of the man and that he will cover what's needed. We can ask ourselves, "Who can I connect this person to? Who will be able to provide the care they need?" Perhaps that person is a counselor, doctor, or even a mutual friend.

You can be a neighbor to whoever crosses your path today. You can make a difference. You can touch a life. Like the Samaritan, do what you can with whatever you have wherever you are.

God, show me how I can love whoever you place in my path today.

· · · ·

What's one way you can help someone today?

GOD WILL NEVER HARM YOU

[God] rescues me unharmed from the battle. (Psalm 55:18)

David is in the heat of war, the middle of a storm, surrounded by trouble. Yet he still says he's unharmed. It is well with his soul.

God doesn't promise we'll avoid hurt. We live in a fallen, broken world and are not home yet. But God will keep us from being harmed—in other words, from being irreparably damaged by what happens in our lives.

It may be unwell with our bodies. It may be difficult with our families. It may be challenging with our work. Yet in all those things we can still say, "It is well with my soul." There's a place within you that this world and the enemy simply can't touch because it's safe in the hand of God, and he has promised never to let go. That's the part of you that will live forever. And while it may be dinged and dented by this life, it can't be permanently damaged.

God is faithful. He may allow hurt in our lives, but *he will not harm us*. God will sustain us until we're home with him. So we can say with the apostle Paul, "I know whom I have believed, and am convinced that he is able to guard what I have entrusted to him until that day" (2 Tim. 1:12). And on that day, we can trust it will be well with our souls . . . and with everything else too.

God, even on the hard days, I entrust myself to you.

. . . .

How is it "well with your soul" today despite
what might be happening in your life?

Day 214

GOD SEES THE REAL YOU

The Lord doesn't see things the way you see them. (1 Samuel 16:7 NLT)

We live in a world that's all about image. Post the perfect picture. Keep up with the latest trends. Have the right car, house, or friends.

Deep down inside most of us carry around this lie: if people really knew me, I wouldn't be loved. So we only show our best selves to the world, the highlights of our vacation, the happy smiles that hide the pain. No one would choose us, we think, if they could see past the polished image we're trying so hard to protect.

But we serve a God who says he doesn't see things the way we see them. When selecting a king for Israel, God picks David—a shepherd and the youngest son. He's not the most impressive or handsome. He doesn't have a fancy résumé or influential relationships.

David isn't perfect; we see him make many mistakes. He doesn't have flawless faith; the Psalms are full of questions and doubts. But what David wants more than image is intimacy with God, and that's why he's chosen to be king.

God sees past the surface in your life. He sees the real, imperfect you. He's choosing you too. You don't have to pretend with him; he knows you fully and loves you deeply just as you are today.

God, thank you for inviting me into true intimacy with you. Give me the courage to show up as I really am today.

. . . .

What's one way you're tempted to create an image, and what helps you choose real intimacy instead?

GOD IS YOUR SUSTAINER

Surely God is my help;
the Lord is the one who sustains me. (Psalm 54:4)

I pull my journal out of the nightstand and begin to write in loopy, early morning script, my eyes still only half-open. The day before comes back to me—the intense meetings, impending deadlines, emails I've yet to answer. In the near-dark it seems God whispers to my searching heart, *Will you let me be your sustainer?*

Sustain means "strengthen and support," and I'm learning, slowly, to lean on Jesus instead of flimsy earthly things that can never hold my weight. They are not bad things; it's simply that we sometimes ask far more of them than they are able to give. A cupcake can't heal my heart. Another episode can't give me peace. They have their place; they can contribute. We need not feel guilty for enjoying them. *But they are only nice supplements and not true sustenance.*

This is the miracle: the God of the universe, the creator of bread, the spinner of the earth, and the maker of our hearts says he is our sustainer. This can feel big and mysterious. But I think it simply comes down to inviting him into our everyday moments, letting his shoulder be the one we lean on, asking his love to be our strength and support.

I sit on the edge of my bed and whisper, "Yes, Lord, be my sustainer today." It is a prayer he always answers, one our hearts can say anytime we're weary.

God, thank you that I can come to you no matter what I need or what kind of day I've had.

. . . .

How do you need God to be your sustainer today?

Day 216

GOD IS YOUR PROVIDER

My God will meet all your needs according to the riches of his glory in Christ Jesus. (Philippians 4:19)

God will meet our needs "according to the riches of his glory in Christ Jesus." This isn't adequate; it's abundant. It's extravagant. It's limitless. Perhaps what matters even more to me is that it's *personal*. When God provides, it's not one-size-fits-all. The one who numbers every hair on our heads knows every desire in our hearts.

This doesn't mean we will get everything we request. God promises instead the only thing better than what we want—what we really need. Here's the secret: he alone knows what that is. We might articulate or calculate, list or describe. But we're still amateurs, guessing and grasping.

When I look back over the requests I've prayed and the wishes I've asked to be granted, I'm grateful that so many of them were met with a benevolent no. Among other things, I would have woken up every Christmas morning to a new pony, monkey, and large tortoise. All of which I had room for in my childhood imagination but not in my actual living room.

Yes, there are other prayers I still go back to and touch with confusion and tears. They will remain a mystery until eternity. With those it's a comfort to know someone does understand. And this someone loves me more than I can comprehend. The God who gave his Son is not holding out or holding back.

God, you know not only my needs but also my desires. Thank you for working out what is best for me even when I don't understand.

· · · ·

What's one way you need God to be your provider today?

YOU CAN TELL GOD ANYTHING

It is God who justifies. Who then is the one who condemns? No one.
(Romans 8:33–34)

Years ago I said to my daughter, "We don't have secrets in our family. I want you to know that there is nothing you could ever tell me that would make me love you less. You can come to me with anything, and there will never be any judgment. And if you feel like anything in your life is ever coming after you, I will stand with you and we will fight it together."

As those words came out of my mouth, it suddenly seemed that the table we were at became holy ground. Because I understood in a way I never had before what Romans 8:34 really means.

What I said to my daughter our heavenly Father says to us today, right here and now: "We don't have secrets in our family. I want you to know that there is nothing you could ever tell me that would make me love you less. You can come to me with anything, and there will never be judgment. And if you feel like anything in your life is ever coming after you, I will stand with you and we will fight it together."

This is what I know is true in a deeper way than ever before, and I hope my daughter and my granddaughter and all my sisters like you know it too: whatever we did yesterday, whatever we're battling today, whatever we may face tomorrow, the love of God for us and the grace of God toward us will never, ever change.

God, you are the grace-giver, the struggle-defeater,
the victory-bringer.

· · · ·

What struggle or secret do you want to share with God today?

Day 218

GOD IS GROWING YOU

Your roots will grow down into God's love and keep you strong. (Ephesians 3:17 NLT)

The walkway to our house is trimmed in vibrant green on a backdrop of black mulch. Emeralds on velvet. I stroll past the familiar leaves of the plants that return all on their own.

My favorites, two chubby hostas, like to tease us. Every year we wonder if perhaps winter got them and then, at the last moment, they pop out of the ground like smiling children.

Other more sinister green always appears too. Weeds that sneak into corners and burrow into shadows until we find them. We would never decide not to plant flowers because of the weeds that would come too. The nature of growth is that it comes with weeds.

Our hearts are much the same. A sin or struggle pops up in our lives and we're horrified. "Oh no!" we declare, "now everything God has done in my life is ruined!" But God is only interested in pulling the weed. It's not a surprise to him. It doesn't change the beauty he's creating in our lives. It doesn't cancel out the growth that we've seen.

My husband tosses the weed over his shoulder. I watch it sink out of sight into the trash can. I turn and look at my man, a smile of pride across his face. The weed has already been forgotten. He says, "Don't you think the hostas look especially good this year?"

I glance down at the green, a few stray bits of dirt the only trace of where the weed had so recently been. I nod my head and agree, "Yes, they're more beautiful than ever."

God, thank you for growing good things in me.

. . . .

What is God growing in your life right now?

YOU'RE NOT THE ONLY ONE

There is only one God and no other. (Mark 12:32 NLT)

You're not the only one. We are all broken. We are all beautiful. We are all in need of grace. We are all glory-reflectors. We are all paradox people. None of us have it together, but we are all better together.

This is what community means—even if the specifics of our lives and stories are different, we both understand what it's like to be human, and we choose to do life with each other rather than apart.

I've also begun saying, "You're not the only one" in another way too. I have said it to myself with capital letters: "You're not the Only One." In other words, "You are not Jesus." Last time I checked, no one else on the planet is either.

This is excellent news because it means we don't have to save the world. We don't have to be perfect. We don't have to take care of everything and everyone all the time. There is Only One who can do those things, and he's quite good at them.

It also means there is Only One who is truly deserving of our glory and our honor and our praise. Our lives are not about us. They are about him. Yes and amen.

Just in case you're facing something hard or scary in your life today, I want to whisper one more time: "You're not the only one. And the Only One who can do the impossible is right there with you."

God, you are the Only One who can get me through every struggle I face.

. . . .

What sometimes makes you say, "I'm the only one,"
and what's really true?

GOD WANTS TO USE YOU TODAY

Go home to your own people and tell them how much the Lord has done for you, and how he has had mercy on you. (Mark 5:19)

The Gospel of Mark tells about a man so controlled by evil that he has to live among the tombs outside town. No one can keep him chained, but he's all bound up inside. Then Jesus goes to the one who is an outcast and casts out the demons within him.

The man wants to go with Jesus. This is the answer: "Go home to your own people and tell them how much the Lord has done for you, and how he has had mercy on you" (Mark 5:19). Five minutes before, this man had been a spokesperson for all that's sinister and dark. His life is a wreck. He seems beyond redemption or rescue. And now, immediately, Jesus is saying, "I trust you to speak for me. I want you to represent me. I have a divine purpose for you."

I might have protested. I might have said, "I need more time to get ready. I need to go to seminary. I need to listen to more sermons. I need to attend some conferences or read a hundred books or have a dozen mentors." But Jesus has only one requirement for being in his service: a willingness to speak the truth of our deliverance.

We are all this man. Because this story is a preview of the resurrection. Jesus came for us. He braved the tombs. He released us. He wants to use us today.

God, thank you for being willing to use me today.
Nothing disqualifies me from serving you.

. . . .

What are you tempted to believe could keep God from using you?

YOU CAN RELY ON GOD

You are my strength, I watch for you;
*   you, God, are my fortress,*
*   my God on whom I can rely. (Psalm 59:9–10)*

We may place our trust in imperfect family members who let us down, confide in friends only to hear our secrets shared, or give our love to someone who says they will stay only to wake up alone one day. Then we wonder, *Is there anyone I can truly trust?* And God whispers quietly, *Yes.*

There's a big difference between God and others who have betrayed us. When we think God has disappointed us, it's usually because our circumstances haven't turned out like we planned. But even in those times, God himself has stayed steady in his love for us. He has not changed. He has not become undependable. He has not let us fall when he promised to catch us. People let us down because they are sinful and broken. But God is neither. That means he is fully trustworthy.

Not only is he reliable, but he understands that nothing else in our lives is the same way. He understands that we'll be disappointed and betrayed. He knows that our expectations will not be met. That gives him great compassion for us. And it's in the very moment we may want to push him away that he wants to say, "Come here. Lean on me. Put the full weight of your need on me. I can handle it. I love you and I will not let you down."

God, you know my disappointments and how that sometimes makes it hard for me to trust. I choose to believe you're there for me.

. . . .

How has God been there for you when someone let you down?

GOD WILL CALM YOUR HEART

When Jesus woke up, he rebuked the wind and the raging waves.
Suddenly the storm stopped and all was calm. (Luke 8:24 NLT)

The Sea of Galilee is known for its violent storms. One minute can bring blue skies, the next fierce winds and rain. The lake is surrounded by hills with steep sides, and cold air rushing over the edges collides with warmer air around the water, causing waves up to ten feet high.

We're going to die, the disciples think as panic floods their minds and water begins to fill the boat. Where is Jesus? Why isn't he doing anything? They find him still sleeping and wake him with a fear-filled question: "Teacher, don't you care that we're going to drown?" (Mark 4:38 NLT).

What Jesus speaks to the wind and waves seems fitting for the hearts of the disciples too: "Silence! Be still!" (v. 39 NLT). The storm suddenly stops, and there is great calm.

God is not distant; he's in the boat with us. No matter how the storm rages, he will not let us drown in our difficulties. He is present and powerful, and he cares about every detail of our lives.

The disciples experienced the complete calming of a physical storm. This side of heaven, the emotional storms we're in may not fully go away. The depression may come back. The panic attack might not stop instantly. The stress in our job could continue. Sometimes the storms calm, and sometimes we find calm in the storm because we know with certainty these two things: God is God in every moment of our lives, and with him we can make it through anything.

God, when storms come, I pray for your supernatural calm.

· · · ·

What's a storm you're facing right now?

GOD WILL GET YOU
THROUGH THE NIGHT

Where morning dawns, where evening fades,
you call forth songs of joy. (Psalm 65:8)

At first the darkness comes softly. Perhaps we get bad news from the doctor. Our marriage begins to feel a little off. Our employer announces there will be changes. But then the twilight deepens until we can hardly see. What happened to the light in our lives? Then it's midnight, and morning seems so far away.

We grit our teeth, cry out to God, and hold on with all our might. We keep loving. We keep persevering. We keep choosing what's hard even though it would be so much easier just to give up.

Then the moment comes, the first sliver of light. Our eyes can hardly take it in because they've been used to the dark for so long. But slowly it appears. At first it's just fingers of light stretching toward us. Then the sun barely slips over the horizon. We catch our breath because we'd forgotten the world could actually be beautiful. Then it hits us: we've made it through the night.

It's in that place—"where morning dawns, where evening fades"—that God calls forth "songs of joy." Those songs are ours because we've survived. They're the sound of our soul declaring God is good no matter what.

You may walk through nights so dark that they seem as if they'll never end. Your heart may seem as silent as a stone. You may forget what it even means to feel joy for a season. But dawn will come. And you will sing again. That's the hope. That's the promise.

God, you bring me through the darkest night and into the dawn.
You are the light in my life.

· · · ·

How has God brought you through a dark time in your life?

GOD INVITES YOU TO STOP STRIVING

The Lord said to her, "My dear Martha, you are worried and upset over all these details! There is only one thing worth being concerned about." (Luke 10:41–42 NLT)

I imagine Jesus looking at Martha as he says these words in a way that makes her feel deep in her soul that *he knows*. He knows how hard she's tried. He knows the pressure she's felt to always be the "good" one. He sees the weight of responsibility that's so heavy on her shoulders. He understands that she's anxious and so tired that all she wants to do is sit down too.

In this story, we see Martha striving, overwhelmed, and acting as if it all depends on her. But later when Jesus arrives after her brother Lazarus has died, there's a noticeable shift. The first thing Martha says to Jesus is "Lord, if only you had been here, my brother would not have died. But even now I know that God will give you whatever you ask" (John 11:21–22 NLT).

What's the difference? When Martha tries to recruit Jesus to rebuke Mary, she is striving for control—of dinner, of her sister, and even of Jesus. She's the bossy older sister. But this time her actions and words express this: *Jesus, you are in control.* She's embraced her identity as the beloved daughter of God.

What we need more than control is to know that someone else is in charge of everything, that he is good and he loves us. We think control will give us invincibility, but what we really need—the "one thing worth being concerned about" (Luke 10:42)—is intimacy with the One who will take care of us no matter what happens.

God, when I start to strive and stress out,
please help me give you control instead.

. . . .

What do you want to give God control of today?

YOU CAN ACCEPT GOD'S GIFTS WITH GLADNESS

Whatever is good and perfect is a gift coming down to us from God.
(James 1:17 NLT)

My grandmother is sitting at my kitchen table. I open a small book filled with questions about spiritual legacy and invite her to give voice to her history.

I love the reciting of the stories and the way she smiles when she gets to the part about me being born, her oldest grandchild. What I don't know is what she would say to me now. "What do you wish someone had told you when you were my age?" I ask. She pauses for a long time, then she says, simply and thoughtfully, "Accept God's gifts with gladness."

She knows me well—that I'm prone to placing pressure on myself, to wrestling with guilt and fear, to making burdens out of blessings.

I think "accepting God's gifts with gladness" is ultimately about humility. It's remembering to say "thank you" more often. It's understanding that the world does not rest on our shoulders but in God's hands. It's daring to experience the most vulnerable of emotions—happiness, delight, freedom. It's living with open hands rather than clenching them in fear or striving. It's having the courage to not let the enemy of our hearts steal the joy of what's ours.

I have a picture of my grandma and me on a shelf in our living room. Life has been hard for her, I know, but in this moment it doesn't show. She looks instead like God has been good to her, like she's a kid at a birthday party who's just pulled the wrapping paper off another present, like she knows a secret she's willing to tell.

God, grant me the courage to accept your gifts with gladness.

· · · ·

What's a gift from God in your life?

GOD IS YOUR PROTECTOR

Because you are my help,
I sing in the shadow of your wings. (Psalm 63:7)

While we often think of God as our heavenly Father, he describes himself in mothering terms at times—especially as a bird who gathers her chicks under her wings. That metaphor is used repeatedly in the Psalms.

I love this picture of God's care for us because at the heart of it is this: the bird with her little ones under her wings is essentially putting herself between her young and any predators. She's saying, "You want to come after my children? You're going to have to come through me first." It's not a distant defensive strategy. It's up close, personal, and powerful. It means that she's willing to die to make sure that those she cares for are ultimately okay.

And that's exactly what Jesus did for us. He put himself between us and our sin, between us and the enemy, between us and this world. He stretched out on a cross, and with his arms spread wide like wings, he said that we could all come there for protection.

We will never know all God has shielded us from, at least not this side of heaven. Will we understand? Probably not. Does that take the hurt away? Not this side of heaven. But it does mean that instead of striving so hard, we can quiet our hearts, nestle into the side of one who loves us, and listen to his heartbeat while we wait for what seeks to destroy us to pass. Maybe sometimes we can even dare to sing.

God, you are my comforter and protector.
I will sing in the shadow of your wings today.

. . . .

What has God protected you from?

YOU ARE UNDER GOD'S WINGS

He will cover you with his feathers,
and under his wings you will find refuge. (Psalm 91:4)

Last year a robin settled down just outside our guest bathroom window in a place where we could watch the whole nesting process unfold. I know from that experience that new birds spend a good bit of time under the wings of their parents.

Then I remembered the words in Psalm 91:4 and suddenly thought, *When we feel we are in the shadows, what if we're actually in the shadow of God's wings?* This is a place of protection and grace, of affection and care.

When we feel unnoticed, when we're tempted to compare, we can reassure our hearts with this truth: *We are never in anyone's shadow but God's.* This means the moments or seasons when we seem to be in the shadows are not failures or disappointments. They can be gifts from God.

This world tells us to seek the spotlight. But David, a man after God's own heart, prayed for the opposite: "Hide me in the shadow of your wings" (Ps. 17:8). All of our hearts need a place to remember who we are, find peace and rest, and be covered by the one who loves us most of all.

In the shadow of God's wings, life isn't about performance; it's about praise. It's not about proving our worth; it's about sharing our gratefulness. It's not about gaining attention, it's about dwelling in the affection of the one who keeps us in the place we most need to be—under his wings, close to his heart.

God, you cover me, care for me, and keep me close to your heart.

. . . .

When have you felt covered by God's love and grace?

Day 228

YOU CAN BE CONTENT

Think about the things of heaven, not the things of earth. (Colossians 3:2 NLT)

If only . . .
If I could just . . .
If they would . . .

The scenarios play out in my mind as I stare at the ceiling, sleep eluding me. I imagine a thousand ways my life could be better. It's like descending a spiral staircase into a dark basement of discontent.

It's always easier to go down than up. It's simpler to escape into what could be rather than embrace flawed reality. It's less difficult to blame my circumstances or other people than to take ownership for my own happiness.

The realization that my patterns of thinking aren't helpful is uncomfortable, but it's also liberating because it means there is an alternative. I can stop telling myself a fantasy would be better and start doing the hard work of making the best of my real life.

This is what I want because each of us is on this planet for only so long. The years are already whirring by, moments melting into decades. This is the life we have. These are the people we love. We can miss out on what we've been given by wishing for something we think might make us a little happier, or we can choose what's right in front of us.

We can embrace today. We can be grateful. We can see the good instead of the gaps. God's name is I Am, so he is not in our fantasies; he is in our real lives—this present and imperfect moment. May he give us the courage to fully and gratefully be in the here and now too.

God, thank you for my real life and that you are with me in every imperfect yet beautiful moment of it.

. . . .

What's one thing you're grateful for today?

GOD ISN'T DONE
WITH YOUR STORY YET

Jesus also did many other things. If they were all written down, I suppose the whole world could not contain the books that would be written. (John 21:25 NLT)

You are living a story today. A story crafted and told by the author of heaven. The star-scatterer. The mountain-mover. The water-walker. It is a story of grace. A story of hope. A story of, most of all, love.

In the day-to-day it doesn't feel like a story. It feels like dishes in the sink. Reports on the desk. Another mile behind the steering wheel of the car. But this doesn't change what's true. Beneath the surface of all that ordinary still lurks the glory.

Sometimes we want to cut a chapter out with sharp scissors. Sometimes we want to be the editors with the red ink. Sometimes we want to skip right to the end just to make sure it says, "and they lived happily ever after."

Instead we are to trust, to wait, to be in the middle of the mystery. There is so much we do not know, that we will not know, but we can be certain of this: the author is good and we are loved.

God is not done with history. He is not finished with the part of it that is your story either. Whatever you are living today, it is not the final page. Hold on, there is a turning coming. There is more than this, more than here and now. We have not yet seen the then and there. And however it may seem, God is still holding the pen.

God, you are writing a story in my life today,
and I trust that it is good.

. . . .

What story is God writing in your life?

YOU'RE OVERCOMING NEGATIVITY

Fix your thoughts on what is true, and honorable, and right, and pure, and lovely, and admirable. Think about things that are excellent and worthy of praise. (Philippians 4:8 NLT)

Why do we often remember negative moments more easily than positive ones? Because of the negativity bias we all have. Our brains are wired to give more weight to negative experiences than positive ones and to hold on to them longer.

The purpose of the negativity bias is to help us learn from our mistakes, pain, and failures. These lessons contribute to our physical and emotional survival. But left unchecked, our negativity bias can also increase our stress and anxiety. A number of studies have found a ratio that neutralizes the unwanted effects of our negativity bias. Whether in personal circumstances or relationships, we need to have five positives for every one negative.[1]

The apostle Paul told early believers to practice focusing on the positive too. He may not have used the term *negativity bias*, but the God who inspired him to write certainly knew that this is a struggle for humans. In Philippians 4:8, Paul offers another way to get to five positives. Ask, "What's one thing in my life right now that is true, honorable, right, pure, lovely, admirable, excellent, worthy of praise?" If you come up with something for each of those words, you'll have eight positives (way to go, overachiever).

God, help me refocus on what's true, honorable, right, pure, lovely, admirable, excellent, and worthy of praise.

· · · ·

What is true, honorable, right, pure, lovely, admirable, excellent, and worthy of praise in your life today?

GOD'S LOVE IS GIVEN, NOT EARNED

Nothing can ever separate us from God's love. (Romans 8:38 NLT)

As a former Pharisee, what Paul writes in Romans 8 is scandalous. He spent his entire life trying to be perfect but now says all we need is God's perfect love. For those of us who have spent our entire lives trying to earn God's approval, this is the answer our souls need.

I want you to read all of verse 38 with your name inserted: "I am convinced that nothing can ever separate [your name] from God's love. Neither death nor life, neither angels nor demons, neither our fears for today nor [your name's] worries about tomorrow—not even the powers of hell can separate [your name] from God's love."

When anxiety tries to tell you God's love is conditional or you must earn his approval, when you hear the echoes of the voices of the Pharisees in your life, cling to this truth: nothing can separate you from God's love—no exceptions. No mistake or shortcoming, no weakness or struggle, no relapse or rule broken. Not even that secret you've never told anyone. Not that battle you lost again yesterday. Not the critical voice in your mind.

You never have to ask, "What can I do to earn God's approval?" because his love is a gift and his grace is a certainty you can count on for all eternity.

God, thank you that nothing can ever separate me from your love.

. . . .

How would you finish this sentence,
"Nothing can ever separate me from God's love, not even _____"?

YOU DON'T HAVE TO HUSTLE FOR GOD'S LOVE

The work of God is this: to believe in the one he has sent. (John 6:29)

I am a completer by nature. Give me a checklist or a project or dishes to put away. I will roll up my sleeves, invite the sweat, and smile with satisfaction. So I'm interested in the answer when someone asks Jesus, "What exactly does God want us to do?" (John 6:28 CEV). I am pulling out my newly sharpened pencil, ready to take notes. Then comes his reply in the next verse: "The work of God is this: to believe in the one he has sent."

I pause, unsure hand hovering over the page, and tilt my head in confusion. Did I hear that right? He only wants me to believe? I should be relieved. Instead I feel inexplicably disappointed. Because if that's it, if that's all, then it's not about me. And it's sure not about being perfect.

Jesus loves me. This is the truest theology. This is the hum and rhythm our souls are made to dance to. We are not workers after all; we are worshipers. We are the broken made whole, the fallen and rescued, the messy and undeserving children jumping in endless puddles of rained-down grace.

May God give us the courage to live as beloved believers today. The ones whose souls have no hard-work calluses. The trusters who trade our pencils for an old wooden cross. The unexpectedly brave who look at the spinning, striving world and dare to say, "He is good. We are loved. That is all."

God, I choose to do the work of believing in the One you sent and trust that is enough.

. . . .

What helps you do the work of believing instead of striving?

GOD WILL GUARD YOUR HEART

His peace will guard your hearts and minds as you live in Christ Jesus. (Philippians 4:7 NLT)

You've probably heard the phrase "guard your heart" from the Old Testament book of Proverbs. In the New Testament, the phrase "guard your hearts" comes just after a passage that encourages us to bring all our worries and concerns to God.

What stands out to me most in this context is that we're not in charge of the guarding. Our role is staying in an intimate relationship with God and trusting him with everything we face. This means we don't have to live reactively, simply trying to defend our territory. We don't have to hide behind fences of our own making, pretending to be strong.

Instead, we can live in freedom and grace. We can take risks. We can reach out. We can dare to follow our dreams. Because God's peace will guard our hearts in the process. Each day we can wake up and say, "God, I trust you to take care of me."

Yes, we're to use wisdom and discernment, have healthy boundaries, and decide what to let in and out of our lives. But we don't have to feel helpless and confined. We're not at the mercy of whatever might come along. Even when life is hard, when the unexpected happens, when we feel vulnerable, we can know that we have a defender.

God, thank you for telling me to guard my heart.
Thank you also that I don't have to do it on my own.

. . . .

What do you need God's peace to protect your heart from today?

YOU ARE NOT YOUR CIRCUMSTANCES

For you have rescued me from my troubles
and helped me to triumph over my enemies. (Psalm 54:7 NLT)

Whether you're at the end of a hard day, in the middle of celebrating, or somewhere in between, there's some truth you need to hear and it's this: you are not your circumstances.

In all the moments of your life, you are a woman of grace and strength. Even when you feel weak, you have divine power within you that is able to get you through anything. And you are loved far more than you can even imagine.

How you feel today, what you're facing, even what others may say doesn't change that—and never can. Who you are is secure forever. And you are a daughter of God, a holy princess, a woman who is chosen and cherished. Nothing and no one can take that away from you.

You have within you a God who is bigger than your bad days and stronger than your circumstances, and he will never let you go. He has promised that nothing will defeat you and no one can stand against you.

So keep pressing forward. Hold your head up high and know that you are loved. Yesterday. Today. Tomorrow.

God, thank you that I am not my circumstances;
I am your beloved child. Help me to remember who I am
and whose I am today, no matter what happens.

. . . .

What's one truth about who you are that you want to hold on to today?

GOD WILL CONSOLE YOU

When anxiety was great within me,
your consolation brought me joy. (Psalm 94:19)

The word *consolation* means "comfort received by a person after a loss or disappointment." What if we think of God as a friend who consoles us, who wants to hear about our week and our worries, our doubts and discouragement, who will bring us from aching to joy?

There is a kind of comfort that sits with someone in the pit. This is good and necessary. But there is another kind that pulls you up out of it, that mysteriously takes you from tears to laughing so hard you cry. What if God wants to offer both to us? Yes, being compassionate and gracious, tender with our hearts, giving us all the time we need to grieve. But also bringing us gifts that delight and inspire us, that remind us that life is still beautiful, that surprise us with wonder.

Sometimes in the darkest moments of my life, it's not something big that gets through to my hurting heart. It's the crazy cardinal that insists on landing on our window ledge and peering into our living room as if he's watching television with us. It's the sound a baby makes when she's sleeping. It's the taste of a piece of dark chocolate. It's dinner with dear friends. All of these seem to whisper to my heart, *There is still good*. I remember that's true and then I start looking for it, start believing again that I can find it.

Yes, God is grand and beyond our understanding. But he is also a friend who consoles us.

God, thank you that you are with me in the big moments,
but you are also there in the small ones.

. . . .

How can you see God's consolation in your life?

GOD WILL DELIVER YOU

From birth I have relied on you;
*   you brought me forth from my mother's womb.*
*   I will ever praise you....*
My lips will shout for joy
*   when I sing praise to you—*
*   I whom you have delivered. (Psalm 71:6, 23)*

Our first delivery happens when we're born. David says in Psalm 71 that God himself brought you forth from your mother's womb. He caught you with unseen hands and welcomed you to the world. And he's been delivering you ever since.

My friend recently had a baby, and she told me about one of the sessions in the birthing class she and her husband did together. She said that every woman who has a child will have a moment when the delivery seems like too much for her.

We need to know that when our hearts are in delivery too. There will come a moment when every truth you've ever heard will seem to ring hollow. By knowing that, we can push through to the other side. We can somehow cling to the promise that God is there and he will deliver us. And that pain really can lead to new life.

God is your deliverer.

He brought you forth from your mother's womb when you took your first breath.

He delivers you in the hard moments when it feels as if you will never catch your breath again.

And he will deliver you from this life to the next when you take your final breath and enter eternity with him.

God, from my first breath to my last, you are the one
I can trust to see me through.

. . . .

What has God delivered you from?

GOD WILL RENEW YOUR MIND

Don't copy the behavior and customs of this world. (Romans 12:2 NLT)

When Paul says, "Don't copy the behaviors and customs of this world," it's easy to imagine a wild party in Las Vegas. But on a deeper level, if we live in a culture motivated by fear, then changing the way we think means learning to be motivated instead by faith.

One way we can do this is by noticing how the news we consume affects us. Does what we're reading, watching, or hearing cause us to experience fear? Who's the source, and do they have an agenda? Is what's being shared actually true and/or as dire as it seems? Even if it *is* true, where will we put our trust—in newsmakers or in the maker of heaven and earth?

When we start living out of faith rather than fear, it may feel strange. We'll likely have thoughts such as, *What if I miss something important?* or *Something bad will happen if I don't know everything.* When we've operated in fear for a long time, it literally forms neural pathways in our minds. As we change how we think the way Paul encourages us to do, our brains actually make new pathways. True transformation takes persistence and perseverance.

When you feel anxiety rising and want to turn on the TV or reach for your phone to check just one more headline, pause, take a deep breath, and say, "Not this time, fear. With God's help, I'm renewing my mind."

God, help me consume news in ways that lead to more peace in my heart instead of having the news consume me.

· · · ·

What helps you live in faith, not fear?

YOU'RE ALLOWED
TO HAVE BOUNDARIES

Then God said, "Let there be light," and there was light. And God saw that the light was good. Then he separated the light from the darkness. (Genesis 1:3–4 NLT)

In the story of creation, we often focus on what's coming into *being*. But the creation story is also full of *boundaries*. God separates light and dark, land and sea, day and night. Why is this needed? Because it makes life on earth possible. Only after these boundaries are in place does God start creating living things.

Years ago I needed to set boundaries in a challenging work situation but I resisted. I worried about being unloving. I thought I wouldn't be reflecting God's heart. Surely, I had to keep giving the best of who I was despite someone else's bad choices.

But I've come to see that godly boundaries do reflect the heart of God. They make life with other people possible. Without boundaries, there is no space for healing, no room for making things right again, no opportunity for growth.

A question inspired by the boundaries God set in Genesis has been helpful to me. When I need to set a boundary I can pause and ask, "Will this boundary lead to something life-giving?" For example, it's okay to say, "If you talk to me that way again, I'll leave the room until you're ready to speak with kindness." This leads to healthy communication and helps relationships thrive.

In the beginning, God created the heavens and the earth. He also created boundaries. He separated light from darkness. It's okay for us to still do the same in our relationships today.

God, give me the wisdom to set healthy,
life-giving boundaries when needed.

. . . .

What's a boundary you might need to set in a relationship?

GOD WILL BEAR YOUR BURDENS

*Praise be to the Lord, to God our Savior,
who daily bears our burdens. (Psalm 68:19)*

We all have times in our lives when what we need to carry through life is just too much for us to handle on our own. We're good at looking strong and trying to hide the fact that we're about to fall over. We wave away offers of assistance and plaster on a fake smile instead. But we're not intended to go through life that way. We need others to bear our burdens, especially when we're hurting. And amazingly, God himself says in Psalm 68:19 that he will daily help us with them.

We're not expected to take on more than we can handle alone. God is committed to carrying our burdens—what we can't carry by ourselves. Often, he does this through other people. But we have to be willing to ask for and receive the help, which can be scary.

Somehow it's easy to confuse *having* a burden with *being* a burden. But the two are not the same. Your burdens are not your identity. They're temporary baggage. It's okay to say, "I can't hold this up anymore. Can you please help me?"

Whatever you're going through, you don't have to bear the full weight of it. God is ready and willing to bear your burdens so you can continue your journey. And he'll send others to help you too.

God, I'm coming to you with a burden I need you to carry for me. Thank you for your help.

. . . .

What burden do you need God to carry for you today?

YOU CAN COME TO JESUS
AS YOU ARE

As she stood behind him at his feet weeping, she began to wet his feet with her tears. Then she wiped them with her hair, kissed them and poured perfume on them. (Luke 7:38)

She's making a spectacle of herself. She's being a bother. She's doing everything wrong. A woman at a dinner party for men. A sinner touching someone holy. An uninvited guest stealing the show. But all that matters to her is that Jesus knows, sees, hears, feels, understands how sorry she is for all the other, greater wrongs that have come before. Repentant tears replace her voice, but Jesus speaks, "I tell you, her many sins have been forgiven—as her great love has shown. But whoever has been forgiven little loves little" (Luke 7:47).

Forgiven. The word explodes in her heart like a burst of light. She weeps even more, but now her tears are ones of joy. She pours out the last drops of precious perfume. It's worth about a year's wages. Quite likely it was her dowry—her hopes for the future. Certainly it is one of the only pure things in her life. And she has given it all to the one who has given her what she needed most. Her Savior looks at her with tenderness and says, "Your faith has saved you; go in peace" (v. 50).

When we offer Jesus our tears, fears, secrets, and hidden treasures, it is beautiful in his sight. Let's dare to pour out our hearts to him. Dare to discover his scandalous mercy. Dare to simply *come.*

God, thank you for letting me come to you just as I am and always forgiving me.

. . . .

What do you need to believe you're really forgiven for today?

GOD CAN USE YOUR
AWKWARD MOMENTS

I came to you in weakness—timid and trembling. (1 Corinthians 2:3 NLT)

The apostle Paul has an impressive spiritual résumé: circumcised on the eighth day, as Jewish law requires; a citizen of Israel; part of the tribe of Benjamin; a Pharisee and religious leader. Then he has an intimate encounter with Jesus, hears the actual voice of God, and is entrusted to share the gospel with the gentiles.

Yet he says, "I came to you in weakness—timid and trembling." We're not used to hearing this from modern spiritual leaders. In our world, charisma, high energy, a big personality, and smooth delivery are often the expectations. But Paul says that our weakness can point people to the power of God.

I once did a workshop at a conference, and halfway through my computer stopped working. I couldn't use any of my slides. At first, I felt flustered (and it showed), but I finally took a deep breath and said, "I'm glad you're seeing this. Because at some point, something like this will happen to you too. And it will be okay. God can use you anyway." At the end of the conference, a woman walked up to me and said, "The most helpful thing for me out of this whole weekend was seeing you mess up. Now I know it's okay if I do too."

The Corinthians didn't need to see Paul give a perfect performance. They needed to see he had been transformed by Jesus. It's okay if sometimes our anxiety shows. Those might unexpectedly be the moments when God shows most in us too.

God, thank you that I don't have to be perfect for you to use me.

· · · ·

When have you felt nervous and the situation worked out anyway?

YOUR LIFE MATTERS

Teach us to number our days,
that we may gain a heart of wisdom. (Psalm 90:12)

I sit in bleachers as sun and storm clouds play tag over a stadium. My beautiful niece will soon walk across the stage to receive her diploma. As students wait, hands on their caps to keep the wind from stealing them, my husband points to glints of light on the other side of the fence. "What's that?" he asks.

We both squint toward the odd shapes stretched out across a green stretch of grass. I finally realize. "It's a cemetery," I say.

The years between that walk across the stage and the walk into eternity will fly by. You and I—we're somewhere in the middle. You are the only you we will ever have. God didn't create a plan B for your life. We need you to be who you are, to do what only you can do. And to do it now, today, in whatever way you can.

We live our lives waiting for the big moments—the "walk across the stage" times in life. But those are few and far between.

I think the folks who have completed the journey would say instead it's the little moments that really matter.

My niece crosses the stage. We cheer as loud as we can.

And I wonder, just wonder, if the same is happening in heaven too. Perhaps it does every time we take a step of faith until we cross that final stage. Not because of how big we are but because it shows how BIG our God is.

Do you think angels ever say, "Woo-hoo"?

God, help me make the most of each day you give me.

* * * *

What's a moment that felt small but significant to you?

GOD IS YOUR REFUGE

Trust in him at all times, you people;
pour out your hearts to him,
for God is our refuge. (Psalm 62:8)

We have a God who calls himself our refuge. And a refuge is where we are to go back to, especially when we're hurt or afraid. This is what I know: our refuge wept at the tomb of a friend. He took a nap on a boat. He tossed the tables of money changers in frustration. He hurt and ached and smiled and laughed. He understands still what it is to be human. Even more, we are made in the image of God and we are created with emotions. So to say faith is only about facts is to amputate the heart of God in our lives. We can never experience the fullness of who he is without embracing the fullness of who we are, of this wild and vivid life of earth living.

Facts are cold-edged and hard. They are granite. They are still and unmoving. To seek comfort in them is like sleeping on the pavement. But Jesus is open-armed and grace-filled. He is fierce in his love and mighty in his comfort. "Pour out your hearts to him, for God is our refuge" (Ps. 62:8). This is the invitation. To bring not our high-minded thoughts but our rawness and weeping, our humanity and brokenness, our soft and tender places.

We can go to God whenever we need to, with whatever we're facing, with all that we're feeling, and know that our hearts will be safe.

God, you are so tender with my heart. You are the safe place
I can always go back to.

· · · ·

How has God been a refuge to you in a hard time of your life?

Day 244

GOD CAN TRANSFORM
YOUR ANXIETY

When anxiety was great within me,
your consolation brought me joy. (Psalm 94:19)

I love that Psalm 94 doesn't just say, "When anxiety was great within me, you calmed me down." Nope. God doesn't take us from anxiety to calm. He can actually take us from anxiety to joy.

How does he do that? Truth can switch the track in our minds. When we remember what God says, we change courses from thoughts that lead to anxiety to those that can instead lead to emotions like courage and even celebration. For example, you might feel fear about an upcoming meeting at work. And yet as you pray and remember that what God has told you is true, you find yourself becoming first calmer and then even filled with confidence and anticipation.

We're human, and for our brains to learn to respond in new ways takes time and practice. But we can begin to change by saying, "Okay, I'm feeling anxious. That's okay. It's the same system that's related to a lot of other things—like enthusiasm and joy. God, please help me pinpoint the thoughts that are causing fear and replace them with faith instead so my emotions can change too." This won't happen instantly, and that's totally fine. God understands. Yet as you practice this transformation, over time you will probably notice a little less anxiety and a little more excitement coming into your life.

Instead of immediately running away, see some of the moments when you feel anxiety as opportunities to retrain your brain. Lean into them. Learn from them. And let them eventually lead you to more joy.

God, you are the only one who can turn my anxiety into joy.

. . . .

What helps when you're anxious?

GOD THINKS YOU'RE BEAUTIFUL

> *My beloved spoke and said to me,*
> *"Arise, my darling,*
> *my beautiful one, and come with me." (Song of Solomon 2:10)*

Just flip through a few television channels and it's easy to see that our culture is obsessed with beauty. Stars get plastic surgery before they grace the red carpet. Makeover shows transform lives and faces. Miss America crowns one girl the fairest of them all. From the time we are young girls, we wonder how we fit into all of this fuss about beauty.

I clearly remember changing outfits at least ten times the evening before the first day of school in fourth grade. I would put one on, parade in front of my parents, and then rush back to my room to stare in the mirror. None of them seemed quite right. I was a wallflower who got few compliments.

The next morning I woke up to find a note beside my bed. It said, "The outfit looks great and so do you. Love, Dad." I don't even think he knew which outfit I ended up choosing. It didn't matter. I belonged to him and that made me beautiful in his eyes no matter what I was wearing.

Our heavenly Father feels the same way about us. He created us and regardless of what the world may try to tell us, he thinks we're beautiful.

Whether we obsess about it or ignore it, we're made to know we're beautiful. That truth can ultimately only come from God. He's waiting to speak to our hearts the words we've always longed to hear . . .

You are beautiful.

> *God, thank you for making me beautiful in ways*
> *beyond what I can see.*
>
> . . . .
>
> What makes someone beautiful to you besides how they look?

GOD IS YOUR GROWER

*So neither the one who plants nor the one who waters is anything,
but only God, who makes things grow. (1 Corinthians 3:7)*

We can't make anything grow. This sounds so contrary to our hustle-and-strive, stress-out, and make-it-happen culture. Yet this truth can bring back our peace, slow down our breathing, and return the joy to our relationships.

Yet just because we can't make things grow doesn't mean we're supposed to hang out on the couch all day. Wise Solomon said, "Sow your seed in the morning, and at evening let your hands not be idle, for you do not know which will succeed" (Eccles. 11:6).

In other words, our role is daily obedience and God's role is results.

We spend intentional time nurturing the hearts of our children even though we can't force them to choose faith.

We do our work well and with excellence even though the outcome of the project is uncertain.

We take the next step in our dreams even when it feels hard and risky.

We can be faithful workers, loving parents, and diligent dreamers. Like farmers who plant and water, we do what's within our realm of responsibility. But in the end, we leave it all in God's hands.

This makes a difference because we don't have to carry the weight of what ultimately happens. Here's truth we can cling to: "If you remain in me and I in you, you will bear much fruit" (John 15:5). There *will* be growth. It may not look like what we planned, but it will come in its season.

*God, it's so easy to live as if everything depends on me.
Thank you that instead I can fully depend on you.*

. . . .

What's God growing in your life right now?

GOD CARES ABOUT
THE LITTLE THINGS

*What are mere mortals that you should think about them,
human beings that you should care for them? (Psalm 8:4 NLT)*

I lift my shoulder, then wince, and my chiropractor says, "Microtears." The stress of a new exercise program has caused tiny bits of damage to my tendons. I need a bit of treatment and recovery time. He adds, "Good thing you didn't push through the pain or wait a lot longer. Then you'd need something a lot more serious."

Yet all through today's workout I kept telling myself, "You should be able to do this." Then when I got home I thought, *Pain is part of the process—I'm just being weak if I stop and get help for this now.*

Have you ever said something similar? Life gives all of our hearts microtears. Yesterday a painful situation made me ache inside. My day was a little busier than is best. I felt stressed about a conflict. None of these were big on their own but together they added up.

Today I can either push through the pain or pause and ask, "What do I need to heal and recover?" The answer might be a nap, a conversation with a trusted friend, or some time for prayer. Nothing big, but without these things what's minor now could turn into something far more serious.

The God who numbers every hair on our heads also cares about every microtear in our hearts. He's our healer and helper, mender and maker, the one who's big enough to handle anything and loving enough to help with even the smallest things too.

God, thank you for caring about everything that causes me pain, no matter the size. I bring all of my hurts to you today.

· · · ·

What's a microtear in your heart you need God to heal today?

GOD WILL HELP YOU FIGHT FOR PEACE

Don't worry about anything; instead, pray about everything. Tell God what you need, and thank him for all he has done. (Philippians 4:6 NLT)

Mark and I went through almost a decade of infertility. At times it felt like being trapped in a dark place, unable to move forward with our dreams. I cried in bathrooms, asked God questions, experienced confusion and frustration. Yet over time, I began to experience "God's peace, which exceeds anything we can understand" (Phil. 4:7 NLT).

It's easy to think peace is something that simply descends on us the first time we ask for God's help. But in my experience, it's something we fight for over and over. Thankfully, Paul gives us a battle plan.

Don't worry about anything. Pray about everything. Tell God what you need. Thank him for all he has done. Repeat, repeat, repeat.

Is this easy? Absolutely not. Will there be times when we *do* worry, even feel despair? Yes, we are human, after all. Will we experience resistance? Every day.

When people asked me how I was doing, I started saying, "I have a peace about it." If they looked at me with disbelief, I'd add, "It's not a cliché. It's the kind of peace that comes after war."

If you have to fight for peace, nothing is wrong with your faith. There is peace that comes from the absence of all pain or difficulty. But there is a deeper, more powerful peace that comes after the heat of battle. Only warriors know this kind of peace. Fight on.

God, when peace requires a battle, give me the strength to fight.

. . . .

How have you fought for peace?

YOU ARE GOD'S BELOVED CHILD

See how very much our Father loves us, for he calls us his children, and that is what we are! (1 John 3:1 NLT)

This is the paradox I so often miss: bravery doesn't come from bravado; it comes from humility. I so often want to impress God when what he wants most is for me to place my hand in his. I can think I'm so much bigger and stronger than I am, than he's asking me to be. Our culture says independence is the ultimate goal, that we're to pull ourselves up by our own bootstraps. But Jesus said the one who is greatest is the one who is the most dependent, the one who knows God alone supports and sustains her. Because like a little child with a parent, when we are depending on him we have access to all his strength and power, all his might and goodness.

About that time the disciples came to Jesus and asked, "Who is greatest in the Kingdom of Heaven?" Jesus called a little child to him and put the child among them. Then he said, "I tell you the truth, unless you turn from your sins and become like little children, you will never get into the Kingdom of Heaven. So anyone who becomes as humble as this little child is the greatest in the Kingdom of Heaven." (Matt. 18:1–4 NLT)

We never have to stand alone. We never have to take the next step by ourselves. We never outgrow our need for a God who holds us up, who cheers us on, who never lets us go.

God, I'm your child, and I never have to take a single step on my own.

. . . .

What's one thing a little one in your life has shown you about what it means to have childlike faith?

GOD IS WITH
THE PEOPLE YOU LOVE

God is . . . an ever-present help in trouble. (Psalm 46:1)

I answer the phone and hear the tears in her voice. I close my eyes and wish I had wings to fly the many miles to her side. I want to be there for the people I love. I imagine you do too.

I don't like the idea of missing even a moment when they might need me. And yet I realize making this happen is impossible. How do I live with that reality? How do I know they will be okay anyway?

The answer came to me through Psalm 46:1, "God is . . . an ever-present help in trouble." There is never a time when God will not be with the people we love. They are not alone even when we can't be with them. They are not without help even when we can't do all we'd like to serve them. We don't have to bear the weight of believing they can't possibly make it unless we're there every second.

And the same is true for us. As much as the people in our lives care for us, they can't always be there for us either. But God is always available.

This is the beautiful truth we can trust for ourselves and others: we are never alone. In the moments when we feel helpless to do anything, we can count on a God who can help more than we can even imagine. He's not even a phone call, email, or hug away—he's right there with us right now, right here, every moment of every day.

God, thank you for being ever-present when
I need you and when those I love do too.

. . . .

Who do you need to entrust to God's care today?

YOU CAN QUIET
YOUR INNER CRITIC TODAY

Get rid of all bitterness, rage, anger, harsh words, and slander, as well as all types of evil behavior. (Ephesians 4:31 NLT)

I'm driving with my husband on a beautiful day, and I remember a recent mistake. My inner critic speaks up with harsh words and suddenly my inner sky turns from blue to gray. One accusation can have the power to darken my whole day. Has this ever happened to you?

In the past, this often would have sent me into a spiral of shame and guilt. But on this occasion, I had a different reaction. Seven unexpected words came to my mind in response to my inner critic: *We don't talk to people that way.*

I've heard moms say this to their children when they speak in hurtful ways. These words are usually followed by three more: "Say you're sorry." For the first time ever, I make my inner critic apologize to me.

It's unexpectedly freeing. The harshness and condemnation disappear and are replaced by compassion and grace. We teach our children not to harm others with their words. Why is it okay to harm ourselves with them?

We speak to others with kindness, encouragement, understanding, and a desire for their good. We extend grace to their humanness, comfort them when they're struggling, cheer them on when they're working hard, and see the best in them even in their worst moments.

In my situation that sounded like this: *You made a mistake but that doesn't change who you are or how much you're loved. You're already forgiven. Let's try again.*

Let's listen to love, not our inner critic, today.

God, help me silence my inner critic and listen to your voice of love.

. . . .

What do you need to say to your inner critic today?

JESUS IS YOUR PEACE

And he will be called . . . Prince of Peace. (Isaiah 9:6)

The lights burn low in the sanctuary, and the voices raise high. Years ago I stood in this church and felt like a warrior who had clawed her way back to her fortress after battle. Bloodied and bruised, armor dented, sword hanging by her side. "I will keep fighting," I told myself then. "I will not give up." Then I slumped inside, spent, and begged, "Jesus, help me."

And he did. He rescued me from the depression and anxiety that threatened to tear me apart, break my heart, and turn every bit of joy into ashes with their flaming torches. In my weariness, Jesus became my strength. He delivered me again and again. With the help of a counselor and a doctor and a circle of close friends, I survived. And now, years later, I am thriving.

When the pastor spoke of peace on this night when we would light the Advent candle for it, I saw it with new eyes. I once thought of peace as only tranquility. The absence of something. But now, here, I knew it as the presence of Jesus.

I told the One who fought for peace on my behalf, "I will not surrender what you have gained for me." I will not define peace as the world does, as weak or even boring, as only a whisper and never a roar.

"Let there be peace on earth," the congregation sings.

I join in on the final note, "And let it begin with me."

God, thank you for being my peace in every circumstance of life.

. . . .

When has God given you peace in the middle of a hard situation?

YOUR IMPERFECT STORY
IS POWERFUL

They triumphed over him
by the blood of the Lamb
and by the word of their testimony. (Revelation 12:11)

Among other things, I think Revelation 12:11 means saying out loud that we are human and God is God. This calls for telling the stories where we don't show up as the prom queen in our pristine tiara, the times when we drop the spaghetti on the white shag carpet, the moments when the orange hairy monsters are scratching our bedposts in the dark, and even though we know better we're just flat-out scared.

I used to think honoring God meant leaving all this out. But I've come to believe instead that authenticity, honesty, and having the courage to own who we are, what we live, and what we feel can mysteriously get him glory.

I think this explains why the stories and the characters in Scripture seem so unedited. It's blue-sky clear there's only one hero in God's story, and it's not us. And this hero calls himself "I am who I am." I wonder if this means we, made in his image, honor him when we have the guts to say, "I am who I am" too. Even when doing so only highlights how very different we are from this beyond-our-imagination God.

Sometimes we think we need to show off.

Because of Jesus, we always and only need to show up.

God, thank you that I don't have to be perfect or perform, impress, or earn approval. I can simply point to you in all we say and do.

. . . .

What's one way God is asking you to simply show up today?

GOD IS STRONG
IN OUR WEAKNESS

Three different times I begged the Lord to take it away. Each time he said, "My grace is all you need. My power works best in weakness."
(2 Corinthians 12:8–9 NLT)

The apostle Paul never shares specifics about the "thorn" in his flesh" (2 Cor. 12:7) that he begs God to take away.

But God told Paul, "My grace is all you need." The first step is letting go of guilt and shame over our struggles, because they only cause us to stay stuck. Instead, we can embrace the freedom of God's abundant grace. Then God said, "My power works best in weakness." This means we don't have to "fix" ourselves. We're invited to bring our struggles to God and ask for his help.

I believe we're to be proactive partners in the process as well. I've learned I need spiritual practices like prayer, physical rhythms like rest and exercise, and social support from those who love me. Each of these helps me align with how God created me to live and moves me away from my struggles and toward my strengths.

God created each of us in an amazing and wonderful way. Because we live in a fallen world, we each have potential struggles and powerful strengths. Yes, we may feel like we have a thorn in our flesh. But sometimes thorns come with beautiful things. As a quote often attributed to author Henry Van Dyke says, "The best rosebush, after all, is not that which has the fewest thorns, but that which bears the finest roses."

God, use my "thorn in the flesh" to bring you glory.

· · · ·

What is a struggle or weakness God can use?

YOU CAN BE REAL

The Lord looks at the heart. (1 Samuel 16:7 NLT)

Sometimes vulnerability is met with clichés or pat answers or misunderstanding. A phrase like "I'm struggling today" can trigger a response of "Well, you just need to trust Jesus more." When this happens, we can experience shame and guilt. But we have done nothing wrong. In that case it's the other person who's not being real. They are hiding behind easy words and safe phrases, likely because they are afraid of life's messes, of what emotions look like close up without mascara.

One of the greatest gifts we can offer each other when someone is real with us is to be real in return, which means offering support and a safe place for our hearts to land. It's always okay to simply say, "I hear you. I am for you. What you're going through matters to me."

I don't think being real requires letting everything about us be out there all the time. What I think it means is that we're willing to go there when God asks us to do so. God isn't looking for good examples; he's looking for imperfect people willing to make it clear why we all need a Savior.

Being real also doesn't mean defining ourselves by our worst moments and deepest struggles. This is another reason why we can be real: it doesn't change who we are. It only gives people a more complete picture of our lives, which offers them the permission to accept all of their story too.

God, you've seen everything about me and you love me still.
Help this to be the true source of my confidence and security.

. . . .

What are you glad God sees about you?

Day 256

YOU CAN HIGHLIGHT THE GOOD

Look after each other so that none of you fails to receive the grace of God. (Hebrews 12:15 NLT)

I have a tendency to see the best in people. I asked God if I might have been fooling myself to see so much good. And this is the whisper it seemed I heard in return: *When you believe the best about people, what you believe is true. It's just not the whole story. But it's still the part worth highlighting.*

I pictured the way I cradle books in my arms and pull out my hot pink highlighter —how I run it over the lines I love most, how when I come back to that book that's what I see first. It's not that the rest of the page doesn't exist, but it's what I focus on before anything else.

People tend to become who we believe them to be, so let's believe the best.

When we see the best in others, we are not naive; we are intentional. We're choosing to see what is good and letting grace cover the rest. I am committed to fighting relentlessly to keep doing so. And, yes, it means sometimes I will be disappointed. But I would rather be occasionally surprised than continually suspicious and cynical.

When we listen to someone else's story, let's put down our swords and pick up our highlighters. Let's be safe places for the wounded to come home to, the voices in their ears and hearts reminding them of who they still are, how strong we know they can be, that we see beauty where they only see scars.

God, give me eyes of grace that see like you do.
Make me a safe place for the hearts of others.

. . . .

What helps you see the best in others?

YOU'RE MAKING A DIFFERENCE TODAY

And if anyone gives even a cup of cold water to one of these little ones who is my disciple, truly I tell you, that person will certainly not lose their reward. (Matthew 10:42)

We carry crock pots into the kitchen and set them on the table. Soup is ladled into bowls. Bread is neatly placed on plates. Dessert stands ready on a counter nearby. Outside hungry people wait. My community group is serving those in need tonight.

Aren't we all in need? Don't we all feed each other?

I'm reminded of this when a coworker pauses to offer a kind word—a little morsel of encouragement. I see it when my friend wraps her arms around her oh-so-tired little one, answering the silent request for comfort and rest. I see it when a stranger on the street flashes a smile like an unexpected bit of chocolate.

If I were with you now, I know I'd see it there too. You're feeding someone today. Who is the hungry heart in your life? Oh, what you do may feel small. It may feel unseen. But it matters. Thank you for what you do. Thank you for feeding the hungry in your life in your own amazing way.

We carry the crock pots back to our cars. Every last bit is gone. We didn't even get to eat, but I don't feel hungry. It turns out those whose bodies we fed did the same for our hearts in return.

And so it goes—round and round. Giving, receiving, in need, meeting needs too. Until we're all so very full.

God, show me who I can feed today and help me receive what I need too.

. . . .

What's one small way you can feed someone's heart today?

GOD IS BIGGER THAN YOUR PROBLEMS

The mountains melt like wax before the LORD,
before the Lord of all the earth. (Psalm 97:5)

God sees the mountains we have to overcome in our lives differently than we do. We look at them and think, *How am I ever going to get past this thing?* while God looks at them and they "melt like wax" before him. God is not surprised, intimidated, or discouraged by your mountains. He has the perspective of all of history as well as eternity. And as intense as what you're facing may feel, he's dealt with far worse and beat it.

Does this mean God tells us to "just get over it"? No, that's the beautiful part. He comes alongside us and encourages our hearts every bit of the climb. He doesn't wait at the top, sipping water and saying, "Well, that was easy," while we struggle.

What mountain are you facing today? Whatever it is, God is bigger. He's strong enough to overcome it, and gentle enough to stay beside you every step.

Yes, God could level that mountain in your life in a minute. Why he doesn't will probably remain a mystery until heaven. But you can know this: your mountain is revealing courage you never knew you had and creating more power within you. The next mountain you face isn't going to feel as steep as this one. Not because it will be smaller but because you will be stronger. And God will be with you all the way to the top.

God, even the tallest mountain in my life is small to you.
Help me see with your perspective today.

. . . .

What's a mountain you faced and overcame with God's help?

GOD IS GENTLE WITH YOU

Be completely humble and gentle; be patient, bearing with one another in love. (Ephesians 4:2)

Gentleness is not weakness or passivity—it's strength under control. Then what is the opposite of gentleness? Harshness. If there is one thing that's true about the guilt voice in my mind, it's this: it is unrelentingly harsh. I realize, suddenly, that this means it can't be the voice of God or anyone representing him.

This feels scandalous and unfamiliar. I become nervous that I'm misunderstanding. But verse after verse affirms it. "Your gentleness makes me great" (Ps. 18:35 NASB). Jesus told us, "I am gentle and humble in heart" (Matt. 11:29 NASB). "He tends his flock like a shepherd . . . he gently leads those that have young" (Isa. 40:11).

I'd assumed the hollering preachers and the Facebook ranters and the rule makers must be practicing righteousness. But this seems not to be the case. I write it down: I will not listen to any spiritual voice that is not speaking from a place of true grace. I'm no longer going to attribute to God what is not in his heart or character. Instead I'm going to embrace that Jesus is my advocate, defender, and Savior.

Next time the critical voice inside me speaks, I will ask for God's help rather than hearing it as if it is from him. He is gentle. He came to set us free. He walks with us as we are. He understands our weaknesses and wandering. He is not a God of guilt but extravagant grace.

God, thank you for your unfailing gentleness and kindness toward me, for the way you speak to my heart with love and mercy.

. . . .

What's a self-critical thought you tend to have?
What's the truth God wants to speak to you instead?

GOD IS YOUR KING

For God is the King of all the earth;
sing to him a psalm of praise. (Psalm 47:7)

Our future is controlled by a God who hung stars in place, who spoke the world into being, who keeps it twirling on its axis still. The One who watches a billion sparrows hatch, who knows the feathers on their wings and numbers the hairs on our heads. The One who went to a cross for us and defeated death itself when he stepped outside an empty tomb.

The future is not dependent on any elected official. The hands that hold us are not the ones of the baby-kissing politicians, not the ones of those who pass the laws or make the campaign promises. No, we are in the hands of the One big enough to contain the mountains and valleys, all the maps and the globes and every country on them.

No matter what the results of any election might be, no matter what is happening in our world when your eyes land on this very sentence, God will still be in charge. He is good and wise and not startled or overwhelmed by any of it.

No matter which leader we may have, which politician may promise or lie, which person seems to hold the power, *we will have the same King.* He is good, wise, and kind. He cannot be defeated. "Let the heavens rejoice, let the earth be glad; let them say among the nations, 'The LORD reigns!'" (1 Chron. 16:31).

God, you are the ruler of my heart and life.
You are the only one who holds all the earth in his hands.

. . . .

What does it mean to you that God is your king?

JESUS GETS THE FINAL SAY
ABOUT YOU

At the name of Jesus every knee should bow, in heaven and on earth and under the earth. (Philippians 2:10)

Like a badge that says, "Hi, my name is . . ." we can let the names people call us or the labels they place on us define who we are. But Philippians offers a different perspective.

God gave Jesus "the name above all other names" (Phil. 2:9 NLT). Have you ever played cards? Then you know what a "high card" means. It's the one that beats all the others. The name of Jesus is higher than all other names—including the ones other people, the enemy of our soul, and even ourselves have tried to give us. In other words, Jesus gets the last say.

The world may try to name us "unwanted," but Jesus calls us "chosen."

The enemy of our soul may try to name us "sinner," but Jesus calls us "forgiven."

The voice in our own hearts may try to name us "victim," but Jesus calls us "victorious."

The One who is the Word takes the power away from the words spoken to us. He is above all names. He is above all labels. He is above all critical comments. He is above all lies. He is above everything that tries to push us down, shut us up, or keep us from being all we're created to be. He alone defines our identity and destiny.

*God, replace any hurtful words said to me
with the truth of who you say I am.*

. . . .

What's a name or label you need to replace
with the truth of God's love?

YOUR MESS CAN MEAN PROGRESS

For every house has a builder, but the one who built everything is God. (Hebrews 3:4 NLT)

As I walked through a building undergoing remodeling one day, a friend remarked, "Mess means progress." For days afterward, her words echoed in my mind. *Mess means progress.* She's an interior designer, so she understands that between the vision and the reality must come the mess.

I thought about how our lives are often that way too. I personally would like to skip that phase. I want to go straight to the completed project, the resolved struggle, the happy ending to the story. I don't like the phase where the dust is flying, the hammers are banging, and the paint is half-finished on the wall.

Yet the mess is necessary for the beauty to happen. So next time we feel ashamed of the mess in our lives, maybe we can pause and say, "Mess means progress." It means worthwhile work is happening in our hearts. It means good plans are coming to be. It means someone is working out a greater purpose in our lives beyond what we can yet see.

Where do we most often find Jesus? Not in the neat, quiet corners of our lives. Not in the Pinterest-perfect parts. Not in any of the places where we think he'd like to be. No, if he is the one doing the work, then where we find him is right in the middle of the mess. He's not afraid of it because he can already see what it will one day become. And he will not quit until it's done.

God, I choose to trust that the mess I sometimes see is part of the progress.

. . . .

Where can you see progress even in the middle of a mess today?

YOU'RE NOT BEING PUNISHED

If we are afraid, it is for fear of punishment, and this shows that we have not fully experienced his perfect love. (1 John 4:18 NLT)

The enemy of our hearts would love for us to believe that when "bad" things happen, we're being punished.

> But [Jesus] was pierced for our transgressions,
>   he was crushed for our iniquities;
> the punishment that brought us peace was on him,
>   and by his wounds we are healed. (Isa. 53:5)

Part of the miracle of the gospel is that Jesus took our punishment for us. It matters that we know this, because otherwise we're tempted to see God as a slightly menacing figure with a lightning bolt in his hand, ready to throw it our way as soon as we do wrong.

Thinking about all that can go wrong in this world makes me want to find a safe place to hide. You too? If so, there's good news. The love of God is the safe haven we can run to when life gets hard.

That's why it matters so much that we don't believe he's punishing us. If we do, we'll distance ourselves when we need him most. The state of the world, the brokenness of our lives, the reality of death, and the losses we endure grieve God's heart too. He is in our hard times *with* us. He is forever *for* us. We serve a God not of lightning bolts but of love, not of meanness but of mercy, not of punishment but of peace.

God, help me experience your perfect love today.

. . . .

What helps you trust God's love when things are going wrong?

Day 264

YOU PLANT SEEDS OF PEACE

Those who are peacemakers will plant seeds of peace and reap a harvest of righteousness. (James 3:18 NLT)

At some time in recent years, it feels like the volume got turned up in our world. The internet in particular can feel like an angsty teenager blaring angry music with no concern for anyone else in the house. Social media is full of rants and arguments, strongly stated opinions and individual manifestos, subtle insults and divisive declarations. Stressful. I imagine you, like me, have sometimes wished for virtual earplugs.

Then this morning I came across these words from Scripture: "Those who are peacemakers will plant seeds of peace and reap a harvest of righteousness" (James 3:18 NLT). It stood out to me that *peace needs to come first*. Sometimes there's an issue we're passionate about, something we're utterly convinced is right (and it may very well be). But then we decide that the *rightness* is what matters most, even more than relationships. Rather than planting seeds of peace, we sacrifice peace for the sake of declaring our position or opinion on a particular subject. We somehow feel doing so is our duty.

What's the alternative? For us to be peacemakers who love others so well that they want to hear what we have to say. To be people who value those who are different from us even if we don't understand them. To build relationships one tiny seed at a time until something strong, beautiful, and righteous grows.

God, when I'm tempted to focus on making sure I'm telling everyone what's right, help me remember what matters most.

· · · ·

What does it mean to you to be a peacemaker?

GOD IS YOUR HIDING PLACE

You are my hiding place;
you will protect me from trouble
and surround me with songs of deliverance. (Psalm 32:7)

We live in a "go out there and be bold" kind of world. But it seems a longing for hiding is built into us. We tuck our faces into the necks of our parents as babies. We play hide-and-seek with our childhood friends. As adults we hide in less conspicuous ways: behind the screen of a computer, in the bottom of a glass, underneath all that makeup. So perhaps it's not about whether we will hide but rather where and how.

And this is the beautiful reality: God himself says he will be our hiding place. He'll be the retreat and the fortress and the silent space in a chaotic, busy world. Where does this mean we are hidden? In love. Because "God is love" (1 John 4:8).

When Adam and Eve fell, they hid. God came looking for them and asked, "Where are you?" (Gen. 3:9). It seems a strange question because, as God, he already knew. Perhaps he needed to ask because *they* didn't fully realize the truth. Maybe he's asking the same of us today. *Where are you?* No matter the answer we may give—"in the middle of depression," "on the battlefield," "at the center of a stage"—he wants us to know that is not our truest, deepest location. Where we belong, where we've been all along, where we always are in some mysterious way is *in him*. Secure. Loved. Known. He is our hiding place; he is our heart's true home.

God, no matter where I am or what I do,
I am always secure and cared for in you.

. . . .

What do you need God to hide you from today?

JESUS IS MAKING SOMETHING BEAUTIFUL OF YOUR LIFE

Isn't this the carpenter? (Mark 6:3)

Jesus knew ordinary. He knew the feel of a splinter in his thumb, the smell of earth and sawdust, the sound of nails against boards. He understood deadlines and demanding customers. He comprehended the common, the kind of day that slips right by without fanfare or fireworks. "As carpenters, Joseph and Jesus would have created mainly farm tools (carts, plows, winnowing forks, and yokes), house parts (doors, frames, posts, and beams), furniture, and kitchen utensils."[1]

Jesus likely would have begun his work as a carpenter while still a teenager. When we consider this, it seems a decade or more of his time on earth could have been used differently. Only ten percent of Jesus's life was spent in public ministry.

I think we need to know this because we will all have "carpenter years." Times when we don't feel like we're living up to our potential. We feel like we could be doing something more, something bigger. We can resist the smallness. We, like the questioning crowd around Jesus, can become disappointed and disillusioned by what doesn't seem as grand as we'd imagined.

So much of God's plan is a mystery. But those "wasted" years in his life, in ours? It seems clear there is no such thing. The master carpenter knows how to make every part useful, every part beautiful.

And he is not done with his work in us yet.

*God, I take comfort in the example of your life. I pray that
I will serve you faithfully wherever you have me.*

· · · ·

How can you see Jesus working in the ordinary moments of your life?

GOD WILL EQUIP YOU TO HANDLE IT

I have learned to be content whatever the circumstances. (Philippians 4:11)

In *Feel the Fear ... and Do It Anyway*, Dr. Susan Jeffers says, "At the bottom of every one of your fears is simply the fear that you can't handle whatever life may bring you."[1]

I can't handle losing my job.

I can't handle getting sick.

I can't handle a loved one leaving.

I can't handle someone being mad at me.

I can't handle the latest news headline.

I can't handle my responsibilities.

I can't handle _____ (fill in the blank with one of your fears).

Paul says, "I have learned the secret of being content in any and every situation" (Phil. 4:12). What is his secret? Most of us have heard it many times: "I can do all this through him who gives me strength" (v. 13). Paul is really saying, "With Jesus, I can handle anything."

With Jesus, I can handle a Roman prison.

With Jesus, I can handle hurt and hunger.

With Jesus, I can even handle death.

Think back over your life and the difficulties you've already overcome. If someone had told you in advance about those, you might have said, "If that happens, I won't be able to handle it." But you had the strength you needed because God gave it to you. You've handled hard times before, and when new challenges arise, you can be confident you'll do so again.

God, no matter what happens, you and I will handle it together.

. . . .

What hard things have you and God handled together?

YOU'RE A CANDLE
IN A FIREWORK WORLD

You are the light of the world. (Matthew 5:14)

The sky stretches inky black above us as we wait for the first spark to light it with color. Whizz. Bang. Suddenly the evening is filled with red and blue and yellow. We ooh and aah as each firework explodes and sends ashes to the ground.

When it's over we walk back into the house—back to the ordinary of dishes, laundry, and conversations about what we'll do tomorrow.

As I drift off to sleep, these words drift across my mind: *Be a candle, not a firework.* In other words, shine brightly for a lifetime, not just a brief, spectacular time.

But how do we do this? Here are three ways.

Live with intention. Fireworks are scattered, a million sparks in a thousand directions. Candles burn with a single flame. We can be thoughtful about how we spend our time, affection, and resources.

Stay steady. We love fireworks because of the thrill and excitement. Candles aren't quite as glamorous but they last much longer. Sure, we can have "firework moments" and that's great. In daily life, we can be quietly faithful to what God has called us to do.

Go for substance, not show. A firework is flashy and draws a crowd. But as a source of light and warmth, well, they don't quite do the trick. We can stay true to our purpose, even when it seems no one notices.

Each time I light a candle and set it on a dinner table or in a window, I'll remember that sometimes being steady, faithful, and intentional can make us shine brighter than we will ever fully realize.

God, help me shine for you in all I do today.

. . . .

Who's a candle in your life?

GOD HAS BENEFITS FOR YOU

Praise the LORD, my soul,
and forget not all his benefits. (Psalm 103:2)

David had served God and Israel for years by the time he penned these words. He'd experienced war, betrayal, and family trouble. What had started as a glorious appointing probably felt routine on many days—especially the hard ones.

We can tend to feel the same about whatever is in our lives. When we first get married, have a baby, or join a new church, it's easy to see the benefits. Then tough times come, and we lose our perspective. It can be time to say with David, "Praise the LORD, my soul, and forget not all his benefits."

In Psalm 103:3–5, David goes on to list the specific benefits that mean the most to him:

God forgives all your sins. Perhaps David thought of his affair with Bathsheba on this one.

God heals all your diseases. Maybe a time of serious illness came to mind.

God redeems your life from the pit. David could have remembered how he came from a low position to become king.

God crowns you with love and compassion. David valued these characteristics of God more than any of the royal perks.

We're human, and we naturally grow used to what's in our lives. It can all seem ordinary until we intentionally refocus on the extraordinary benefits God gives us. Sometimes taking a few minutes to adjust our perspective can turn our everyday work into joy-filled worship again.

God, you're good to me in ways beyond what I can even comprehend.
Help me remember your benefits.

· · · ·

What's a benefit God has given you?

YOU BELONG TO GOD

Know that the LORD is God.
It is he who made us, and we are his;
we are his people, the sheep of his pasture. (Psalm 100:3)

We're not only God's people but also "the sheep of his pasture." In ancient times, the members of a shepherd's flock were a lot like his children. Without his loving attention, protection, and provision the sheep would get lost, become malnourished, or even die. A good shepherd, like a parent, loved his sheep so much that he would even be willing to lay down his life for them.

In hard times, we can take comfort in knowing we are watched over by someone who loves us. We're not drifting through life on our own. We're not orphans or sheep without a shepherd. We have a home. We have an identity. We have someone who is committed to our care. That means we don't have to try so hard to fend for ourselves. We don't have to go through life believing no one will be there for us. We don't have to carry the weight of our own existence.

Instead we can come to our heavenly Father, our Good Shepherd, and say, "I belong to you. You've promised to take care of me. Will you please help me?" He will always answer that prayer. And you have many other brothers and sisters, fellow sheep in the flock, who can come alongside you too.

You're not on your own.

You're deeply loved and cherished as part of a family and flock forever.

God, I'm so glad I belong to you. I'm grateful for your care, and it brings me so much comfort to know that I will never be on my own.

. . . .

What do you need from your Good Shepherd today?

GOD TAKES THE PRESSURE OFF

Make it your goal to live a quiet life, minding your own business and working with your hands, just as we instructed you before. (1 Thessalonians 4:11 NLT)

Make it your goal to... Imagine for a moment how our modern world would finish that sentence.

Make it your goal to be busy all the time.

Make it your goal to be successful and productive.

Make it your goal to look good.

Think of how some contemporary spiritual leaders might finish it too. Or how you might finish it yourself on the days when you feel not good enough.

Make it your goal to help everyone.

Make it your goal to change the whole world.

Make it your goal to be a spiritual hero.

What Paul, Silas, and Timothy decide to say is surprising: "Make it your goal to live a quiet life."

So what does a "quiet life" mean? It's easy to think it's about a *lack* of something. Fewer activities. Not as many commitments. Less noise. That can certainly be part of it, especially in seasons when we need restoration, but a quiet life is really about abiding in the presence of Jesus. It's about grace silencing the voices in our minds that pressure us to do, be, and have more. In their place, we begin to experience the joy, peace, and contentment only Jesus can give.

Let's keep learning together. Let's remember how much we're loved. Let's make it our goal to lead a quiet life.

God, give me the courage to embrace a quiet life.

· · · ·

What does God want to say to your heart today?

JESUS IS YOUR CORNERSTONE

See, I lay a stone in Zion, a tested stone,
a precious cornerstone for a sure foundation. (Isaiah 28:16)

It was common in the construction of first-century buildings to lean a building into itself. This meant that one part of the structure would have a greater amount of pressure on it than the rest of the structure. . . . This became known as the cornerstone and was the one part of the building on which the rest of the structure depended absolutely."[1]

One word in that description especially calls out to me: *pressure*. I think back over my busy day. There have been deadlines, emails, phone calls, and requests. Hurting friends to comfort, dinner to cook, and socks like a gang of feral cats in need of corralling on the laundry room floor. I have felt it all like a weight: the expectations to be so many things to so many people, to get it all done perfectly and right now. I want someone to take what I can't possibly bear. Maybe you can relate.

We all need a cornerstone. Not a vague architectural term lost mostly to history, but the One who is our living, breathing, daily reality. God will remind us that "in him all things hold together" (Col. 1:17). On him all things depend. We can rest on this truth, this promise. We don't have to carry the weight of this world—or even just our little lives. We only need to keep leaning into love.

God, thank you for being sure, strong, and true in a world
that can seem uncertain and chaotic.

. . . .

What's one way you need to lean into Jesus today?

THE BELT OF TRUTH PROTECTS YOU

Stand firm then, with the belt of truth buckled around your waist.
(Ephesians 6:14)

The belt described here, the kind worn by a Roman soldier, would have been eight to twelve inches long and made of thick leather. It covered much of a soldier's torso, offering not only protection but security and stability. It was the first piece of armor to be put on and held many of the others together.[1]

In ancient times the part of the body the belt covered (described as "the bowels") was seen as an important part of emotions. This is somewhat similar to how we might talk about feeling something in our "gut" today. I did some research and discovered this is true and that this meaning persisted in some Bible translations up until the early seventeenth century. If this is so, I pondered, then perhaps part of the purpose of the "belt of truth" is to help guard our emotions.

Experiencing emotions, even unwelcome ones, isn't an attack. But hearing things like "God is holding out on you" and "You're missing out" that impact our emotions can be. Those words are ruthlessly aimed at the most tender parts of who we are. Lies wound and destroy; truth protects and defends.

I am choosing to put on the belt of truth. I need its strength. I need its protection. And the really good news? This belt is available to all of us and goes with everything.

God, today I choose to put on the belt of truth.
I will believe what you say. I will stand firm.

. . . .

What's a lie you're battling today and the truth
that will defend your heart against it?

YOU HAVE GOOD NEWS SHOES

For shoes, put on the peace that comes from the Good News. (Ephesians 6:15 NLT)

Every ancient soldier knew that stability, being able to stand firm, is the most important part of footwear. But they didn't accomplish that goal through fancy tennis shoes. Instead soldiers wore leather sandals that had something like small spikes attached to the soles. More similar to soccer cleats, these shoes allowed them to hold their ground when the enemy attacked. Paul said, "For shoes, put on the *peace* that comes from the Good News so that you will be fully prepared" (Eph. 6:15 NLT).

The peace that comes from the Good News is knowing we have been made right with God and he is on our side. "The God of peace will soon crush Satan under your feet" (Rom. 16:20 NLT). We don't have to fight the attacks alone. Victory isn't up to us. We are simply told to "stand firm" (Eph. 6:14 NIV). God will do it. He will deliver us. He will bring us through the battle. The peace we have *with God* means we can have peace *within us* regardless of what happens around us.

The most powerful warrior is the one who can hold on to peace even in the middle of the battle. Oh, our knees may knock and our hands tremble. There will be tears and sweat and hard days. That's okay. Peace is not simply an emotion. Instead peace is a position we take of standing on who God is, what he has promised, and who he tells us we are no matter what happens.

God, you are my peace and the one who brings victory in my life.

. . . .

When have you experienced peace in the middle of a difficulty?

GOD GIVES YOU HIS RIGHTEOUSNESS

Stand firm then . . . with the breastplate of righteousness in place.
(Ephesians 6:14)

The breastplate (also known as body armor) protected the vital organs, especially the heart. In some instances it was literally called a "heart guard." What strikes me most about the breastplate in the armor of God is how it's described: "the breastplate *of righteousness*."

You and I can't create our own righteousness. "As the Scriptures say, 'No one is righteous—not even one'" (Rom. 3:10 NLT). We need someone to impart their righteousness to us. This is what happens when we place our trust in Jesus. "I no longer count on my own righteousness through obeying the law; rather, I become righteous through faith in Christ. For God's way of making us right with himself depends on faith" (Phil. 3:9 NLT).

This goes against our human nature, our desire to strive and earn and prove. Someone once said to Jesus, "We want to perform God's works, too. What should we do?" (John 6:28 NLT). Jesus replies, "This is the only work God wants from you: Believe in the one he has sent" (v. 29 NLT).

Believing. Trusting. Surrendering our desire to prove we're good enough. The righteousness we receive *through Jesus alone* is our heart's hope and defense. We take what's his as ours, and then he empowers us to live it out.

God, you are my heart's hope and defense now and forever.

. . . .

What's one area of your life where you especially need God
to guard your heart today?

Day 276

YOUR FAITH IS A SHIELD

Take up the shield of faith. (Ephesians 6:16)

When I looked closer at the elements of ancient shields, I almost fell out of my chair because while soldiers likely never realized it, I see God so present throughout each layer.

First, the shield itself was made out of wood. When we take up the shield of faith, we are placing ourselves behind the protection and redemption of the cross, who Jesus is, and what he has done on our behalf.

Then the wood was covered by leather, by animal skins—a reminder of sacrifice. God gave his only Son on our behalf, and it is this sacrifice that saves us.

The leather of the shield was frequently rubbed down with oil or soaked in water, which was the invisible secret to extinguishing flaming arrows. This sounds a lot like anointing and baptism, both of which are related to the Holy Spirit. It is the truth imparted to us by the Spirit that quenches the fiery arrows that the enemy shoots at us—the lies, accusations, and temptations.

Taking up the shield of faith means simply placing our trust in who God is and what he has done for us. When an ancient soldier was under the most intense attack, the best position to be in was *on his knees*. That's when the shield was most effective because in that position it covered the entire soldier. This is the battle-winning secret: when we don't have the strength or will or wisdom to fight, we don't have to; we only need to be still and let God cover us.

God, help me to take up the shield of faith and trust you today.

. . . .

What's an area of life where you feel under attack
and need your shield of faith?

SALVATION IS YOUR HELMET

Put on salvation as your helmet. (Ephesians 6:17 NLT)

The helmet of salvation is mentioned in two other places in Scripture as well. God himself is the first to wear it. In the Old Testament, "He . . . placed the helmet of salvation on his head" (Isa. 59:17 NLT). What this tells me is that the helmet we put on is not our own. Salvation isn't something we earn or invent. Instead it's something always and only given to us by God.

In the second mention Paul tells us to live "wearing as our helmet the confidence of our salvation" (1 Thess. 5:8 NLT). Yes, this confidence in our salvation is about eternal hope, but the armor of God passage in Ephesians is clearly about the here and now, about the battlefield we find ourselves on today.

When we're confident in God's love for us, we can come to him in the middle of the battle, in the hardest places. We can tell him what concerns us and trust he will take care of us. We can live in gratitude because we know he is faithful. Then his peace will guard our minds—even in the midst of all-out war.

We need a defense for our minds, and God offers us one. We don't have to let worry or fear win today. Oh, this doesn't mean it will be easy. We're talking about a battle after all. About fighting hard. About sometimes getting knocked down. God understands this, but he also knows the identity and destiny he's given us. We are not worriers; we are warriors.

God, you are the one who gives me salvation for eternity and what I need now too.

. . . .

What battle are you fighting in your mind that you need God's help with today?

YOU FIGHT WITH
THE SWORD OF THE SPIRIT

Take . . . the sword of the Spirit, which is the word of God. (Ephesians 6:17)

In the armor of God there's only one piece that's used not just for defense but for fighting back. This is not the kind of shiny silver sword carried by princes in cartoon movies. The kind of weapon mentioned in this passage is more like a small dagger used in hand-to-hand combat. The "word" in this verse doesn't mean big, broad truth. Instead in the ancient language it's *rhema*, which more accurately describes "a particular truth for a particular situation."[1]

This description makes me think of Jesus overcoming temptation during his forty days in the wilderness (see Luke 4:3–12). The exchange that happens between Jesus and the devil during that time reads like a hand-to-hand combat scene where words are the weapons.

The devil said to him, "If you are the Son of God, tell this stone to become bread."
Jesus answered, "It is written: 'Man shall not live on bread alone.'"
[The devil] said to him, "If you worship me, it will all be yours."
Jesus answered, "It is written: 'Worship the Lord your God and serve him only.'"
"If you are the Son of God," [the devil] said, "throw yourself down from here."
Jesus answered, "It is said: 'Do not put the Lord your God to the test.'"

Jesus won this showdown by knowing and declaring specific spiritual truth. To be prepared for what we may face from the enemy, it's essential for us to spend time in God's Word. We have a real God who equips us with everything we need for victory.

*God, you are the living Word, the one who gives me
the truth I need for victory.*

. . . .

What is one of your favorite Scripture verses?

GOD HAS GOOD THINGS FOR YOU

Let them give thanks to the LORD for his unfailing love
and his wonderful deeds for mankind,
for he satisfies the thirsty
and fills the hungry with good things. (Psalm 107:8–9)

God promises that he will satisfy the thirsty and fill the hungry with good things. Yet sometimes what he places on our plates may not be what we wanted. So we turn our heads like toddlers and declare we will not eat our broccoli. Then we blame God when we walk away from the table still feeling hungry. Yet he knows that to give us what we want—even if it seems to us like a very good thing—would actually not be what's best.

Deciding to "eat our broccoli" is an act of faith. It doesn't taste better when we put it in our mouths. It's not suddenly transformed into ice cream just because we've been obedient. It's often hard to swallow. But over time we begin to reap the benefits. We become healthier, stronger, and more whole.

Only he knows what our hearts truly need to eat. We can compare what's on our plates to those around us at the table and decide we got the bad end of the deal. Can't I just have what she's having? It's in those moments God asks us to trust that he knows what's good—what will truly satisfy our hunger and nourish us. When we do so, he promises to fill us up.

When your heart is hungry, come to God's table. You're always welcome. And you'll always be served with love.

God, you are the only one who truly knows what my heart needs.
Help me be content with what you have for my life.

. . . .

What's something your heart has hungered for that God has satisfied?

Day 280

YOUR DESIRES MATTER

*When the queen of Sheba saw all the wisdom of Solomon and the
palace he had built, the food on his table, the seating of his officials,
the attending servants in their robes, his cupbearers, and the burnt
offerings he made at the temple of the LORD, she was overwhelmed.
(1 Kings 10:4–5)*

The queen of Sheba could have turned back at this moment when she was
overwhelmed. But the desire of her heart for wisdom prevailed, and "she
came to Solomon and talked with him about all that she had on her mind" and
he "answered all her questions" (1 Kings 10:2–3).

The queen of Sheba shows us we're to identify what we want, and when it
aligns with God's will to audaciously go for it. Jesus said, "Ask and it will be given
to you; seek and you will find; knock and the door will be opened to you" (Matt.
7:7). When we do so, we are creating an opportunity for God to use us to bless
others too. "King Solomon gave the queen of Sheba all she desired and asked
for, besides what he had given her out of his royal bounty. Then she left and
returned with her retinue to her own country" (1 Kings 10:13).

When the queen went home, she didn't go empty-handed. She brought lavish
gifts from Solomon, wisdom that would help her rule well, and a new faith in
the one true God. All of those benefited her people. God is inviting us to enjoy
our fill of his abundant goodness. And as the queen of Sheba found, we will have
plenty to share with others too.

God, help me boldly pursue the desires you have put in my heart.

. . . .

What is a desire of your heart?

YOUR STRUGGLES AREN'T YOUR IDENTITY

But you are a chosen people, a royal priesthood, a holy nation, God's special possession. (1 Peter 2:9)

I curled up on my couch, phone tucked between my ear and shoulder, listening to my friend share about a challenge in her life. At some point she said, "I guess this is who I am now. I am the girl who struggles with this thing."

I sat up straight, grabbed my phone so I could speak as loudly and directly into it as I could, and ceased nodding. I said, "No, that is not who you are now. That is not who you are ever. This is your current circumstance. It is what you are fighting. It is not and will never be your identity." Long after our call was over, I kept thinking about those words. Yes, they came from my mouth, but I knew they also came from God's heart.

The enemy of our hearts would love to convince us that we are our struggles or our failures, our mistakes or our secrets. If we let this happen, then shame wins and we hide. But we are never ever defined by what we do. We are always and only defined by what Jesus has done for us. Because of his death on the cross and his resurrection from the grave, sin has been defeated, death has been overcome, and even the darkest moments of our lives can't diminish his light within us.

Let's never stop shining. Let's never stop speaking of what he has done for us. Let's never believe our circumstances are more powerful than the grace of our Savior.

God, you created me and saved me, and only you get to say who I am.

. . . .

What has shaped how you see yourself and what's really true?

GOD CARES ABOUT IT ALL

Praise be to the God and Father of our Lord Jesus Christ, . . . the God of all comfort, who comforts us in all our troubles. (2 Corinthians 1:3–4)

D o you want me to kiss it and make it better?"
      I've heard those words from the lips of countless moms. They've taught me this: no hurt is too small for attention or affection. I believe that reflects the heart of our God. He is "the God of all comfort, who comforts us in all our troubles." There's no disclaimer. No exceptions. No fine print at the end of the sentence.

That's hard for me to grasp sometimes. I don't have trouble bringing God the huge tragedies. But the bumps, scrapes, and bruises of everyday life are trickier. I tend to think, *This isn't important enough for God's attention. He has bigger things to worry about than my little pain.*

But in those moments, I'm forgetting God has limitless resources. Unlike us, he doesn't have to manage his time or energy. He never grows tired, and he has all of eternity. Our needs can't diminish him in any way.

I'm also forgetting how much I'm loved. Those moms aren't kissing boo-boos because someone is forcing them to do so. They're comforting their children because they care. And God loves us even more than the best mama.

We don't have to deal with life's troubles on our own. With childlike faith we can come to God and simply ask, "Will you love on me and make it better?" No matter the size, situation, or circumstances, the answer is always a compassionate, affectionate *yes*.

---

*God, thank you for caring about everything in my life,
whether big or small.*

. . . .

What hurt do you need God to make better today?

YOU CAN HAVE HOPE
EVEN IN HEARTACHE

Even in laughter the heart may ache,
and rejoicing may end in grief. (Proverbs 14:13)

On a fall morning over a decade ago, I sat in a circle of women whose ages and stories varied. We clutched coffee cups and held in our emotions, no one wanting to be the first to share. What did we all have in common? Being part of a class at my church called "Interrupted Expectations." I, as a counseling intern and cofacilitator, felt the pressure to say something brilliant but instead stared at the carpet.

Our leader pulled out a box of twenty-four crayons which, she said, represented our emotions. She showed us the whole range of colors but only pulled out two, black and white. Most of us, she says, were only allowed to experience or express a narrow range of emotions. But what about all the rest?

Everyone in the group had experienced some kind of loss, whether of a person, job, or dream. I was struggling with infertility. "Loss leads to grief," Jan said, "and grief leads to messy emotions that aren't black and white." Disappointment is one of those emotions.

I used to worry sometimes that disappointment was a lack of faith. But that's not true—it's simply a human reaction to life not turning out the way we hoped. It's an emotion, a crayon in our box, that helps us make sense of loss.

God's love is big enough to handle all of our emotions, strong enough to see us through hard seasons, faithful enough to never let us go, near to us when we need it most, and beyond our expectations.

God, thank you for all of my emotions. Help me to embrace each of them.

. . . .

What emotion is hardest for you to feel?

Day 284

YOU'RE BEARING GOOD FRUIT

I am the vine; you are the branches. If you remain in me and I in you,
you will bear much fruit. (John 15:5)

The other day a fruit stand on the side of the road caught my attention. As I approached it, a weather-worn farmer who looked to be in his eighties gave me a bright smile.

He extended his hand, which held a gorgeous peach, and asked, "Would you like to try my fruit?" I accepted and it was delicious. The farmer smiled with satisfaction and said, "It's good, isn't it?"

Jesus said we'll bear fruit when we remain in him. But unlike the farmer, I often hesitate to share the fruit God produces in my life with those around me. I think it's not good enough. I'm afraid they won't like it. So I hide it away.

But what if the farmer did the same? His peaches were delicious, but they weren't perfect. There were bumps, bruises, and scrapes in some places. He could have hidden them in his barn out of shame and fear until they rotted away. Then I, and many others, would have missed out on something wonderful.

So I'm challenging all of us today to offer our fruit. Whatever gifts God has entrusted to us, let's share them. Whatever talents he's blessed us with, let's use them. Whatever words of encouragement he's placed within our hearts, let's speak them.

Those who receive our fruit will be blessed. And perhaps our heavenly Father will smile with satisfaction as he sees the fruit in our lives and says, "It's good, isn't it?"

God, help me abide in you today and share
the fruit you grow through me.

. . . .

What can you share with someone else today?

GOD WILL UPHOLD YOU

Though they stumble, they will never fall,
for the LORD holds them by the hand. (Psalm 37:24 NLT)

"Jesus." I whisper his name because this is all I can muster in terms of a prayer. I will confess to you that it's flat-out hard to believe he is there. You have those moments too, don't you? The ones where faith feels like a mirage, like a story you've made up to make yourself feel better.

God knows our human selves can't feel what's spiritual sometimes, and he will hold us up when our faith feels frail, our hearts grow weary, and we're not sure we can keep standing firm.

When life begins to go downward or when I slip up, I fear I will never be able to recover. I will slide, slide, slide, and I will land in a place where there is no light or hope or coming back. But this is the promise we have: "Though they may stumble, they will never fall, for the LORD holds them by the hand" (Ps. 27:24). I'm finding God's hand has many forms, many fingers, but it is ever-present if I reach for it, look for it, let it be the soft place where I land.

His nail-struck hands uphold us. His hands catch the tears streaming down in the shower. His hands set us on our feet over and over again. Yes, we will falter, *but we will not fall.* Not because we can hold it all together. But because we are always, mysteriously, held.

God, I'm so grateful for the security I have in you.
It's reassuring to know you will hold me up.

. . . .

How has God held you up when you felt weak?

YOU DON'T HAVE TO DEFEND YOURSELF

God, have mercy on me, a sinner. (Luke 18:13)

It used to feel like there was a courtroom inside of me. No matter how hard I tried, it seemed the verdict came out the same: "Guilty, guilty, guilty. Peace confiscated. Sentenced to shame."

These days I've started to pray two simple prayers that are my only defense. First, "God, have mercy on me, a sinner." This prayer was uttered by a tax collector while a Pharisee stood by praying in a way that made a case for himself, including his good deeds and how he was better than others. Jesus said the tax collector rather than the Pharisee "went home justified before God" (v. 14). The second prayer I've come to love is simply declaring, "Jesus is Lord, I am loved, that is all."

There's no case the enemy of my heart can make against those truths. Yes, I *am* a sinner. But I'm also forgiven, transformed, redeemed, and a new creation. My true identity is in not my mistakes but what God speaks over me. What Jesus has done on my behalf is irrefutable, his love for me unchangeable.

We don't have to defend ourselves. "If anybody does sin, we have an advocate with the Father—Jesus Christ, the Righteous One. He is the atoning sacrifice for our sins" (1 John 2:1–2).

Our lives are a paradox. We're guilty and entirely covered by grace. We're accused by the enemy and affirmed by our Father. We're lawbreakers made wholly righteous by what Jesus did for us.

God, thank you for your grace that is stronger than any accusation the enemy of my heart may try to bring against me.

· · · ·

Which of the two prayers in today's reading speaks most to you?

GOD IS YOUR GREAT REWARD

Do not be afraid, Abram.
I am your shield,
your very great reward. (Genesis 15:1)

One thing I love about the Bible is that the heroes are so very fallible, so uncensored and rough-edged, so unpolished and in progress. Like the moment when God came to Abram (later called Abraham) and said, "I am your shield, your very great reward." The moviemakers would have the voice booming from the sky, Abram dropping to his knees in worship, the music rising in holy crescendo. But this Abram, the forefather of our faith, said instead, "Sovereign Lord, what can you give me?" (Gen. 15:2). Hadn't God just answered that question? Hadn't he just offered Abram his very self?

God seems to lean in and listen as Abram explains this question. He has no heir. He's confused. He's afraid. Then God took Abram outside and told him to look at the sky. God explained and reassured, promised and affirmed. And Abram believed him.

I think we need to know this story just like we need to know what we'd like the answer to be when we ask, "God, what can you give me?" Pause for a moment and think about it. None of us are above this question. The response is most likely a longing of our hearts—love or acceptance or belonging.

Whatever it is, I believe God is still giving this answer: "I am your very great reward." He is acceptance. He is belonging. He is courage and hope and grace. Truth and strength and healing. Power and security and everything we long for most.

God, help me bring all my hopes and longings to you,
the only one who can truly fill them.

. . . .

What do you desire for God to give you today?

YES, YOU'VE GOT WHAT IT TAKES

Seek the Kingdom of God above all else, and live righteously, and he will give you everything you need. (Matthew 6:33 NLT)

My hands grip the steering wheel of my car tightly as I think about the road ahead for my life. It has been a season of open doors and answered prayers. Yet I'm experiencing the same emotion I've felt in more difficult times: fear.

I'm confused until I suddenly realize it's because a familiar question is echoing in my heart: Will I have what it takes? We've all wondered that at some point, haven't we? In the quiet of my car, it seemed God whispered to my scared-silly soul, *What matters isn't if you will have what it takes. What matters is if you will have what needs to be given. And you will. Because I will provide it.*

In that moment the pressure lifted from my shoulders. I wasn't required to be perfect. I didn't have to make everyone happy. I didn't need to turn into superwoman to accomplish God's purpose for my life. I just needed to believe and receive.

God would give me the strength. He would love others through me. He would do it. As I pulled into a parking spot, my worried thoughts finally came to a standstill as well. God was with me, for me, and able to empower me. Whew.

No matter what we're facing, the same is true for all of us. When fear comes, we can pause and say, "Yes, I have what it takes because I belong to the God who gives all I need . . . and more."

God, thank you that in you I will always have what it takes because you give me everything I need.

. . . .

What do you need God to give you today?

GOD HAS NOT GIVEN YOU A SPIRIT OF FEAR

For God has not given us a spirit of fear and timidity, but of power, love, and self-discipline. (2 Timothy 1:7 NLT)

Paul writes 2 Timothy 1:7 as reassurance that no matter what's ahead, Timothy won't have to handle it on his own. We don't have to either. We'll have everything we need through God's spirit.

Power. The original word is *dynamis*, and it's where we get the modern word *dynamic*. The power Paul speaks of is not human but supernatural. Fear tells us we are weak; God's spirit makes us strong.

Love. This is *agape*, divine love. It's not what we see in romantic comedies. It's the fierce, wild love of God in and for us. Fear tells us to withdraw; God's spirit empowers us to reach out.

Self-discipline. The word *sophronismos* can also be translated as "sound mind." It's an inner alignment with truth, a deep knowing that makes us brave. Fear tells us lies—we can't do it, we're not enough, we're going to fail; God's spirit assures us we will prevail.

We don't have to fake or force anything. We've been given a Spirit who lives within us and empowers us. We can turn Paul's words into an affirmation: God has not given me a spirit of fear and timidity, but of power, love, and self-discipline.

Saying these words doesn't mean our fear will magically go away—Paul compares the life of faith to a fight, after all. But it will remind us that we, like Timothy, have everything we need to move forward in faith and finish strong.

God, thank you for giving me a spirit not of fear but of power, love, and self-discipline.

. . . .

When have you experienced the Spirit's power, love, and self-discipline in your life?

TRUTH CAN
BRING YOU FREEDOM

Love does not delight in evil but rejoices with the truth. (1 Corinthians 13:6)

Jesus told us, "The truth will set you free" (John 8:32), and yes, I believe this applies first and foremost to the gospel. But I think it also means that when we speak the truth of our struggles and stories, we help set each other free too.

I picture being across from a friend and clearing my throat, finally putting words to the darkness I've been battling. I think of the freedom that comes when she says, "Me too." I imagine coming across sentences in a book that put words to something I thought no one else had ever faced, the shock and joy of "I'm not the only one" breaking the chains around my heart.

I also remember moments when I've bit my tongue, when I've smiled and said the polite words, and how I felt tangled up in my soul. I can recall holding back, holding it all in, and how silence seemed like a prison.

I'm not advocating that we go around sharing all things with all people. That would be unwise and downright dangerous. What I'm saying is that there is a time and a place and a people with whom speaking truth can bring true freedom.

I want to be a woman who speaks the truth of her story. I want to be a woman who brings God glory. I want to be a woman who helps set her sisters free.

God, give me the courage I need to speak my story and the wisdom to know when it's time to be silent too.

. . . .

How has hearing someone's story encouraged you
or helped set you free?

SELAH FOR YOUR SOUL

Meditate within your heart on your bed, and be still. Selah (Psalm 4:4 NKJV)

The word *selah* appears over seventy times in the book of Psalms, and yet in many ways it remains a mystery. Some translations of Scripture leave it out because there is no English equivalent. Author and worship pastor Jason Soroski says, "Many commentators think that Selah meant 'to pause' or 'to reflect.'"[1]

Our God didn't design us just for productivity. We need eight hours of sleep a night. Three meals a day. We're far slower than cheetahs. Less industrious than ants. We so easily forget this and often think we're on this earth to do as much as we can as quickly as we can. But the God who spoke the world into being in six days has no trouble with his to-do list.

Selah is placed with intention throughout the Psalms. We can also place it intentionally throughout our days. It's tempting to think we need to wait until we go on vacation or even retire to slow down. But selah tells us the peace of God can be found in the here and now, wherever we are. Selah goes well with morning coffee and the cozy corner of a couch, with prayer closets and carpool lines. Anywhere we can find a sliver of time. Selah doesn't demand hours. It asks only for a deep breath, a few moments, a pause in the middle of the rush. Those little bits of time can make a big difference in our lives.

God, when I'm tempted to hurry through my days,
draw me back to your heart.

. . . .

What's a recent moment when you experienced selah?

GOD IS THE ULTIMATE TRAINER

Physical training is good, but training for godliness is much better, promising benefits in this life and in the life to come. (1 Timothy 4:8 NLT)

We likely know how to exercise our bodies, but how do we do the same for our spiritual lives as Paul encourages Timothy to do? One simple way that actually has similar benefits to physical exercise is meditation. Some of us have been taught that *meditate* is a scary word, but it actually just means intentionally thinking deeply or focusing. It's like a workout for your mind. The Psalms give us three areas that can work well for meditation:

- *God's love.* "We meditate on your unfailing love" (Ps. 48:9).
- *God's ways and truth.* "I will meditate on your decrees" (119:23 NLT).
- *God's character and power.* "I will meditate on your majestic, glorious splendor and your wonderful miracles" (145:5 NLT).

Here's a basic meditation to try: Find a comfortable, quiet space to sit or lie down. Start a timer for five minutes. Then mentally repeat a Scripture such as, "I can do all things through Christ who strengthens me" (Phil. 4:13 NKJV), and emphasize different words each time. (*I* can do all things. I *can* do all things. I can *do* all things. I can do *all things*.) Take deep breaths in through your nose and out through your mouth while you do so.

The two things that set exercise apart from everyday movement and meditation from simply thinking are intentionality and consistency. If you exercise ten minutes a day and meditate for five, it's enough to have anxiety-reducing benefits.

Train your body. Train your brain.

God, help me to train my body and mind so that
I can fully use them to serve you and others.

. . . .

What's one small way you can train your body and mind today?

YOU CAN CAST
YOUR CARES ON JESUS

Casting all your cares on him, because he cares about you. (1 Peter 5:7 CSB)

A fisherman like Peter would have had a personal cast net about eight to fifteen feet in diameter. Attached to the center of this net would have been a line, which the fisherman held in his left hand. Then he would have hurled the net toward the sea with his right hand. The net would have spread wide, landed on the water, then fallen like a parachute, capturing all the fish below.

Sometimes we put pressure on ourselves to cast our cares on God, then feel like spiritual failures when we need to do so more than once. But Peter would have known that casting takes many tries. He didn't just cast his net once; he did it over and over again. We may need to do the same.

Releasing our cares isn't a one-time event. It's a lifelong process. We can come to the shore of God's faithful love again and again, as often as we need. We are always welcome to give him whatever weighs us down so that we can continue our journey with freer, lighter hearts.

Like throwing stones in a lake, casting our cares is more than just a tentative letting go—it's a hurling, tossing, complete release. This is the offer of God: to let him take our anxieties as the lake takes our stones, fully and completely. There is enough room to hold one care or a thousand. We can let them all sink beneath the surface of his endlessly deep love.

God, I'm grateful for the invitation to cast my cares on you.

. . . .

What care do you need to release to God today?

Day 294

YOU HAVE A DEEPER KIND OF PEACE

The peace I give is a gift the world cannot give. (John 14:27 NLT)

"I have peace about it." I've heard this phrase many times, and I understand the good intentions behind it. We want to be sure we're doing what's right and following God's will.

But I can think of many times when a biblical character didn't have any human peace in a situation. When Jesus was in the garden of Gethsemane, he felt deep distress and prayed, "Father, if you are willing, please take this cup of suffering away from me. Yet I want your will to be done, not mine" (Luke 22:42 NLT).

Imagine if Jesus had said, "I don't have peace about going to the cross, so I'm not going to do it." History, and our story, would be very different. Emotional peace and spiritual peace are not the same.

Emotional peace says, "You'll be fine."

Spiritual peace says, "No matter what happens, God will see you through it."

Emotional peace says, "You don't have anything to be afraid of."

Spiritual peace says, "Yes, there is much to fear, but God will make you brave."

Emotional peace says, "This will be convenient and easy."

Spiritual peace says, "This will be inconvenient and hard, but nothing is impossible with God."

Emotional peace says, "Quit when it gets to be too much."

Spiritual peace says, "Persevere because God has promised you victory."

Instead of saying, "I have peace *about* it," perhaps we can say, "I have peace *within* me." Peace that is beyond our humanity. Peace only the God of eternity can give.

God, give me wisdom to know when peace is external and when it is eternal.

· · · ·

How would you describe the differences between human peace and supernatural peace?

MUSTARD-SEED FAITH

If you had faith even as small as a mustard seed, you could say to this mountain, "Move from here to there," and it would move. Nothing would be impossible. (Matthew 17:20 NLT)

Mustard seeds are tiny, like little grains of sand. Some people interpret this passage to mean our Savior is telling us, "You need to grow your faith!" But if this is so, why not use something big as the metaphor? Why not tell us to have faith as big as the ocean or as high as the sky? When Jesus says the apostles only need faith like a mustard seed, the tiniest of all, it seems clear to me he's expressing, "Size is not the problem."

I think Jesus is trying to help us understand that it's not about our faith but who we place our faith in. To tell anyone their faith is the controlling factor in a situation is to put them in the place of God.

Having faith also doesn't mean things will turn out the way we want. Jesus prayed for the cup of suffering to pass but still went to the cross. His mother prayed one of the most beautiful prayers in all of Scripture and then watched her beloved son die. But God also resurrected Jesus. He sustained Mary. Faith isn't about a result; it's about a relationship.

Let's never allow anyone to convince us our faith isn't big enough, that if we can only increase it, all we want will be ours. Instead, let's wholly put our faith in a God who is bigger, stronger, and more loving than we could ever imagine or measure.

God, thank you that I can always put my faith, trust, and hope fully in you.

. . . .

What is something you're trusting God with today?

YOU HAVE THE REAL SECRET OF SUCCESS

Commit your actions to the LORD, and your plans will succeed. (Proverbs 16:3 NLT)

I'm doing a final review of a project when an unexpected wave of fear sweeps over me. I begin to ask, "How can I make sure this goes well?" The words from Proverbs 16:3 pop into my mind. I pause and consider: Is this a guarantee from God that everything will go the way I'd like? Life experience and the rest of his Word would seem to tell me otherwise.

Slowly I begin to see the true meaning of that verse: success isn't about outcome; it's about obedience.

The "success" this verse talks about is set in motion not when the results are in but as soon as we say, "God, I give this to you." He thinks differently than we do. To him, every obedient yes is already a success.

The real relief is that when I commit something to God, I no longer have to carry it. I don't bear the weight of the expectations, fears, and pressure. I can faithfully do what he's asked and know he will take care of the rest.

I return to my project and the familiar fear fades with this realization: who I'm turning this over to matters more than how it all turns out. God's got this. He's got me too. And whatever happens next, in his eyes it will be a success.

God, I commit to you all that I do, trusting that you will make it a success in your eyes.

. . . .

What do you need God's help to make a "success" today?

YOU HAVE ADVOCATES

I will ask the Father, and he will give you another advocate to help you and be with you forever. (John 14:16)

S ometimes a word flashes up from the pages of my Bible as if it's lit up from the inside, a holy neon arrow or divine underlining. That happened this morning when I read the word *another* in John 14:16, because it made me ask myself, "If the Spirit is *another* advocate for us, then who are the others?"

It turns out we have all *three* members of the Trinity on our side. Job said about God, "Even now my witness is in heaven; my advocate is on high" (Job 16:19). Then John tells us, "We have an advocate with the Father—Jesus Christ, the Righteous One" (1 John 2:1). And Jesus affirmed, "The Advocate, the Holy Spirit, whom the Father will send in my name, will teach you all things and will remind you of everything I have said to you" (John 14:26).

"God is for us" (Rom. 8:31). Jesus and the Holy Spirit are too. *All of divinity is an advocate for us in all our humanity.* This is a mystery and wonder to me. In the kingdom, we are God's children. You. Me. Us. We are cherished and spoken up for and supported. Not because we are perfect or have earned it. Simply because of what our advocates have already done for us, what they are doing even in this moment, and what they have promised to always do.

God, Jesus, and Holy Spirit, it is so powerful to know you are for me, my strong and loving advocates.

. . . .

How have you seen God be an advocate
who supports and defends you?

GOD IS A JOY-BRINGER

You will fill me with joy in your presence. (Psalm 16:11)

My grandmother has a sign on her wall that reads, "Joy is the most infallible sign of the presence of God." French philosopher and scientist Pierre Teilhard de Chardin said these words. He lived from 1881 to 1955, which means he endured two world wars, the Great Depression, and the Spanish flu epidemic.

When I read that sign, I always thought, *Whoever said that must have had an easy life.* I pictured joy like a party with glasses clinking and people laughing. But the events of the last few years in humanity's history have given me a deeper understanding. Teilhard de Chardin is not talking about the joy of perfection but the joy that comes into our hard places and broken hearts.

I struggle with anxiety and depression, so joy isn't always something I feel. It's something I choose to believe is real. And I don't know if joy is the most infallible sign of the presence of God. Some of the times I've felt God nearest have actually been in moments of despair. But I do think joy is one sign.

I'm learning joy isn't something we're supposed to force or fake. Instead it's something that finds us—often in the most unexpected places. I've known joy in hospital rooms just as surely as watching the sunset on a beautiful beach at the end of a glorious day. Wherever it comes to us, joy is the whisper of God saying, *Hold on, I'm still here.*

God, help me to find joy in unexpected ways and places today.

. . . .

When have you been surprised by joy?

JESUS SHOWS YOU WHO GOD IS

The Son is the radiance of God's glory and the exact representation of his being. (Hebrews 1:3)

The author of Hebrews tells us that Jesus is the "exact representation" of God, and the original meaning of this phrase is "replica." This truth about God's nature seems obvious as I'm typing it, but when I read it in Hebrews, I realized I had thought there were some subtle differences between Son and Father. Sometimes I believed . . .

Jesus is always compassionate. God is impatient.

Jesus is always with me. God can be distant.

Jesus is always accepting of my humanity. God is exasperated by my imperfections.

But to see who God is, I only need to look at who Jesus was when he was on this earth.

The compassion of Jesus is the compassion of God.

The gentleness of Jesus is the gentleness of God.

The love of Jesus is the love of God.

When God sent his Son to Earth, he sent not just a *representation* but also a *replica*. Every brushstroke the same. Every line and curve repeated. God took all of his grandness and mystery, wrapped it in skin, laid it in a manger, walked it through the dusty streets of Jerusalem, hung it from a cross, and raised it from a tomb. He took the eternal and invisible and made it earthly and tangible.

This is the miracle, the truth that's beyond forgery: all of who God is dwelled in Jesus, who dwelled with us, who now dwells in me.

God, when I wonder who you are or what you're like, help me remember to look to the replica you gave me of yourself.

. . . .

What's a characteristic of God and Jesus you love?

WHEN WE FEEL OVERWHELMED BY ALL THE NEEDS

*Certainly there were many needy widows in Israel in Elijah's time.
... Yet Elijah was not sent to any of them.... And many in Israel had
leprosy in the time of the prophet Elisha, but the only one healed was
Naaman, a Syrian. (Luke 4:25–27 NLT)*

Whenever I hear about any injustice, natural disaster, new diagnosis, charity lacking funds, family in crisis, or community in conflict, I can start feeling like I need to save the world.

But Luke 4:25–27 shows every need doesn't automatically equal an assignment. In our individualistic culture we often forget we are part of the body of Christ. That means we don't have to do everything. We only need to do our part.

We're to ask, "God, who do you want to send me to?" Being "sent" doesn't necessarily mean going across the world. It can mean crossing the yard to our neighbor's house. Or the hallway between the kitchen and our teenager's room. What matters is not distance but that we are taking obedient action.

What God asks us to do won't overwhelm us with guilt and shame. Yes, it will be hard at times. But it will also be a joy as he uses us to serve in ways only we can. God already knows the good things he wants us to do, and he has equipped us to do them.

*God, send me where you want me today; I release everything
and everyone else to you.*

. . . .

Who is one person God wants to send you to today?

YOUR WORTH ISN'T IN YOUR WORKS

So don't be afraid; you are worth more than many sparrows. (Matthew 10:31)

The laundry is still unfolded, the emails unanswered, the to-do list undone. I sigh and ask myself, "Have I been productive at all today?"

Anxiety and accusations are the only response. So I pray, "God, what lie am I believing? And what's the truth that replaces it?" This is a new habit I'm practicing. It's uncomfortable and hard.

Yet in that quiet moment it seems my heart hears a reassuring whisper . . .

Life isn't about being productive. It's about being purposeful.

I've often believed the lie that God's first priority is what I can produce. But I'm learning that just because something doesn't have tangible results, it doesn't mean it doesn't have eternal impact.

I'm no longer going to ask myself whether I've been productive. Instead I'm going to ask, "Have I been purposeful today?" To me that simply means living in love. Sometimes love looks like laundry and answering emails and checking off what's on my list. Those are good and worthy things. But often it looks like the exact opposite, like we've done nothing at all. And that's okay too.

Our work doesn't determine our worth. Our accomplishments don't earn us God's acceptance. Our value isn't validated by our hustle. We are already and always loved.

God, thank you that whatever seems big in the eyes of this world is still small to you, and whatever is small in my life is still big to you.

. . . .

What's one small way you're living in love today?

Day 302

GOD WANTS TO HELP WHEN YOU DON'T KNOW WHAT TO DO

The fear of the LORD is the beginning of wisdom;
all who follow his precepts have good understanding.
To him belongs eternal praise. (Psalm 111:10)

When we see the word *fear* in Psalm 111:10, we can feel as if we should be afraid to come to God and ask for help. But this kind of fear is about awe and respect. It's recognizing God knows far more than we do and he alone is the source of what we need. The psalmist shares the progression that unfolds when we enter the process of truly seeking God:

Wisdom. We go to God for help and insight with a specific situation.

Understanding. We realize God truly knows what's best for us.

Praise. We joyfully affirm that God is good and he has helped us.

Whatever is on your mind today, you can bring it to God. You can freely say to him, "I don't know what to do. Will you please help me?" He may answer in many different ways—through his Word, through other believers, or from an entirely unexpected source. It may seem as if your heart knows in an instant what to do, or it may take a long time for the solution to come. He might grant you what you ask or take you on an entirely different path. *But God will answer.* And when he does, you can trust it will be what your heart has truly been searching for all along.

God, thank you for being the source of all wisdom.
I'm glad I can come to you when I'm not sure what to do.

· · · ·

What's a situation you need God's wisdom for today?

YOU'RE WANTED, CHOSEN, AND LOVED

God decided in advance to adopt us into his own family by bringing us to himself through Jesus Christ. This is what he wanted to do, and it gave him great pleasure. (Ephesians 1:5 NLT)

I scroll through the photos of adopted children. Each one has a caption below it with a message from the parents who chose them. The phrases jump out at me . . .

The best gift ever.

We are blessed that we could adopt her.

She has brought so much joy to our lives.

I nod in understanding because God brought us our daughter in an unexpected way as well. While every adoption story is different, they all have this in common: adoption is about choice and celebration, not obligation.

That's how God sees his relationship with us as well. God wanted us. He pursued us. He delighted in making us his forever. On the days when we can't understand why anyone would love us, it can seem impossible to believe God would see us that way. But his Word says it's true.

His affection for us isn't based on anything we do. Adoption isn't earned—it's received. Those kids didn't win their parents over by being perfect. They weren't selected because they were the best at something. They didn't get a family as a reward for following all the rules. Adoption is a wild act of grace. It's saying, "I want you as you are. And I will love you all your life—no matter what."

It gave God great pleasure to make us part of his family. And it still does today.

God, thank you for adopting me as part of your forever family.

· · · ·

What do you need from God today as his beloved child?

YOU'RE STRONGER
THAN YOU THINK YOU ARE

I thank Christ Jesus our Lord, who has given me strength to do his work. (1 Timothy 1:12 NLT)

It's early in the morning, and I'm at one of the last places I feel like being—the gym. I've done squats and presses, box step-ups, and a series of other exercises whose names I can't yet remember. I'm awkward and sweaty, already anticipating how sore I'll be tomorrow.

My friend Heather is in my class, and she's been coming for years. I tell her good job, and she says to me, "You're stronger than you think you are." At those words, I feel my spine straighten, my shoulders go back, my head raise.

When we're challenging ourselves, it's never going to feel easy or comfortable. We're not going to think, "Oh, yeah, I've totally got this." We're going to feel uncertain and hurt in places we didn't know we could. We're going to consider hiding in the bathroom or walking out the door. We're going to fixate on how far we still have to go instead of on all we've gained since we began.

This place of challenge is the growth zone. It's the bridge between what we can do today and what we're capable of tomorrow. If we avoid it so we never feel like we're not enough, then we're missing out on all we can become. Feeling weak isn't failure; it's the precursor to embracing our God-given power.

You're stronger than you think you are.

*God, thank you for giving me strength beyond
what I could ever have on my own.*

. . . .

How is God strengthening you today?

GOD HAS A DIFFERENT PERSPECTIVE

*"My thoughts are nothing like your thoughts," says the L*ORD.
"And my ways are far beyond anything you could imagine."
(Isaiah 55:8 NLT)

There's a fancy psychological word called *reframing*. Counselors and authors Linda and Charlie Bloom explain, "When we change our point of view on any given situation, the facts remain the same, but a deliberate shift is made in how we see it."[1] Reframing has been shown to contribute to better mental health, decreased anxiety, and increased resilience.

As believers, we can choose to see ourselves and our circumstances from God's perspective.

We see ourselves as broken. He sees us as beloved.

We see our circumstances as impossible. He sees a bigger plan.

We see our sin. He sees what Jesus did for us on the cross.

We see what's temporary. He sees what's eternal.

We see our limits. He sees how we can do anything through him.

When we find ourselves struggling with our thoughts, we can pause and ask, "God, how do you see me right now? How do you see my circumstances?"

Because of what Jesus did for us, God looks at us with love and grace. He is relentlessly *for* us. He is not looking for our flaws; he's looking for our best features—the ones he created, the ones he wants to use for a purpose. He's also looking at our best future, the one beyond our current situation and concerns that he's working out even now.

God, realign my view with yours.
Bring me peace through a new perspective.

. . . .

How do you see yourself right now? How does God see you?

Day 306

GOD WILL ALWAYS
COME FOR YOU

I will not leave you as orphans; I will come to you. (John 14:18)

God always comes for us. He came for Adam and Eve when they were hiding in shame. He came for his people when they were enslaved in Egypt. He came to Bethlehem. He's coming again.

He doesn't wait for us to get it together. He comes right into the garden while the fruit is still half-eaten on the ground. He finds us where we are hiding in fear and wrestling with regret. He comes to the places where we feel trapped, where it seems no matter how much we want change we just can't be free. He comes to the humble and mundane—not to the fancy, prepared inn but to the manger, to the places we deem far too improper and unlovely for him. He will come for us today and tomorrow and on our last day when we take our last breath.

Why? Because that's what love does. It comes when we are unworthy. It comes when we are overwhelmed. It comes when we are weary. It comes when we are insecure. It comes when we are doubting. It comes when we are broken. It comes when we just need a hug.

We do not need to earn our way to God. We only need to open our hearts and see that he is already here with us and he's told us, "Never will I leave you; never will I forsake you" (Heb. 13:5).

Love came for us. Love will always come for us. And, no matter what, he's not leaving.

God, thank you for always coming for me.
I am so grateful for your faithful love.

. . . .

What's one way you've seen God's love in your life lately?

GOD IS IN THE BEGINNING, MIDDLE, AND END

*From the rising of the sun to the place where it sets,
the name of the LORD is to be praised. (Psalm 113:3)*

I tend to be a "rising of the sun" praise-giver. When something is brand-new, I'm excited. I can clearly see God's hand, and I'm willing to follow wherever he's going. Then high noon comes and I'm hot, tired, and ready to be done. The praise I offered when the day began can quickly turn into discontent. And when the sun goes down on a dream in my life? I can get downright whiny.

God and I are working through this together. He's gently saying to my heart, *I'm equally present in all phases of the process. I'm there when you begin. I'm there in the difficult or glorious middle. I'm there when it comes to an end.*

God wants me to praise him through the whole process because it affirms that though my circumstances may change, *who he is stays the same*. We desperately need to know this, especially when the relationship is unraveling, the dream is fading, or the world around us is growing darker.

When God wants us to praise him, he's actually doing something deeply loving for us. We're human. We get scared. We don't like uncertainty. So by asking us to praise him even in our most difficult moments, God is creating a safe space for our hearts. He's reminding us that we are loved, we don't have to control everything, and there's a good plan for our lives.

God, you are my Savior from the rising of the sun to the setting of the same, even in the hard moments.

. . . .

What can you praise God for today?

YOU'RE NEVER "OVER THE HILL"

Though outwardly we are wasting away, yet inwardly we are being renewed day by day. (2 Corinthians 4:16)

My Grandpa Hollie showed me being "over the hill" is just a myth. In the ways that matter most, he was still going strong at ninety-three when he went home to Jesus. When I look at Scripture, I see that pattern too.

Our culture has sold us a lie. It tells us we peak in middle age. But I don't see that reflected anywhere in God's Word. Moses was eighty when God called him from the burning bush. Sarah was ninety when the promised Isaac was born. Anna was eighty-four when God let her be one of the first to recognize Jesus as the Messiah.

Rather than seeing ourselves as "over the hill," our journey toward Jesus can be one steady, faithful, continual, mysteriously glorious climb. We don't have to coast, count ourselves out, or compare now to then. Instead we're to press on and keep preparing for whatever God has next for us.

If you're still in the first half of life, then make choices now that will help put you in a position to finish strong. If you're in the second half of life, then realize God is not done with you. In fact, he may just be getting started. You are needed, valued, and you have more to offer than ever before.

Only God gets to decide when we're done. He will sustain us. It's not about being "over the hill" but being in the center of his will.

God, thank you that I will never be "over the hill" but instead always moving onward and upward with you.

. . . .

What's one way you've become stronger or wiser as you've gotten older?

GOD GIVES YOU PERMISSION TO LAUGH

Our mouths were filled with laughter,
our tongues with songs of joy. (Psalm 126:2)

When we're going through a hard time, we can begin to feel as if we don't have the right to laugh or feel joy anymore. But laughter in difficult moments, when it's done with sensitivity and grace, can help sustain us as well as others who are hurting too.

Laughter reminds us that we are not our circumstances.

It gives us a glimpse of a better future ahead.

It builds resilience—it's like exercise for our souls.

Laughter also tells the world that God has been good to us. And there is no time that's more powerful than when our circumstances seem to be truly bad. Does this mean we need to force cheerfulness when our hearts are breaking? Not at all. Honest grief gives God glory too. It shows we trust him with our pain. We just don't have to feel limited to always staying in sorrow. Lighter moments can help with heavy burdens.

Our bodies release feel-good chemicals when we laugh. God has designed you to benefit from giggles as well as tears. Both help us in hard times. Some of my favorite moments with people I love have started with tears of sadness and ended in tears of joy. There's something healing about experiencing the whole range of emotions together. "There is a time for everything . . . a time to weep and a time to laugh" (Eccles. 3:1, 4).

God, thank you for the gifts of tears and laughter. You have given us
so many ways to express our emotions.

. . . .

What's something that recently made you laugh?

GOD'S LOVE FOR YOU IS PERFECT

There is no fear in love. But perfect love drives out fear. (1 John 4:18)

The true meaning of the word *perfect* in the Bible is different from how we often think of it. It's about wholeness and completion. Here John is saying that when we fully know we're loved, we're no longer afraid.

John also says we can "know and rely on the love God has for us" (1 John 4:16). I've written my own versions of this, and I imagine you have too. I know and rely on the power of brownies to make me feel better. I know and rely on the comfort of a good ol' pity party. I know and rely on my ability to keep trying harder until I prove my worth. Amen? God doesn't condemn us for this; he loves us completely and as is. But he does whisper to our hearts, *I have something better for you.*

When we're anxious, we can ask ourselves, "What's one thing I can do that will help me know and rely on God's love for me?" We might tell a trustworthy friend or counselor we're not okay and let them speak encouragement to us. We may go for a walk in nature so we can see how God cares for the birds, the flowers, and us. We could pause to pray, listen to music that calms us, or embrace the gift of rest through a much-needed nap.

John discovered a heart-freeing truth we can embrace today. Even in our fearful moments, two things never change: God's love and our true identity. We are fully and always beloved.

God, help me know and rely on the love you have for me today.

· · · ·

What's one way you see God's love in your life today?

GOD SEES THE MAKINGS
OF A BEAUTIFUL MIRACLE

We know that all things work together for the good of those who love God, who are called according to his purpose. (Romans 8:28 CSB)

My mother-in-law stretches a newly finished quilt across the bed. "It's fantastic!" I tell her as I run my fingers along the careful stitching. She brushes off my compliment, "Oh, it's just a bunch of scraps put together."

As I consider this, I also think of how my life can sometimes look to me like a pile of scraps. I often don't see the possibility of beauty or usefulness in it. I see small. I see ordinary. I see leftover or left out. But in that moment, I suddenly realize God doesn't share this perspective. The maker of the universe, the One who is so big we can't even fathom his beginning or end, dares to endow our little scraps with the divine. He is the sewer of our stories.

This is the truth every tattered heart needs: there are no scraps in the hands of God, the One who works all things together for our good. Every little piece will one day have a place and a purpose. The things in your life you want to throw out, that you consider unworthy, that you try to hide, might be the very ones God wants to use.

Nothing in our lives is wasted.

Bit by bit, God is making something beautiful out of all of it—and all of us.

God, take every bit of what I go through—what's hard, happy, and everything in-between—and use it. Give me eyes that see from your perspective today.

. . . .

What is God making into something beautiful in your life?

YOU CAN GO AND SHOW

As he entered a village there, ten men with leprosy stood at a distance, crying out, "Jesus, Master, have mercy on us!" He looked at them and said, "Go show yourselves to the priests." And as they went, they were cleansed of their leprosy. (Luke 17:12–14 NLT)

I find so much hope in the story of the ten lepers in Luke 17. It's a gift for every human who is still a work in progress. "Jesus, Master, have mercy on us!" they cried. His answer? "Go show yourselves to the priests."

It's what happens next that amazes me. "And *as they went*, they were cleansed." It's tempting to hold back and stay stuck because we think we have to be completely healed before we *go and show*. We want our story to already have the happy ending, the bow to be tied around the package, the scars to be faded into invisibility. But I've found, as the lepers did, that the healing often happens along the way.

You don't have to wait for your healing to be complete before you start moving forward. You don't have to be whole before God sends you out. Of course we want healing to be a one-time, instantaneous event. We can even feel guilty if it's not. But I've found healing is more often a process. Sometimes when we ask God to move, he's asking us the same.

Nothing has the power to hold you back.

You are already worthy.

And God is already at work.

God, thank you that I don't have to be perfect to be part of your plan. You aren't asking me to hold back until my healing is complete.

. . . .

How has God healed you, whether emotionally, physically, or spiritually?

GOD CAN FREE YOU
FROM LIFE'S PRESSURE

When hard pressed, I cried to the LORD;
he brought me into a spacious place. (Psalm 118:5)

W e're not made to live under continual pressure. Our culture tries to tell us otherwise. We're supposed to pursue success, keep a busy social calendar, and have all the latest and greatest products on the market. We can even turn our faith into a part of the pressure we feel. We have to be at church every time the doors are open, pray more, and try harder.

But eventually something happens. Either we explode or we become completely deflated. Here's a reality of the universe whether we're talking about inanimate objects or our hearts: ongoing pressure simply isn't sustainable.

The day we realize we just can't do it all can feel like our biggest moment of failure. But it's actually the first step to true success. Saying "Enough!" isn't a word of weakness. It's one of the most powerful ones you can utter. It means that you believe God has a better way. It means you're not trying to gain the approval of others but rather you've decided to live for the joy of your master. It means you believe who the Creator made you is good and your identity is secure in him.

Only God knows what you truly need, and he will give you the power to do his will. Over time you'll find that instead of the world pushing in, you'll be living from a new space of strength and resilience deep within.

God, sometimes my life can feel so full of pressure.
I pray you would replace that with your freedom and power.

. . . .

What pressure do you need God to help you break free from today?

GOD DOESN'T EXPECT
YOU TO BE "FINE"

*I trusted in the L*ord *when I said,*
"I am greatly afflicted." (Psalm 116:10)

For years I believed that if I ever came to a place where I couldn't muster up the strength to say, "I'm fine," it would be a crisis of faith. So when I read the verse above, it stopped me in my tracks. I stared at the sentence and kept repeating it again and again in my mind. Something didn't seem right.

"I trusted in the Lord when I said, 'I am greatly afflicted.'"

I thought it should say instead, "I trusted in the Lord when I said, 'I'm doing great!'"

Yes, of course we can honor God by praising him in the happy times of life. But we also bring him glory by saying, "I'm having a really hard time right now." Coming to that place means we've stopped trying to protect ourselves. And that shows we believe we have a protector. It means we have stopped trying to be perfect. And that reflects our belief that God loves us just as we are. It means we're admitting we don't know what the future will hold. But we're confident that there is One who will hold us no matter what happens.

You don't have to be as strong as you think you do. You don't have to pretend. You don't have to put up a good front for God. He can handle where your heart really is today.

God, it's wonderful to me that I can be honest with you. I'm not "fine"
all the time, and there are some things I want to share with you.

. . . .

What do you want to tell God today about how you're really doing?

GOD WILL HELP YOU TRY AGAIN

I will instruct you and teach you in the way you should go;
I will counsel you with my loving eye on you. (Psalm 32:8)

Psalm 32 is one David wrote after confessing his affair with Bathsheba. If we think God's will is a tightrope, he has taken an epic tumble. But even then God does not say, "You've irrevocably blown it. I'm done with you."

Instead it's as if he's taking David by the hand, lifting him up, and saying, "Try again." Perhaps David felt paralyzed with fear. Certainly he felt he couldn't trust himself. But God is there to be the one David can trust as a guide who will "instruct you and teach you in the way you should go."

Then there's the most astonishing line of all: "I will counsel you with my loving eye on you." My loving eye. Not my judgmental eye. Not my harsh and condemning eye. Not my "I saw that coming" eye. No, even in the moments when we least deserve it God is watching over us with love.

Sometimes we put far more pressure on ourselves to know exactly what God wants us to do next than is really needed. If we are trying to be obedient, then God sees our hearts, and he can gently redirect us along the way. Our role is simply to be willing to move forward in faith as best we can with what we know. It's God's responsibility to make sure we get there.

God's will isn't a tightrope after all. It's a journey with someone who loves us.

God, instruct me and teach me in the way I should go.

· · · ·

What is the next step God is inviting you to take?

YOU CAN WORK WITH
ALL YOUR HEART

So we rebuilt the wall till all of it reached half its height, for the people worked with all their heart. (Nehemiah 4:6)

The wall around Jerusalem is broken down. Threats abound. One man, Nehemiah, decides that things must be different. It's time for change. With the help of others, he sets about repairing and restoring. In the face of many obstacles, progress continues to be made. One reason? Because they worked with all their heart.

On the journey to our goals, especially in our logical culture, we can leave our hearts out of the process. We intellectually create task lists, take measurements, and carry on without taking time to listen to our hearts. Why does your heart *really* want to achieve a goal?

The deeper answer is more likely to be something along these lines: "To have more energy to invest in the relationships God has placed in my life" or "To be able to meet more practical needs in the lives of others through giving."

When you find your heart answer, you'll know it because everything within you will say a resounding yes, and you'll feel a strong desire to push forward no matter what. Keep pressing in until you find the heart motivation that energizes you. Ask God to reveal it to you as well. He knows your heart better than anyone—even you.

Nehemiah and his workers finished the wall. What seemed like an impossible task became a reality. Yes, it required their hands. But if that was all it involved, they would have given up when the going got tough. Instead their hearts pushed them through, and they saw God do more than they could even have imagined.

God, help me to work with all my heart today.

. . . .

What's a goal in your life?

YOUR WATERS WILL RECEDE

But God remembered Noah and all the wild animals and livestock with him in the boat. He sent a wind to blow across the earth, and the floodwaters began to recede. (Genesis 8:1 NLT)

At the end of a long day, I tell God all the things on my mind—the worries and fears, questions and concerns. I stand at the window and look out over a gray afternoon. Then I see it in the distance—a rainbow. I turn to my whiteboard and I write something new: Write, Pray, Wait. As soon as I do it feels like my heart sighs in relief.

I think then of Noah after the flood when the first rainbow appeared. Surely as soon as the last drop of rain fell he was ready to get off that boat. But it took time for the waters to recede. So he stayed where God had placed him. He prayed. He waited. Then finally, the time was right to leave the ark, to embrace what God had next for him.

When we've had a flood in our lives—a significant change or a loss or even a new opportunity that threatens to overwhelm us—it can be tempting to want to get back to "normal" as quickly as possible. But it takes time for the waters to recede in our lives too. And even when they do, things never go back to the way they were before. We learn a new normal, a different way of being. Sometimes the bravest move is to stay where you are and simply see what God will do.

God, give me the wisdom to know when to move forward and when it's time to simply be still and wait for you.

. . . .

What are you waiting for right now?

IT'S OKAY IF YOU GET LONELY

Each heart knows its own bitterness,
and no one else can fully share its joy. (Proverbs 14:10 NLT)

Loneliness is a hard thing to talk about in this era of friending and liking and sharing with the entire universe. But there's no shame in being lonely sometimes.

Loneliness is really a desire to be completely connected to someone else. And, in this world, that's simply not possible. Yes, there are friendships made at summer camp and in boardrooms. There are marriages that last over half a century. There are sisters we are born to and those of our own making. But even then, even those don't mean that sometimes we won't feel lonely. I say this not to be discouraging but to help us stop taking loneliness personally.

I think loneliness tells us better than perhaps anything else what we really want from community. If I'm always lonely in groups, then I am probably craving one-on-one time, a meaningful conversation over coffee. If I always leave the coffee shop feeling disconnected, then perhaps what I really need is to play and have fun with a lively tribe. Loneliness also makes us appreciate the people we do have in our lives. And loneliness draws us closer to Jesus, the only one who knows us completely and fully.

Loneliness doesn't have to be a secret we keep from each other. Instead it's something we all have in common that can bring us together. We all live with these two truths: Yes, sometimes we are lonely. Yes, we are always loved.

God, when I feel alone, remind me you are
with me and comfort my heart.

. . . .

Who in your life might be lonely today?

GOD IS SHAPING YOUR HEART

We are the clay, you are the potter;
we are all the work of your hand. (Isaiah 64:8)

I'm sitting in a pottery class for beginners with my daughter. The instructor says, "This is your clay. Today we are going to shape it into hearts." We trace outlines on the surface with a thin stick, then dig deep. All that is not necessary or useful is stripped away.

"Now you can design them however you'd like." This work is intimate and personal. There is no mass production. No uniformity or conformity. It would be impossible to replicate one of these hearts. If we ever wonder if God wants us to be like someone else, ever worry he's disinterested in the details of our lives, ever fret he's after machine-like perfection with us, then all we need to remember is that he is a potter.

After we shape our clay, we paint it. But before this comes a disclaimer from the instructor: "When the clay goes through the fire, it will come out white." This is beautiful and familiar to me, the way trials bring out something unexpectedly lovely and strong in us.

This clay has but one role: to yield itself to my care. It has nothing to worry about, to fear, to strive for as long as it remains in my hands. The same is true of our hearts. We are dirt and we are the crafts of divinity. We are dust and delight. We are in progress and already perfectly loved.

God, thank you that the burden of becoming doesn't rest on me;
you will complete the work you are doing in my life, in my heart.

. . . .

How is God shaping your heart in this season of your life?

GOD WILL BE FAITHFUL TO YOU

Let us hold unswervingly to the hope we profess, for he who promised is faithful. (Hebrews 10:23)

Here's my official definition of faithfulness, courtesy of my Southern roots. Faithfulness is what folks around here like to call "stick-to-it-iveness." It means you see it through, stay committed, hold on in the ups and downs. It's the "for better or worse" in the vows. It's a relentless resilience that simply will not give up, give in, or let go—no matter what.

This is how God loves us. His commitment to us doesn't waver based on how "good" we are on any given day. It doesn't depend on our performance or perfection. Our divine partner isn't waiting to walk out and slam the door behind him because we forgot the milk or burned the toast or hogged the sheets. Or much, much worse.

And God asks that we, in return, be faithful to him too. That we don't shred our commitment when the prayer isn't answered or the plans don't work out or we just can't feel his love for us even though it's as real as the sun above us.

We'll share a lifetime with God, followed by forever. Faithfulness happens one moment, one day, one eternity at a time.

God, help me stay fully devoted to you. And thank you that you promise you will be fully faithful to me too.

. . . .

How has God been faithful to you?

WHEN LIFE GETS HARD

We share in his sufferings in order that we may also share in his glory. (Romans 8:17)

When we think of God's will for our lives, it's easy to picture a path that takes us away from suffering rather than into it. Yet Scripture shows us again and again that suffering is part of the journey. That means when life gets hard, we don't have to say, "I must be doing something wrong." Instead, we can find comfort in knowing that Christ himself faced suffering as he fulfilled his mission of redeeming the world.

Sometimes we go to the other extreme and believe we must suffer all the time in order to be godly. But Scripture makes it clear that God desires a life of joy for us. Suffering is intended to be temporary—whether it is resolved in this life or when we enter eternity. God wants us to thrive. Even Jesus endured the cross "for the joy set before him" (Heb. 12:2). So we are not to be surprised by suffering, yet we're also not to simply accept it as the way things must be forever. We can ask God, "What is your purpose in this?"

You will have hard days. You will face disappointments. You will experience setbacks. Yet, in the middle of this, you can trust that God's purposes will prevail and you are truly, deeply loved.

God, thank you that I can trust you even in the middle of suffering.

. . . .

Who in your life is going through a difficult time
and needs encouragement?

GOD LOOKS AT YOU THROUGH EYES OF LOVE

She gave this name to the LORD who spoke to her: "You are the God who sees me," for she said, "I have now seen the One who sees me." (Genesis 16:13)

When we imagine how God might look at us, it can seem as if he must do so with the cool stare of a professional photographer, as if he's analyzing us, finding the faults and flaws. But no, he is looking at us as a camera-toting dear friend would. The psalmist says, "The LORD watches over all who love him" (Ps. 145:20). In Genesis 16, Hagar discovered this when she found herself alone in the desert with her child, sure they would soon die. God met her there, and while she felt as if she was seeing him for the first time, she realized he had seen her all along.

Wherever we are today, God sees not only our skin but also our souls, our strengths, and our scars. What we choose to show the world and everything we hide from it. And he loves every part of us. Not because we are perfect but because when he looks at us he also sees what Jesus did on the cross. Our sin has been washed away, the darkness has been defeated, and we have been restored to the beauty for which we were formed.

One day when we enter heaven, we will say with Hagar, "I have now seen the One who sees me." Until then, someone is always watching over us with love.

God, you are the one who watches over me.
Thank you for looking at me through eyes of love.

. . . .

Who reflects the heart of God in your life
by seeing you through eyes of love?

YOU'RE A WORLD-CHANGER

Serve one another humbly in love. (Galatians 5:13)

Being a world-changer simply means touching the heart of one person at a time through whatever gifts we've been given right where we are today. That one person for you might be a friend, coworker, someone in your family, or a stranger on the street.

Your gift might be words or encouragement, organizing or baking, leading or creating spreadsheets. We can be equally impactful holding a microphone or heating mac-and-cheese in the microwave for the people we love. We can make a difference from a downtown office or the driver's seat of a minivan.

This is the lie the enemy would like us to believe: only certain people are world-changers, the kind who seem to do big, extraordinary things. But God alone is big and extraordinary. He uses small, ordinary people to change the world every day because that's the only kind there are, the only kind there will ever be. That includes you and me.

So if, like me, you've ever wondered if what you're doing matters, if you've been unsure you're making a difference, if you've been tempted to compare, then let's pause together and realign our perspective with God's heart. He has placed us here for such a time as this, and he is working in and through us in ways beyond what we can see. What seems like nothing at all in this moment might just change all of eternity.

God, thank you for giving meaning to every moment of my life, whether big or small.

. . . .

What's one way you can love God and others today?

GOD HAS WORDS FOR YOUR HEART TO HOLD ON TO

Give thanks to the LORD, for he is good.
His love endures forever. (Psalm 136:1)

The phrase "His love endures forever" appears thirty-six times in Psalm 136. The psalmist describes all kinds of circumstances the Israelites have faced. Some challenging and others joyful. After each one he reaffirms the love of God. The chosen people of Israel have been through many changes, and yet this one thing remains the same: God's love endures forever.

There are particular truths we each personally need more at certain times. Like the psalmist repeating the phrase "his love endures forever," those truths can add stability in the shaky circumstances we're experiencing. They can also influence our actions. When we find ourselves unsure of what to do or how to respond, they give us a place to go back to where we can stand firm.

The specific truth we need for a certain time in our lives often starts with a whisper in our hearts. Then God reveals it in other ways too—through his Word, wise friends, and even unexpected avenues. Our part is primarily to keep our ears and hearts open to receive what he has for us. Then we build on it by living it out.

What truth keeps coming back to your mind and heart? Turn it into part of the foundation for your life that will give you a firm place to stand no matter what happens.

God, help me to hear what you're saying to me
and show me how I can apply it.

. . . .

What's a truth you want to remember in this season of your life?

GOD ISN'T HOLDING
ANYTHING AGAINST YOU

If you, LORD, kept a record of sins,
Lord, who could stand?
But with you there is forgiveness,
so that we can, with reverence, serve you. (Psalm 130:3–4)

God keeps no record of wrongs. He doesn't have a file with your past in it. He's not racking up fines for you to pay when you get to the gates of glory. We're changed by love, not the law. And at the center of love is forgiveness.

When we deeply, truly believe we're forgiven, then we begin to respond from a new place. We have appreciation for the One who has canceled our debts, and we long to serve out of joy. So if you've been worried that the hard times you're facing are simply because you "have to pay your dues," then you can let that fear go.

God doesn't work that way with us. When he forgives us, he means it. We may face natural consequences, of course. But God is not saying, "Oh, you're asking me for a blessing today? Well, I'd love to give that to you, but it looks like you still need to pay for something you did years ago." What's done is done.

Today we truly can "approach God's throne of grace with confidence, so that we may receive mercy and find grace to help us in our time of need" (Heb. 4:16). Your Savior is always willing to give you grace.

God, your forgiveness is more than I can comprehend or ever deserve.
I'm so glad you keep no record of wrongs.
Instead you want to give me grace and bless my life.

· · · ·

What do you need to receive God's grace for today?

GOD WILL WIPE EVERY TEAR FROM YOUR EYES

He will wipe every tear from their eyes, and there will be no more death or sorrow or crying or pain. All these things are gone forever.
(Revelation 21:4 NLT)

The moment when God wipes all the tears from our eyes will also be the end of our hurt. We will never again experience fear. We won't worry, doubt, or second-guess ourselves. We'll live with complete peace, joy, and love. We catch glimpses of that in this life, perhaps when we're laughing with friends on a summer evening, watching a bride walk down the aisle, holding a baby in our arms, creating art that lights us up inside, watching a bird soar or a dolphin swim. They're moments when we have no self-consciousness, when we're caught up in something bigger and wilder than we are, when the critical voice inside us goes silent in awe. We're no longer anxious; we're fully absorbed in the moment.

In heaven, we will live like this always. John doesn't say we'll stand around singing forever (so you can stop feeling bad if you thought that actually sounded pretty boring). We'll first sit down to a feast, to a grand celebration. We'll meet Jesus face-to-face. We'll reconnect with people we love. We'll fully become who we were created to be all along. All our fear will finally be gone. Close your eyes and imagine it for a moment.

Between now and then, we're all just on a journey home.

God, thank you for the journey I'm on with you.

· · · ·

What's a truth you want to remember today?

YOU ARE ALREADY ACCEPTED

Christ accepted you. (Romans 15:7)

I remember standing on the edge of a neighborhood yard, watching as a group of kids played catch. All I wanted was a ball tossed my direction. I remember surveying a high school lunchroom full of giggly teenage girls chatting about their weekends. All I wanted was a seat at the table. I remember sending out book proposals to publishers whose doors seemed locked to new, unknown authors like me. All I wanted was a key.

But what I really longed for in those situations was acceptance. My heart yearned to know I had a place and to be assured I was loved, for someone to say, "I choose you." It took me a long time to learn that someone had already done all those things.

Jesus called my name as a little girl and tossed the ball of faith in my direction. He gave me a place on his team. Jesus gave me strengths, gifts, and ways to serve others. He created a plan and purpose for my life. He had a seat at his table no one else could fill. Jesus revealed that his mission for me doesn't require someone else opening a door. Instead it's about keeping the door of my own heart open to how he wants to use me each day.

I used to believe acceptance was something someone else had to give me. I'm starting to see it's about embracing what's already mine. I am already accepted. You are already accepted. Our stories may be totally different, but that heart-freeing truth is the same for all of us today.

God, thank you for accepting me. Help me to fully receive that gift today.

. . . .

When have you felt most accepted?

YOU CAN TRUST GOD'S PLANS

This foolish plan of God is wiser than the wisest of human plans.
(1 Corinthians 1:25 NLT)

There's nothing wrong with planning. What causes trouble is when I start trusting in my plans rather than God's purposes. I know the symptoms: weariness, discouragement, stress, staring at the ceiling at night, working way too long. I've discovered my planning tendencies go into overdrive for one reason: fear. I'm worried that things won't work out the way I hope. I'm feeling insecure about my calling. I'm forgetting that God has brought me this far and he will not leave me now. I think that I have to figure everything out. I need to make it all happen.

What I'm forgetting is that what God does hardly ever makes any sense at all. Making a shepherd boy the greatest king to ever rule Israel. Sending the Savior of the world to a manger. Choosing an uneducated, inexperienced group of men to spread the gospel. No one would have put those on their whiteboard in a meeting. No one would have added them to a PowerPoint. No one would have thought them worthy of a bullet point in a strategic plan. *But God did.*

This is what I'm coming to understand: life isn't about our plans; it's about God's purposes. He will make sure they happen even in our weakness, in our wandering, in our uncertainty. That's what makes us brave, what gives us the strength to keep going, what our hearts can trust in today and always.

God, your purposes are good, and I choose to trust you with my future.

. . . .

What plan do you need to place in God's hands today?

YOUR AWKWARDNESS IS WELCOME

We belong to each other, and each needs all the others. (Romans 12:5 TLB)

Our world tells us to post the perfect pictures on Instagram. Work the crowd. Craft an image. Create an audience instead of meaningful relationships. Avoid all the awkward.

But despite its difficulties, I'm falling in love with the awkward. It's where we find out which one of our friends laughs so hard she snorts. It's where we discover how lovely the ugly cry can be. It's where we remember we are not God—and that is a very good thing. It's where we learn to believe we're loved for who we are and not who we sometimes wish we could be.

Awkward is the price of admission for authentic connection. It costs us; oh, how it does. It costs us our pride and our desire to be seen as perfect and sometimes our comfortable place on the couch.

The people who impress me most these days are not the ones on stages or those with the most likes on their social media pages. I'm impressed with the folks who show up in the everyday and say, "Here I am. There you are. Let's figure out how to love each other." That is a brave, beautiful, world-changing thing.

Jesus didn't come to a throne but to a manger. He didn't seek a spotlight but a cross. He didn't stay at a distance but instead walked the dusty, messy roads with us. In other words, he could have made everyone love him, but instead he pursued hearts one by one. He still does.

May he give us the courage to do the same.

God, give me the courage to show up as I am and love like you do.

· · · ·

What gives you the courage to show up as you are?

GOD IS NOT TIRED OF YOU

He will not let your foot slip—
he who watches over you will not slumber;
indeed, he who watches over Israel
will neither slumber nor sleep. (Psalm 121:3–4)

God doesn't sleep. Not a wink. While you're safely dreaming, he's watching over you. While you're going about your day, he sees every detail. He never needs to lean back in his chair to shut his eyes for a moment. He doesn't nod off in meetings. He won't miss your call for help because he's snoozing on the sofa.

Not only does God not sleep, he doesn't even get tired. He always has enough energy to engage with you. He always has enough time to listen to your heart. He always has the power to meet your needs. It doesn't matter what time of the day or night it may be—God is ready to respond.

God is not tired. *And he is not tired of you.* No matter how many times you've brought the same request to him. No matter how often you've asked for help with the same struggle. No matter how frequently you've needed to just sit and cry with him. He can handle all of it. You are not too much for God.

Not only that, he *wants* to be there for you. He's not responding to you because he has to—he's doing so because he loves you. His love is not one of obligation. It's a love of choice. He chose you. He delights in you. He invites you to come to him anytime, day or night.

God, it's such a relief to realize you never grow tired.
You always have enough time and energy for me.

. . . .

What does your heart need or want from God today?

GOD IS YOUR FOREVER HUSBAND

> *For your Maker is your husband—*
> *the LORD Almighty is his name—*
> *the Holy One of Israel is your Redeemer;*
> *he is called the God of all the earth. (Isaiah 54:5)*

A relationship with a man in this life was never supposed to be the fulfillment of the desire in our hearts for a perfect husband. It is only a preview and prototype of what we're created to experience with God in eternity.

God uses marital language to describe his relationship with his people. He is the bridegroom. We are the bride. He is the husband. We are the wife. He woos us. He cherishes us. He pursues our hearts. He stays faithful to us always. We are truly, deeply loved.

We may get lovely glimpses of that in this life, but for now our vision is limited. We live out that grand love story in the day-to-day. When we react by demanding that those around us fulfill all the needs within us, we set them up for failure. And when we expect everything to be perfect in the here and now, we set ourselves up for disillusionment.

We are the in-between people, the bride walking down the aisle, which on this earth sometimes seems more like a long dirt road. Still we press on in our white lace. We put a flower in our hair. We set our eyes on the horizon of this life. Because we are the hopers and the hopeless romantics, the ones who scandalously believe our forever-and-ever love story is only just beginning and the best is yet to be.

> *God, there is a longing inside me for perfect love,*
> *and you are the only one who can fulfill it.*
>
> . . . .
>
> How has God loved you like a husband?

JESUS IS YOUR PERFECTER

By one sacrifice he has made perfect forever those who are being made holy. (Hebrews 10:14)

In our modern world and language, *perfect* means "flawless." But in biblical terms, it is different. It is something more like "whole" and "complete." When Scripture says perfect, it's more like a tree growing, roots going deeper, branches spreading wider, fruit ripening in the afternoon sun.

Hebrews tells us, "By one sacrifice he has made perfect forever those who are being made holy." When Jesus died on the cross, he said, "It is finished." So when we receive what he did on our behalf, we are instantly and eternally *positionally* perfect in God's eyes. It is done. We are the broken made whole. Yet we live on this earth, and we are still learning to live out who we already are; we are being made more like Jesus every day.

We don't need a list of rules to keep. We need a Savior. We don't need to get our act together. We need a loving God who acts on our behalf. We don't need to be without flaws. We need to understand that perfect is always and only about faith. It's not something we do; it's something we believe and receive through Jesus's death on the cross and his resurrection.

This is our story and our truth and our sure hope: we are imperfect people who are perfectly loved by a perfect God.

---

*Jesus, thank you for what you have done
and are still doing in and for me.*

. . . .

How is Jesus making you more like him in this season of your life?

GOD WILL TRAIN YOU TO DO BATTLE

Praise be to the LORD my Rock,
who trains my hands for war,
my fingers for battle.
He is my loving God and my fortress,
my stronghold and my deliverer,
my shield, in whom I take refuge. (Psalm 144:1–2)

David says that God "trains my hands for war" and then adds that God is "my stronghold and my deliverer." How do those two fit together? It seems there are times when God asks us to go to the front lines. What David recognizes is that God never sends us into those situations unprepared. He teaches us what we need to know for victory. He also equips us with armor to protect us.

There are other times when God knows we're too weary or wounded to go to battle. When we can't fight, he does so on our behalf. "The LORD will fight for you; you need only to be still" (Exod. 14:14). He's not going to send you into a situation where you can't win.

We can ask God to show us if it's time to fight or be still. You can say to God, "I know you have promised me victory. Please show me the way you want that to happen. Give me courage if it's time to fight, and give me patience if it's time to wait for you to act on my behalf." He'll show you what to do, and he'll be with you through the battle. You're already more than a conqueror, and you can never lose with God on your side.

God, you are the one who gives me victory.
You train me for war, and you also fight for me.

. . . .

What battle do you need God to fight for you today?

YOUR LOVE IS
A POWERFUL WEAPON

*Then Simon Peter, who had a sword, drew it and struck the high
priest's servant, cutting off his right ear. (John 18:10)*

What happens when you cut off someone's ear like Peter did? The person can no longer hear you. This means so much more has been cut off too—communication, understanding, reconciliation, relationship.

I might say, "I would never cut off someone's ear!" But haven't I done it? My swords have been self-righteous words, criticism, judgment, dismissal of those I might be tempted to label "the enemy." We swing the sword of our words in defense of what we believe is right, but there are unintended consequences. This is not the way of the kingdom. "Jesus commanded Peter, 'Put your sword away!'" (John 18:11).

I don't think this means we aren't to fight the darkness. But I do believe it means we are to understand there's a time and place and different way to do so. After Peter swung the sword, Jesus still got arrested. He went to trial, stretched out on a cross, rose from the grave. In doing so, he fought (and won) the greatest battle ever. Here's what stands out to me: none of this involved ear-slashing, shouting, or even sneaky finger-pointing.

Instead Jesus fought with love. Not the fluffy, cotton-candy kind. No, the sort that is willing to be laid wide open, to sacrifice, to reach out to even our enemies. Love is still the most powerful weapon in the world.

In this world we can choose what kind of warriors we will be. Let's fight with love and gentleness and kindness. In other words, let's fight like Jesus.

*God, love through me today in ways
that change the world one heart at a time.*

. . . .

How have you seen love be powerful?

GOD IS YOUR BUILDER

For every house is built by someone, but God is the builder of every-thing. (Hebrews 3:4)

Building is a *process*. The site must be cleared. The foundation laid. There's the plumbing, the framing, the electrical wiring. Here is the secret every builder knows: the house cannot make itself. It must have an outside force to bring forth its potential. We think that we have to "build" ourselves by being good and trying hard, but all the while Jesus is simply saying, "All you need to do is let me do my work in you."

Does this work always go smoothly? Oh, no, sometimes the house resists. The wall tilts sideways. The pipe bursts. The concrete floor gets a crack right through it like a little canyon. When this happens, the builder doesn't say, "Well, this house isn't perfect anymore. Might as well give up and start on the one next door." No, a builder understands such complications are bound to be part of getting to the finish. A builder sets the wall right, fixes the leak, repairs the foundation. Because to a builder, these problems are not a disqualification; they are only a delay.

I think of God, the builder, creating the heavens and the earth, Adam and Eve. He looked at his handiwork and said, "It is good." He has not stopped building since. When this life is over, we'll stand before him, complete, and I believe he'll say, "It is good" again on that day.

God, you are the one who makes me who I am.
Thank you for the work you're doing in my life.

. . . .

What is God building in your heart and life today?

GOD DOESN'T WANT YOU TO STAY BROKEN

*He heals the brokenhearted
and binds up their wounds. (Psalm 147:3)*

God doesn't want us to stay broken in any area of our lives. He's not an insurance adjuster holding out until the last minute before he's willing to repair the damage. He wants us to be whole. He wants to heal our hearts. He wants to restore what has been damaged.

We can come to him and say, "I'm tempted to believe this is small and I shouldn't even bother you with it. But I can see this hurt is there, and I need your help." He's ready and willing to answer.

If we don't ask for him to repair our souls as we go, we can find ourselves full of broken places. We don't have to let that happen. Every time we need to, we can stop and say, "Ouch. Lord, please heal my broken heart and bind up this wound."

On our journey together you've been learning to live in new ways. I hope you're discovering it's okay to go to God as often as needed. It's okay to share your feelings with him. It's okay to stop trying so hard and lean on his grace instead.

Keep pursuing more wholeness in your life in whatever ways you need to. Seek out more resources, see a counselor, or confide in a trusted friend. When you say, "I will not live with ongoing brokenness," it's not an admission of weakness. It's an act of great courage.

God, you are the God who sees every part of me. You know the broken places in my life, and you want to make them whole again.

· · · ·

What's a broken place in your life you want
to ask God to make whole again?

GOD CAN FILL IN
THE GAPS FOR YOU

Human hands can't serve his needs—for he has no needs. He himself gives life and breath to everything, and he satisfies every need. (Acts 17:25 NLT)

It's okay to cut back sometimes. It's all right to say, "At another time I would love to do that, but I simply can't right now." It's allowable to admit, "I really need some extra rest right now." You're not a human treadmill, and you can't sustain the same pace all the time. That's simply not how we're created.

When we think about pulling back or slowing down, instantly we can feel the fear. What will happen? The answer: whatever needs to happen. Because God will fill in the gaps for what you lack right now. Jesus turned a few fish and loaves of bread into a meal for thousands. He can turn whatever you have to offer into enough too.

Sometimes we need to step back to realize, in the best possible way, that the world doesn't rely on us as much as we think. It does our hearts good to have a little "reality check" once in a while. When we rest, we're reminded that we're not God.

That means knowing we're not responsible for the universe. It's believing God can turn whatever we have to give into what's needed—even if we believe we should be able to do more. It's trusting that we are not on this earth for striving and work but for worship.

You have permission to slow down, do less, and rest more today.

God, thank you that you are taking care of everything, including me.

. . . .

What's one thing you can say no to or do less of today?

Day 338

GOD GIVES YOU PURPOSE

But the plans of the LORD stand firm forever,
the purposes of his heart through all generations. (Psalm 33:11)

What's my purpose? When we ask this question and silence seems to be the answer, we often go searching. *My purpose is out there somewhere,* we think, *and one day I'll find it.*

We live in a culture that tells us the purpose of life is about *us*. We must find that *one thing* we are here to do and then all will be well; we will be whole. But when I look closer at how *purpose* is used in Scripture, there's a different story. Over and over when purpose is described, it comes from God and belongs to him. What changes everything is when we understand that a meaningful life is not just about finding our purpose but joining God's.

If we want to be part of God's purposes today, then we simply love him, others, and ourselves. That means standing at the kitchen sink washing dishes can be worship. It means that another diaper changed can be an act of sacred service. It means the work project done well can be an offering. It means we don't have to find purpose only "out there." It can also be "right here."

The square of earth you are standing on is the only place in all of history and the entire universe where both you and God are right now. It's where his purposes and you, a person created by him, come together. This is not small or inconsequential. It is beautiful and powerful. It is holy, meaningful ground.

God, you are the one who is working out his purposes
in all of history, eternity, and me.

. . . .

How can you find purpose in your ordinary life today?

GOD GIVES WHAT YOU NEED

*Better to have one handful with quietness
than two handfuls with hard work
and chasing the wind. (Ecclesiastes 4:6 NLT)*

In a season of striving, I read this verse in Ecclesiastes and sensed God asking me, *Can you be satisfied with one handful?* Because here's how we're meant to live: with one hand holding tight to what God has given us—love, joy, peace, grace, goodness—and the other hand empty and open for whatever else he would have us receive. Two handfuls mean we're clenching our fists through life. We're gritting our teeth. We're hanging on with all our might. Two handfuls mean we're tired.

We live in a world that tells us more is always better, but that's not true. Sometimes more is overwhelming. Sometimes more weighs us down. Sometimes more is too much. We're not made to have it all. We're made to have exactly what our good God provides for us. He alone knows the right amount, the perfect timing, and what will truly satisfy our souls.

Thankfully, God generously offers us what all tired people need. Even if the world around us keeps unavoidably spinning—the toddlers keep throwing Cheerios, the projects keep coming, the calendar keeps filling—we can wrap our fingers around God's provision in every moment. And we can let go of all we've grasped that was never meant for us. We can reach out and take hold of the inexplicable peace that has been promised us today. And we can let go of our striving so we can receive what's infinitely better: God's unconditional love and grace.

*God, give me the wisdom to receive what you have for me
and the courage to let go of the rest.*

. . . .

What do you want to receive from God today?

GOD IS YOUR HEALER

By his wounds we are healed. (Isaiah 53:5)

To call God "Healer" is a brave thing because he is mysterious in his ways. It's tempting to say, "You are good only if you heal in the way and time we want."

Sin-sickness, rejection infection, ravages of addiction, scratch marks of fear, limp of loss, fracture of relationships—humanity is a walking hospital filled with the wounded. God is in the halls and in every room, caring about and tending to every bit of it. From the faintest sneeze to the shattered soul. Our pain is never too small or too big for him. His relentless desire is to bring us into complete wholeness and health. He proved it by stretching out on a cross, by taking our pain and making it his. It is "by his wounds we are healed."

The verb in this verse is present tense—"we *are* healed." It has already happened. It is already true. This means when we pray for healing there is never an "if," only a "when" and a "how." Some in eternity, some now. What God does is about his eternal purposes and faithfulness, not our efforts or the size of our faith. We don't have to try hard or be good to get the answer we want. God is not a manipulator; he is a comforter and miracle-maker.

So we wait. We pray. We wrestle. We hope. Sometimes we rejoice. Sometimes we weep. And always we give ourselves over to the only healer with healed, nail-scarred hands.

God, please bring healing in the ways you know are best even when it's beyond my understanding.

. . . .

How have you seen God be a healer?

GOD INVITES YOU TO CELEBRATE

They celebrate your abundant goodness. (Psalm 145:7)

When a runner receives a gold medal in the Olympics, it seems like it's only about one step across a finish line on a particular day. And yet it's really the culmination of a journey of a thousand steps with many milestones along the way.

As we pursue change in our lives, it's easy to become fixated on the "gold medal"—whatever we ultimately want to accomplish. But life isn't about achievement. Instead it's about an intimate journey with Jesus.

In the Old Testament God often told Israel to set up tangible reminders of what he'd done for them. In other words, they were to pause and reflect. Through the feasts he commanded, they were also to celebrate. Celebration has gotten a bad rap in today's Christian culture. It's often overlooked as frivolous or even worldly. Yet it's unmistakably present in the story of God's people.

When you and God accomplish something together—whether it's conquering an obstacle, overcoming a struggle, or facing a fear—then take time to celebrate with him. You can do so in a variety of ways. For example, you could . . .

Have a meal at your favorite restaurant.

Record your victory in a journal.

Purchase a small item that reminds you of how far you've come.

What matters is a tangible expression of this moment in time. Doing so gives us strength to move forward and also leaves a trail of reminders for us to look back on when things get tough.

What brings you joy? How do you celebrate? Dare to celebrate along the way rather than waiting to cross the finish line.

God, thank you for inviting me to celebrate with you.

. . . .

What can you celebrate with God today?

GOD WILL MAKE YOUR STEPS FIRM

The LORD makes firm the steps
of the one who delights in him. (Psalm 37:23)

The ice spread across the sidewalk in a thin layer. I tried to be brave and navigate the few steps to my driveway. I should have known better. It only took a moment for me to lose my balance. I called for my husband and he quickly came to my rescue. As soon as I stumbled, a strong hand under my elbow held me up.

That's essentially what changes when we begin to walk with Jesus. Life is still precarious. We'll have slick situations and challenging circumstances to navigate. But even when we feel a bit unsteady, we no longer have to worry about falling. Someone bigger and stronger than we are is right by our side to keep us standing.

I didn't even see the patch of ice I slipped on that day. "Black ice" can be invisible until you're right on top of it. Even when the surface of our future seems smooth, there can be more ahead than we think. Only Jesus knows where the slick spots are and how we can make it through them.

The best time to ask for help is before our footsteps falter. But even if we find ourselves in the middle of an unexpected challenge, it's never too late to ask for help. Jesus is always ready and willing to hold us up when we start to stumble.

God, life can be more challenging than it seems on the surface.
When I begin to slip, please hold me up.

. . . .

What's an area of your life where you could easily slip or stumble?
How is God helping you stand firm?

JESUS IS YOUR LIVING WORD

The Word became flesh and made his dwelling among us. We have seen his glory, the glory of the one and only Son, who came from the Father, full of grace and truth. (John 1:14)

When we think of Jesus being the "Word," we can picture dusty old Bibles with red letters and thick ribbon bookmarks, the kind that are set on coffee tables or shelves. But the Word is "alive and active" (Heb. 4:12) because the Word is a person. This has always been so.

"In the beginning was the Word, and the Word was with God, and the Word was God. He was with God in the beginning. Through him all things were made; without him nothing was made that has been made" (John 1:1–3). The Word created peacocks and tomatoes and the freckles on noses. Then the Word came into that creation. He took on flesh—he had eyelashes and elbows and pinky toes. He walked dirty streets and ate fish roasted over open fires and napped on the deck of a boat. In other words, *the Word has always been about the spiritual becoming the tangible, the divine entering our everyday lives.*

The Word is more than lines on a page. He is the narrator of our lives. He is the beginning and the end and the middle of the story. He is still creating, still coming into the ordinary moments, still speaking to every heart willing to listen.

God, you are the one who knows my heart best,
and you are the Word I need in every circumstance.

. . . .

What is the Word speaking to your heart today?

YOU ARE INCOMPARABLE

Don't compare yourself with others. (Galatians 6:4 MSG)

I wish I could say comparison never stole from me, snatched my joy or time or presence of mind. But we both know that's not true. Because I'm a daughter of Eve, descended from the woman in Eden who heard a serpent hissing lies, the implication being, "You are not enough" and "God is holding out on you."

The lies of comparison still hiss at my heart, especially through social media. It's so easy to make an "ideal life" collage in our minds with her vacation and someone else's cute kids, that woman's dream job and this one's redbrick house in the suburbs. But it's fantasy because it's the highlight reel of fifty different people. Meanwhile the perfect kids are throwing spaghetti at the ceiling and they all got the stomach flu on the cruise and the contractor just told them about the crack in the foundation.

This is what's real and true: we have strengths, skills, and gifts no one else does. God has a mission for our lives only we can fulfill. There never has been and will never be another us. And when there is only one of something, it simply can't be compared. Our maker gets to choose who we are. He gets to decide which doors open for us and which stay closed. He is the Creator and the Savior and the one who looks at us and calls us beloved. God doesn't want us to be more like anyone but Jesus.

God, when I'm tempted to compare, remind me of who you've made me and how much I'm already loved.

. . . .

What helps you when you feel tempted to compare?

YOU CAN BE A WORSHIPER, NOT JUST A WORKER

In quietness and confidence is your strength. (Isaiah 30:15 NLT)

I'm stressed out," I confessed to friends over lunch one day. "What's going on?" they asked. I shrugged and said, "I don't really know." They hugged me and promised to pray.

That night I pulled out my art journal, plugged headphones into my ears, and grabbed a Sharpie. I wanted to think through my life—and especially my work. I planned to put "Writer" at the top of the page because that's my title. But as I leaned toward the paper, I felt a bit of hesitation and silently asked God, "What do you want me to write in that spot?" And it seemed I heard one word in response: *worshiper*.

And suddenly I knew why I was so exhausted. *I'd switched from being a worshiper to a worker.* This isn't the first time it's happened. Throughout my life when I've felt pressure mounting and expectations building, I've tended to have one response: try harder. It's a heart reflex I've had since high school. Be more. Do more. Go more. I carry on like that until I get worn out and a bit rebellious.

Yes, I should have caught on more quickly to that pattern by now. But I'm a bit of a slow learner in this area, it seems. Maybe you have one of those areas in your life too? Thankfully, we serve a God of grace. A God who chases us down right in the middle of all our wild and weary-making running. A God who speaks life and peace and rest into us. A God who wants our hearts more than our hands.

God, thank you for continually bringing me back to what matters most.

. . . .

What do you need to give God today?

NO ONE CAN
TAKE YOUR PLACE

We who are many are one body in Christ. (Romans 12:5 CSB)

I tentatively smile at the women surrounding the table. We've gathered to study God's Word, and yet beneath my calm expression I feel a twinge of anxiety. What if I don't fit in?

My fears are confirmed as those around me begin to share and I realize we're different in many ways. With a sinking feeling I think, *These are not my people.* Then just as quickly it seems God whispers to my heart, *But they are* my *people. And that's what matters.*

God created the body of Christ to be full of differences. It's his beautiful plan for us to need, help, and serve one another. What if when we discover we're the only one like us, it doesn't mean we don't belong? What if it just means we've found where we're needed most?

I decided to stick with the group of women who seemed so unlike me. Over the next few weeks, we learned from each other and grew together. To my surprise I discovered that because we weren't the same, I wasn't the same by the end of our time together either.

In Jesus, it's our differences that can really make the difference. You have something to contribute. You are needed. Be who God made you to be.

God, when I'm tempted to think I need to be more like everyone else, help me remember I only need to be more like Jesus.

· · · ·

What's something you've learned from someone
who is different from you?

YOU HAVE JOY AHEAD

For the joy set before him he endured the cross. (Hebrews 12:2)

Stanford psychologist Kelly McGonigal discovered people are better able to deal with stress when they're pursuing a goal.[1] We can endure the discomfort and pain of now when we think of future benefits—*the joy set before us.* When we find ourselves experiencing stress, we can pause and ask ourselves two questions.

We first ask, "What is the joy set before me?" When I run, it's uncomfortable, but I know it will make me stronger. If someone chooses to overcome an addiction, it's challenging, but there's freedom at the finish line. If we take on a project at work because we believe in the good it can do, we're driven to make the sacrifices needed to turn it into a reality. If we envision the people our children will one day become, the dirty diapers and sleepless nights can be meaningful, not just mundane.

We then ask, "If I can't think of any joy set before me and this stress is optional, do I need to eliminate it from my life?" Yes, we will all experience stress and face challenges. But as women, we often do things out of guilt, obligation, a desire to please people, fear, or a false belief we have to be perfect. We put ourselves at higher risk for burnout, depression, and anxiety. Sometimes the most spiritual response to stress is persevering and sometimes it's walking away.

Let's dare to start asking each other, "What's the joy set before you? What's the joy set before me?" Then let's take the next brave step God has for us without guilt, shame, or apology.

God, show me how to look for the joy set before me.

. . . .

What joy can you see set before you today?

YOUR HEART NEEDS A GATE

Above all else, guard your heart,
for everything you do flows from it. (Proverbs 4:23)

We're sitting in a living room with robin's egg blue walls, a lovely fragile color, and clean white trim. My friend asks a question tentatively, as if throwing a pebble at a window. She doesn't want to break anything. She just needs to release this question into the universe. "What if allowing yourself to be loved means someone may hurt you?"

We have been talking about how and why letting love in can be so hard. About how it seems we can all be in the business of constructing walls that seem like they will keep us safe. We know how to build barriers. But really, this is not what any of us want.

I say slowly as it comes to me like the slow light of sun over the horizon, "I think what makes a difference is making sure we have a gate in the wall." We don't shut ourselves completely off but we don't leave ourselves wide open either. This is the paradox of what it means to "above all else, guard your heart" and at the same time follow the example of a Savior who stretched his arms wide on a cross.

Here's a check for us too: Are we safe for others? Yes, even in the relationships we value most we will sometimes have disagreements and misunderstandings. But overall, the pattern is to be love as God defines it.

God loves us and wants to be with us where we are, as we are, today. He will give us the courage and wisdom to guard our hearts. We are worth protecting.

God, give me the courage and wisdom to guard my heart.

· · · ·

What's one way you can guard your heart today?

JESUS STAYS THE SAME

Jesus Christ is the same yesterday and today and forever. (Hebrews 13:8)

It is the nature of humans to be fickle. We put rings on each other's fingers and then signatures on divorce papers. We are employee of the month and then find ourselves on the layoff list. We are dear friends and then time and space and life make us drift until we're looking back at old photos and thinking, *I haven't seen her in a while.* Yet we keep searching, hoping, longing for that person who will stay. The constant who will never go away.

In these moments, it comforts me to know "Jesus Christ is the same yesterday and today and forever." He isn't going to pick someone else on the playground. He isn't going to bring us roses and then forget to call the next day. He won't recruit us for the pet project and then neglect to invite us to the celebration party. He won't use us up and then throw us out, pull us close and then push us away, whisper in our ear and then lose our phone number. Because his love for us isn't based on our charm; it's rooted in his character. It doesn't come from his emotions but instead from an eternal commitment. It isn't dependent on what we do for him but on what he's already done for us.

Jesus has been the same since the beginning of time, since the moment you took your first breath. He will be the same until you take your last breath too and for all eternity.

Jesus, it's so comforting to know that who you are and your love for me will always be faithful and steady.

. . . .

How has Jesus always been there for you?

JESUS IS YOUR
BRIGHT MORNING STAR

I am ... the bright Morning Star. (Revelation 22:16)

The planet Venus is also known as the Morning Star. Here is its mystery and beauty: Venus is known for rising in the darkest part of the night, just before dawn.[1]

Jesus said, "I am ... the bright Morning Star." This means he's not afraid of the deepest dark. He isn't frightened by the secret places in our hearts that haven't seen daylight for years. He isn't running scared from the tragedies in our lives. He isn't backing away from the brokenness or the bitterness. He isn't intimidated by the monsters under our beds or inside our minds. He isn't avoiding our struggles or saying, "This is too much for me."

He isn't afraid to step right into the night. Not afraid to even dwell in the middle of it. Because he is light and in him there is not darkness at all. This means darkness can surround him and he cannot be defeated or diminished by it. He came as a baby into a midnight world and announced his arrival with a shining star. He conquered death in a dark tomb and rolled the stone away, making a way into the brightness for all of us. In the thickest gloom, *the Morning Star rose*.

The Lord's mercies are new every morning (Lam. 3:22–23). Even the deepest night will lead to dawn. The dark cannot win; the light will never be overcome.

God, you truly are the light who comes into our darkest places.
Thank you for your faithfulness and for the promise
that no night will last forever.

. . . .

How is Jesus bringing light into your dark places today?

YOU'RE A WATER-WALKER

When he saw the strong wind and the waves, he was terrified and began to sink. "Save me, Lord!" he shouted. (Matthew 14:30 NLT)

John Ortberg says, "Your boat is whatever represents safety and security to you apart from God himself. Your boat is whatever you are tempted to put your trust in, especially when life gets a little stormy."[1]

In the biblical story, Peter decides to take the risk of walking on water with Jesus. We often stop the story when Peter begins to sink and Jesus reaches out his hand to save him. But I'm fascinated by what happens next. "When they climbed back into the boat, the wind stopped" (Matt. 14:32 NLT).

One day I had a huge aha moment: Peter *did* successfully walk on water. He did so with Jesus all the way back to the boat! And when they made it, the storm subsided.

Jesus may be asking you to step out of the boat in some area of your life today. You look around and think, *Not now, Lord! Wait until things settle down!* You're not sure about walking on water in general, but if you're going to do it, you'd probably much rather have the lake be as smooth as glass and not even a breeze blowing.

But if you dare to take that step of faith despite your fear, it may be the very thing that brings you closer to Jesus, lets you experience more than you ever imagined with him, and perhaps even leads you to the moment when the storm finally subsides.

God, please give me the courage to step out and come to you.

. . . .

What's a step of faith you took in the past?

GOD DESERVES
YOUR PRAISE FOREVER

Let everything that has breath praise the LORD.
Praise the LORD. (Psalm 150:6)

It's not about you. It's not about me. It's about God.

When our world doesn't make sense and hard days come, that truth can set our hearts free. As long as we believe it's about us, we carry the weight of making everything okay. If it's about us, then there's no room for mistakes. If it's about us, then this life is all there is and our stories don't have a happy ending.

But it's not about us. It's about a God who loved us so much that he sent his Son to die on our behalf. It's about a God who greets us with a sunrise every morning and watches over us as we fall asleep every night. It's about a God who can see all of eternity and has promised us that we will be with him forever.

Psalm 150:6 is the final verse in the book of Psalms. It seems fitting that the close to this beloved book of the Bible is a simple phrase: praise the Lord.

It's the one phrase we can always go back to, no matter what.

When we are tired, *praise the Lord.*

When we're not sure what's going to happen, *praise the Lord.*

When we're celebrating, *praise the Lord.*

Praise brings us home to the place where our hearts can heal and find joy. It replaces the lies we hear with the truth we need. It lifts our hands and helps us lay down our burdens.

Let's praise God together. On the happy days. On the hard days. Today. Tomorrow. Forever.

God, this life is not about me. It's about you. I choose to praise you today.

. . . .

What do you want to praise God for today?

GOD IS YOUR REST

Truly my soul finds rest in God;
my salvation comes from him. (Psalm 62:1)

We see a thread of rest woven all through Scripture. In Genesis, just after creation, God rested as a model for us.

He brought his people out of the striving of Egypt to the promised land of Canaan, which means "the resting place."[1]

He is the Good Shepherd in the Psalms who makes us lie down in green pastures, leads us beside still waters, and restores our souls.

In the Gospels, Jesus offers rest: "Come to me, all you who are weary and burdened, and I will give you rest" (Matt. 11:28).

And at the end of time, "there remains, then, a Sabbath-rest for the people of God" (Heb. 4:9).

Rest, not rushing, has always been and will always be God's desire and design for us. In our culture, we define rest narrowly. We see it as simply stopping our work. But to God it is so much more. Rest is a state of peace and security. Yes, sometimes it is an actual, tangible pause, but it is also a way of living differently no matter what we're doing. Our bodies need regular rest, but I think that is only the first layer, the very surface of what God wants for us.

Rest is not simply the lack of activity but the presence of trust. Because trust is a kind of inner leaning, an intentional reliance on someone else. God himself is our true rest.

God, help me pause in this moment and lean into where I belong,
a place of peace and rest in you.

· · · ·

How do you need God to be your rest today?

GOD WILL HELP WHEN YOU WANT TO QUIT

"I have had enough, Lord," he said. (1 Kings 19:4 NLT)

Elijah challenged four hundred prophets of the false god Baal to a show-down. "Immediately the fire of the Lord flashed down from heaven. . . . And when all the people saw it, they fell face down on the ground and cried out, 'The Lord—he is God! Yes, the Lord is God!'" (1 Kings 18:38–39 NLT).

After this victory you'd expect Elijah to be on a spiritual high. Instead "he went on alone into the wilderness, traveling all day. He sat down under a solitary broom tree and prayed that he might die. 'I have had enough, Lord,' he said" (19:4 NLT). Then Elijah falls asleep.

I love this scene because it's so ridiculously human. I love that God included it in Scripture. I love even more that God doesn't rebuke Elijah. He lets him nap, then sends an angel with divine room service and this deeply spiritual message: "Get up and eat!" (v. 5 NLT).

Victory in our lives is wonderful and exhilarating; having God use us in powerful ways is thrilling. It's also flat-out exhausting. In those moments we can show the same kind of compassion to ourselves that God does to us.

Elijah "got up and ate and drank, and the food gave him enough strength to travel forty days and forty nights to Mount Sinai, the mountain of God" (v. 8 NLT). His meltdown in the wilderness didn't disqualify him from the next victory.

Here's what I'm learning: In our highest highs and lowest lows, God and those around us remember we are human. We're wise to do the same.

*God, thank you for understanding I am human
and giving me what I need.*

. . . .

What helps when you feel like quitting?

YOU'RE GOING TO WIN
YOUR BATTLES TODAY

I am weary, God,
   but I can prevail. (Proverbs 30:1)

This one goes out to all the warriors in yoga pants or tennis shoes, the ones strolling through the grocery store or scrolling on social media. When you look in the mirror today, you might see an ordinary human, messy hair, maybe even dark circles under your eyes. But you're a champion in disguise.

Don't let what's on the surface fool you. It's not the whole story. Inside you are fire and tenderness, fierceness and tenacity, resilience and a roar that can shake the world. You are doing hard things. You are taking territory. You are saying "no more" to the darkness. You are kicking butt and taking names (or naps), loving people and refusing to quit, and pushing forward when it would be easier to play it safe.

You sometimes think of how much more you wish you could do, the gap between what is and what you want to be. But don't let that vision make you miss what an overcomer you are TODAY. Right here. Right now.

Remember how far you've come, how much you've learned, all the little ways you've won. Forgive yourself if you didn't know how to do it better back then. You know now, and you are stronger, wiser, more courageous for it.

Fighting perfectly is not the point.

Fighting until you prevail is what matters.

You and God are winning battles today.

God, you are the one who empowers me to prevail. I pray that you would give me the strength and courage I need today.

. . . .

What's a battle that you won with God's help,
and what are you facing today?

YOU'RE ALLOWED TO GET ANGRY

Be angry, and do not sin. (Ephesians 4:26 NKJV)

As I've tried to understand anger and how to handle it in healthier ways, these three discoveries have helped.

Anger is armor. Conflict resolution specialists say, "Anger is often called a secondary emotion because we tend to resort to anger in order to protect ourselves from or cover up other vulnerable feelings."[1] It can help to ask, "What did I feel just before I got angry?" or "What am I afraid of or trying to protect?"

Anger is related to our values. A dear friend has a daughter with special needs, and an unfair decision based on a hospital policy kept her from getting care. My friend was furious and yet kept saying, "I shouldn't feel this way." I told her, "You're mad because you value your daughter's well-being, and that is a beautiful thing." To find the source of our anger, we can ask, "What value of mine is being violated right now?"

Anger is informative. Ephesians 4:26 says, "Be angry, and do not sin." But many of us would say, "Don't be angry, because it's a sin." Those are two *very* different meanings. Emotions make great messengers but bad bosses. We can ask, "What is my anger telling me?" and then "What action is God asking me to take?"

When God created our human minds and hearts, he gave us anger along with all the emotions we need to process life. And when we give our anger back to him, he can use it in powerful, healing ways.

God, I acknowledge my anger and give it to you.

· · · ·

What helps you handle your anger in healthy ways?

YOU'RE PART OF PEACE ON EARTH

Glory to God in the highest,
And on earth peace, goodwill toward men! (Luke 2:14 NKJV)

We've read the story and know the scene. The unshowered shepherds with their flock. The shock, then awe. The angels declaring the good news. The star and the manger. The baby and the hope.

There's a lot God could have chosen to say that night. He could have dealt with politics (which had their troubles then too). He could have made moral proclamations. He could have taken a tone like a ruler-tapping teacher and told us all to get our acts together. But, instead, he blessed us. He spoke words of encouragement and hope.

What if the whole world did the same? What if we all put down our opinions and picked up grace? Shut our mouths and opened our doors. Pulled back our judgments and reached out our hands. Banished our angry words and brought out the welcome mat for kindness and mercy.

It's scary, I know. Because it might seem as if everything will go wrong if we dare to make ourselves vulnerable. But if that's what God chose to do, can't we?

Sometimes we forget that someone already came to save the world. That job has been taken. That task marked complete. It is not on our shoulders. And this is what Jesus told us will continue that mission: "A new command I give you: Love one another" (John 13:34).

Peace on earth, goodwill toward men.

Let's make this day all about love. All about peace, goodwill toward men. Which is really just another way of saying let's make it all about Jesus.

God, make me a messenger of peace and a bringer of hope.

. . . .

How can you help bring peace where you are today?

JESUS IS THE NAME ABOVE ALL NAMES

God exalted him to the highest place
and gave him the name that is above every name.
(Philippians 2:9)

Honor roll. Sports rankings. Election outcomes. Get your name to the top of the list, this world says. Our hearts have their own lists too. Be the most popular. The best mom. The hardest worker.

We have an inner drive for meaning, for affirmation, and for validation. We want to know we matter. We count. We are doing it right. What better way than to push our name to the top? Yes, spell it out in black and white so I can see my worth. Then everyone else will believe it too.

In all our well-intentioned striving, we can miss one thing: the top spot on every list is already taken. Jesus has "the name that is above every name" (Phil. 2:9).

We don't have to make a name for ourselves because we belong to the One with the highest, best name. When we are tired, afraid, or overwhelmed, our hearts can find rest, hope, and strength in God's name. "The name of the LORD is a fortified tower. The righteous run to it and are safe" (Prov. 18:10). When we are filled with joy, celebrating and standing in the middle of unexpected blessings, we can rejoice in God's name. "Now, our God, we give you thanks, and praise your glorious name" (1 Chron. 29:13).

Every moment of our lives, every circumstance we face, every emotion we feel—there is a name of God to meet our needs.

Jesus, your name is above all names,
and you are the one I choose to serve.

. . . .

What is a name of God or Jesus that is comforting to you today?

YOUR HELP IS ON THE WAY

Therefore, we may boldly say,
The Lord is my helper;
I will not be afraid.
What can man do to me? (Hebrews 13:6 CSB)

In the documentary *Won't You Be My Neighbor?* beloved television personality Mr. Rogers says, "When I was a boy and I would see scary things in the news, my mother would say to me, 'Look for the helpers. You will always find people who are helping.'" The film makes it clear he not only looked for the helpers, he chose to become one.

We all have our own way of helping. Maybe you teach, lead, raise children, make beautiful spreadsheets. Maybe you're walking with someone you love through a hard season so they won't be alone in it. Maybe you pray in the quiet where no one is watching. This is all helping. Never underestimate the worth of it.

And the reassuring truth we all need is that God is a helper too—more than that, he is *our* helper. On the days when we become a bit tired, when it all seems like too much, he says to us, "I will strengthen you and help you" (Isa. 41:10). Fred Rogers, an ordained minister, knew this to be true.

Let's keep looking for the helpers. Let's keep being the helpers too.

God, you are the helper who is always with us, always for us,
always working on our behalf. I pray that I would reflect
your heart by helping others too.

. . . .

How has someone been a helper to you,
and how can you be a helper to someone else today?

GOD HEARS WHAT
YOUR HEART HAS TO SAY

Before a word is on my tongue
you, LORD, know it completely. (Psalm 139:4)

God knows what we're going to pray even before we do because he knows our hearts. "The mouth speaks what the heart is full of" (Matt. 12:34). That means prayer isn't about information—it's about intimacy. It builds our relationship with God when we speak to him and listen for his response.

Because God knows us so completely, we also don't have to feel pressure to have just the right words. We've all heard fancy prayers that make us wonder if we should ever dare to speak to Jesus again. But what matters to him is not our language but the meaning behind it. "Help me, Jesus" is one of the most powerful, pleasing prayers you can ever say.

So when you're struggling, it's okay if you're not sure how to express what you're feeling to God. You can simply tell him, "You know my heart. You know what I need. I love and trust you. Please do what is best."

God knows we don't have the same perspective he does. He understands we don't have the wisdom of eternity. He remembers that we are finite, limited beings. So you don't have to fear getting in trouble for asking for the "wrong thing" when you pray. Just be honest, surrender your will, and ask Jesus and the Spirit to intercede for you.

God's presence is a place you can always come to and trust you'll be accepted, cherished, and fully known in a way that's beyond words.

God, it's a beautiful gift to be able to connect with you through prayer.
You know my heart and all that I long to say.

. . . .

What's a short prayer you sometimes pray, like "Help me, Jesus"?

GOD IS NEW AND THE SAME

For I am about to do something new.
See, I have already begun! (Isaiah 43:19 NLT)

The sun is a debutante this morning, wearing a dress of crimson and gold laced with clouds. I stand on the beach to watch the sunrise. I love that the ocean is two things: absolutely consistent and never the same. The tides come in and out in intervals so steady, a chart predicts them by the minute. Yet what the waves bring in is a continual surprise—starfish, sand dollars, an abundance of shells, driftwood that could tell you a long, beautiful story about all the places it's been.

God's heart, character, and ways do not vary. We can count on them not just by the hour but by the minute. But how he shows up, what he brings to us, his mercies and miracles—these are always brand-new, never repeated. Worry reverses these truths. It tempts us to believe God has changed. He is not as reliable as we'd hoped. He might not be who he says he is. We hear an echo of the enemy of our hearts from Eden who hissed, "Did God really say . . . ?" Worry tells us that things will always be the same, that our circumstances will not and cannot change.

But what worry says isn't true. Our God is bigger than the ocean, more faithful than the waves, and at the start of each new day, we can trust him all over again.

God, you are forever the same and yet always
doing something new in my life.

· · · ·

What's one part of God's character you're grateful is always the same, and what's one new thing you see him doing in your life?

TAKE HEART IN JESUS

I have told you these things, so that in me you may have peace. In this world you will have trouble. But take heart! I have overcome the world. (John 16:33)

I take things to heart. This is one of my greatest strengths. It makes me a caring daughter, a kind friend, a thoughtful wife, a compassionate writer. But on some days, it's also one of my greatest struggles. I'm disturbed by the news stories. I worry about those I love. Sometimes I can't sleep because I just want everyone and everything to be okay.

I have a realization: God never asked me to take everything to heart. He did tell me, "In this world you will have trouble. But take heart! I have overcome the world" (John 16:33).

When I take something to heart, I believe it's all on me.

When I take heart in Jesus, I remember he's in control.

When I take something to heart, I feel like I'm alone.

When I take heart in Jesus, I know he will never let me go.

When I take something to heart, I lose my hope.

When I take heart in Jesus, I find him at work even in the hardest circumstances.

Taking heart simply means taking whatever concerns me to Jesus. My challenges remain, but my perspective has changed. Whatever this day brings, I don't have to carry it on my own. I can give it to the only one strong enough to take it.

God, when I'm tempted to take everything to heart, help me remember that, instead, I can take everything to you.

. . . .

What are you taking to heart today?

YOU'RE GETTING STRONGER EVERY DAY

Pursue righteousness and a godly life, along with faith, love, perse-verance, and gentleness. (1 Timothy 6:11 NLT)

Each day in my exercise group, we complete a different workout. Some involve weights, others resistance bands, and all of them mean I have to do tough, awkward things.

There is always the temptation to listen to the tiny voice in the back of my mind that whispers, *Skip the workout, eat a brownie, and sit on the couch. Nothing will happen.* But that voice is a liar, because something *will* happen. Unless I choose to get stronger, over time I will become weaker.

When I push through a workout, it hurts and it's hard. But when I persevere, the next time I can do a little more for a little longer. Over time, this actually changes my body and who I am. I get stronger and know I can handle more than ever before.

This is the emotional process God invites us into as well. We need to lift the "weight" of life, because that's how we become resilient. Again, I'm not talking about doing so to the point of injury. I'm talking about the normal pain and annoyances of life in an imperfect world. We can avoid them in many ways, but we can only overcome them by not taking the easy way out.

When I get to the end of a workout, I'm sweaty and exhausted. But I've done more than I thought I could. I didn't give up. I didn't walk away. I showed up and gave it my best today. And that's enough to make me stronger for tomorrow.

---

*God, fill me with the power I need to persevere. I will not give up.
I am getting stronger every day.*

. . . .

When has doing something hard made you stronger?

YOU HAVE VICTORY

Thanks be to God! He gives us the victory through our Lord Jesus Christ. (1 Corinthians 15:57)

Yesterday morning I sat across from a friend in a coffee shop. The sun slanted through the windows and bounced off the surface of the table between us. She ordered a cinnamon roll the size of my face. She let me have part of it. Because this is what friends do.

We'd both just come through weeks of turmoil and a few tears. We felt battle worn and a bit weary. But we also felt strong and brave and true. "Years ago we wouldn't have done this," we said to each other. "We would have hidden. We would have backed down. We would have let fear win."

But not now. Not anymore.

A few minutes ago I talked with another friend who is still right in the middle of the surge. She is afraid and she wants to quit, but she keeps saying, "I have to see this through because it's about more than just me." I know that she will.

When I think of all three of our situations, and so many more I see in my real life and online, I realize that we are a generation of warriors. We may not ever be recognized as such. Because we fight not with anger but with grace. We defend not with force but with kindness. And we know this secret—that God himself *is* love and nothing is impossible with him.

We are followers of Jesus who are here for such a time as this. We are strong, brave, and loved.

God, I will face hard things, but I can take heart because you are the great Overcomer.

. . . .

When has God brought victory in a circumstance or situation in your life?

JESUS IS YOUR AMEN

These are the words of the Amen, the faithful and true witness, the ruler of God's creation. (Revelation 3:14)

*A*men means "so be it." It is a force word, a setting into action, a powerful alliance between us and heaven's will. Amen is also a name of Jesus. He is *the* Amen. So when we pray, when we say this word, we are actually calling on him.

When we ask God for a Savior, Jesus in the manger is the Amen.

When we beg for forgiveness, Jesus on the cross is the Amen.

When we need new life and hope, Jesus exiting an empty tomb is the Amen.

When we long for comfort, peace, joy, and all that belongs to us as believers, Jesus in our everyday lives is the Amen and Amen and Amen.

This doesn't mean we will automatically get what we want just by invoking this word. It is both a frustration and a relief to realize *amen* doesn't mean "so do it" but "so be it." Ultimately, when we say "amen," we are praying for God's best and yielding to his will. Sometimes this is wonderful. Sometimes it is hard. Most often it's a bit of both.

What God does can be trusted because no matter what we ask for, his love for us through Jesus is the heart of the answer. This is what I know now, what I'll know forever: Amen is more than where a prayer ends. It's where every answer begins—always and only with Jesus.

Jesus, you are the answer to everything I need.
You are the yes to every promise God has made.

. . . .

What are you saying "amen" to in your life today?

Acknowledgments

Mark, thank you for being my biggest encourager, business partner, and best friend. I love sharing life with you and look forward to what's ahead!

Mom, Dad, and Granny Eula, thank you for the legacy of faith you gave me and all your love, support, and prayers through the years.

Lovelle, David, Eula, and Clement, thank you for making me not only Mom but Nana too. I'm so grateful for the family story God is writing for us.

Jennifer Leep, Andrea Doering, Wendy Wetzel, Amy Nemecek, Kelli Smith, and Eileen Hanson, thank you for not only being my publishing team but friends I treasure too.

Kaitlyn Bouchillon, thank you for being my content manager, virtual assistant, trusted friend, and the one who makes so much of the magic happen for the creative work I do.

Thank you to every dear friend who lived one of the stories in this book with me, listened to me process over coffee or lunch, or cheered me on as I wrote. I'm so grateful to share life with you!

God, thank you for letting me be part of your unending creative work and for continuing to remind my heart of what's true. I love you.

Notes

Day 16 Jesus Is the Author of Your Story

1. *Merriam-Webster*, s.v. "Author," accessed April 28, 2017, https://www.merriam-webster.com/dictionary/author.

Day 18 God Will Meet You Where You Are Today

1. Brené Brown, *The Gifts of Imperfection: Let Go of Who You Think You're Supposed to Be and Embrace Who You Are* (Center City, MN: Hazelden Publishing, 2010), 9–10.

Day 44 You Will Be with God Forever

1. "Life Expectancy by Country 2023," World Population Review, accessed October 16, 2023, https://worldpopulationreview.com/country-rankings/life-expectancy-by-country.

Day 68 Your Perspective Is Powerful

1. Martin E. P. Seligman, Susan Nolen-Hoeksema, Joan S. Girgus, "Learned Helplessness in Children: A Longitudinal Study of Depression, Achievement, and Explanatory Style," *Journal of Personality and Social Psychology* 51, no. 2 (1986): 435–42.

Day 70 You're Called to Love

1. Ali Rogin, "Researchers Find Strong Relationships Protect Long-Term Health and Happiness," PBS News Weekend, November 26, 2023, https://www.pbs.org/newshour/show/researchers-find-strong-relationships-protect-long-term-health-and-happiness.

Day 72 Jesus Is Your Counselor

1. Henry Cloud, *The Power of the Other: The Startling Effect Other People Have on You, from the Boardroom to the Bedroom and Beyond—and What to Do about It* (New York: HarperCollins, 2016), chap. 2, Kindle.

Day 86 God Will Satisfy Your Soul Thirst

1. Susan Schoenian, "Feeding and Watering Equipment," Sheep 201: A Beginner's Guide to Raising Sheep, accessed December 7, 2020, http://www.sheep101.info/201/feedwaterequip.html.

Day 101 God Created Fun Too

1. Katrina Nannestad, *When Mischief Came to Town* (New York: Houghton Mifflin Harcourt, 2015), 162–63.

Day 102 God Is Greater Than All Your Fears

1. Chuck Swindoll, "Proverbs," Insight for Living Ministries, accessed December 15, 2021, www
.insight.org/resources/bible/the-wisdom-books/proverbs.

2. William D. Eisenhower, "Fearing God," February 7, 1986, *Christianity Today*, https://www.christi
anitytoday.com/ct/1986/february-7/fearing-god-those-who-have-never-trembled-from-head-to-toe.html.

Day 103 God Is Your Good Shepherd

1. W. Phillip Keller, *A Shepherd Looks at Psalm 23* (Grand Rapids: Zondervan, 2007), 97.

2. Keller, *Shepherd Looks at Psalm 23*, 102.

Day 124 God Alone Knows Your Future

1. Eva M. Krockow, "How Many Decisions Do We Make Each Day?" *Psychology Today*, September
27, 2018, https://www.psychologytoday.com/us/blog/stretching-theory/201809/how-many-decisions
-do-we-make-each-day.

Day 132 You Can Make Friends with Frustration

1. Gretchen Rubin, "Podcast 270: Very Special Episode with Great Advice for Graduates," *Happier with
Gretchen Rubin*, April 22, 2020, https://gretchenrubin.com/podcast-episode/270-vse-advice-for-graduates.

Day 143 God Is Your Abba

1. Matthew George Easton, "Abba," in *Easton's Bible Dictionary* (Nashville: Thomas Nelson, 1997),
http://www.biblestudytools.com/dictionaries/eastons-bible-dictionary/abba.html.

Day 157 Your Dormant Seasons Have Value

1. Eileen Campbell, "How Do Trees Survive Winter?," Treehugger, updated May 10, 2020, https://
www.mnn.com/earth-matters/wilderness-resources/stories/how-do-trees-survive-winter.

Day 158 Your Shepherd Will Care for You

1. Chuck Wooster, *Living with Sheep: Everything You Need to Know to Raise Your Own Flock* (Lan-
ham, MD: Lyons Press, 2007), chap. 9, Kindle.

Day 203 God Catches Your Tears

1. Sheila Walsh, "A Bottle of Your Tears," FaithGateway, August 4, 2015, http://www.faithgateway
.com/bottle-of-your-tears/#.WQPAwhT_trp.

Day 207 You Can Be a Friend

1. Janet Kornblum, "Study: 25% of Americans Have No One to Confide In," *USA Today*, June 22,
2006, www.usatoday.com/news/nation/2006-06-22-friendship_x.htm.

Day 230 You're Overcoming Negativity

1. Hara Estroff Marano, "Our Brain's Negative Bias," *Psychology Today*, June 9, 2016, https://www
.psychologytoday.com/us/articles/200306/our-brains-negative-bias.

Day 266 Jesus Is Making Something Beautiful of Your Life

1. Ted Olsen, "The Life and Times of Jesus of Nazareth: Did You Know?," *Christian History* 59
(1998), http://www.christianitytoday.com/history/issues/issue-59/life-times-of-jesus-of-nazareth
-did-you-know.html.

Day 267 God Will Equip You to Handle It

1. Susan Jeffers, *Feel the Fear . . . and Do It Anyway: Dynamic Techniques for Turning Fear, Indecision, and Anger into Power, Action, and Love* (Santa Monica, CA: Jeffers Press, 2007), 24, Kindle ed.

Day 272 Jesus Is Your Cornerstone

1. Elmer Towns, *The Ultimate Guide to the Names of God* (Bloomington, MN: Bethany House, 2014), 228.

Day 273 The Belt of Truth Protects You

1. Brandon Cox, "Getting Dressed for Battle," Facebook, April 15, 2018, https://www.facebook.com/gracehillsnwa/videos/1654419854640969/.

Day 278 You Fight with the Sword of the Spirit

1. Brandon Cox, "Getting Dressed for Battle," Facebook, April 15, 2018, https://www.facebook.com/gracehillsnwa/videos/1654419854640969/.

Day 291 Selah for Your Soul

1. Jason Soroski, "What Does Selah Mean in the Bible and Why Is It Important?," Crosswalk.com, October 10, 2018, https://www.crosswalk.com/faith/bible-study/what-does-selah-mean.html.

Day 305 God Has a Different Perspective

1. Linda Bloom and Charlie Bloom, "Reframing: The Transformative Power of Suffering," *Psychology Today*, December 14, 2017, https://www.psychologytoday.com/us/blog/stronger-the-broken-places/201712/reframing.

Day 347 You Have Joy Ahead

1. Kelly McGonigal, *The Upside of Stress: Why Stress Is Good for You, and How to Get Good at It* (New York: Avery, 2016), 143.

Day 350 Jesus Is Your Bright Morning Star

1. Richard Talcott, "Venus Shines at Its Brightest before Dawn," Astronomy.com, January 31, 2014, http://www.astronomy.com/observing/sky-events/2014/01/venus-shines-at-its-brightest-before-dawn.

Day 351 You're a Water-Walker

1. John Ortberg, *If You Want to Walk on Water, You've Got to Get Out of the Boat* (Grand Rapids: Zondervan, 2001), 17.

Day 353 God Is Your Rest

1. "Rest," in *Baker's Evangelical Dictionary of Biblical Theology*, ed. Walter A. Elwell (Grand Rapids: Baker Books, 1996), http://www.biblestudytools.com/dictionary/rest/.

Day 356 You're Allowed to Get Angry

1. "Anger: A Secondary Emotion," Conflict Resolution Education, accessed December 15, 2020, http://creducation.net/resources/anger_management/anger__a_secondary_emotion.html.

Holley Gerth

loves humans, words, and good coffee. She's the *Wall Street Journal* bestselling author of many books, including *The Powerful Purpose of Introverts* and *What Your Mind Needs for Anxious Moments*. Holley has served women as a life coach and counselor, cofounded the groundbreaking online community (in)courage, and cohosts the *More Than Small Talk* podcast. Find out more and connect with Holley at HolleyGerth.com.

CONNECT WITH HOLLEY:

- HolleyGerth.com
- @HolleyGerth
- @HolleyGerth
- @HolleyGerth

My Notes